Alienated
America

Alienated America

Why Some Places Thrive

While Others Collapse

Timothy P. Carney

HARPER

NEW YORK • LONDON • TORONTO • SYDNEY

HARPER

A hardcover edition of this book was published in 2020 by HarperCollins Publishers.

HarperCollins books may be purchased for educational, business, or sales promotional use. For information please email the Special Markets Department at SPsales@harpercollins.com.

FIRST HARPER PAPERBACKS EDITION PUBLISHED 2020.

Library of Congress Cataloging-in-Publication Data has been applied for.

ISBN 978-0-06-279712-4

20 21 22 23 24   LSC   10 9 8 7 6 5 4 3 2 1

Seek the well-being of the city to which I have carried you into exile. Pray to the Lord for it, for in its well-being will be your well-being.

—JEREMIAH 29:7

Contents

Preface

We could start a book about the death of the American Dream in a million different places. We could start in Smitty's Bar and Restaurant in a dead steel town outside Pittsburgh, or we could start in the Bishops' Storehouse in Salt Lake City. We could go to Iowa and start in Glory Days Sports Bar in Council Bluffs, or at a Christian college in Sioux Center. We could start at the shuttered Methodist churches in rural Iowa or the bustling basement of the Islamic Center of Greater Toledo. We could start standing in line at a Trump rally or camping out at Occupy Wall Street.

We will get to all those places on this journey, but we will start the story in the Pediatric Intensive Care Unit of Children's National Hospital in Washington, D.C.

It was about four a.m. I had just gotten two hours of decent sleep, relatively speaking, sitting in a spartan armchair, my head leaning against the metal bars of the PICU crib. My daughter Eve, eleven months old, was the patient, and she slept soundly, despite the prongs of the nasal cannula up her nostrils, the pulse–oxygen saturation monitor taped to her toe, the three electric wires stuck to her chest and back, and the fact that she couldn't really breathe.

The breathing was done by a machine next to her crib that slowly won my awe.

Infected with a respiratory virus, Eve's alveoli were too clogged with mucus for her to get sufficient oxygen into her lungs. The local urgent care center I had sprinted to (with her in a jogging stroller) couldn't get her enough oxygen. My wife rode in the ambulance with

Eve to Holy Cross Hospital, where Eve had been born and where our kids had made many emergency room visits. Holy Cross's oxygen pumps also couldn't get enough into her lungs. She was getting paler by the minute.

However, the PICU at Children's had this magic high-powered machine, which could pump up to five times as much oxygen into her lungs as the ordinary "wall oxygen" hospitals normally rely on. That machine, along with an unerringly excellent nursing staff, was saving my daughter's life.

At four a.m., though, that machine and the PICU nurses had to share my attention and gratitude. My thoughts were filled in that hour with the help we were getting from friends and neighbors during our stay, which would stretch from Sunday to Thursday.

My colleagues on the opinion page at the *Washington Examiner* had barbecue (my favorite) delivered to me for lunch on Monday. One colleague delivered beer and dark chocolate to the PICU to make the stay more bearable for my wife, Katie, and me. One friend in Virginia had so much food delivered to our house from the Corner Bakery— sandwiches, salads, chips, cold cuts—that we ate dinner and lunch from the platter for more than a week. America's Future Foundation, an organization of young conservatives and libertarians on whose board I had served for years, sent a gift card for ordering dinner from GrubHub (a food delivery service) for our whole family.

My mother-in-law brought a chicken potpie to our house for dinner one night. She also repeatedly came to watch the kids while my wife or I drove to the hospital to trade off shifts with Eve. Katie's younger sister and her husband also sat a shift with our kids, as did other friends in our parish, and another neighbor.

With us unable to fulfill our carpool duties, the other parents took on extra trips, and even went out of their way to pick up our son.

We got so many offers of help or food that I felt guilty about my inability to field them all. "My cup runneth over," was the Bible verse that crossed my mind.

In the moment, waking up at four a.m. with a sore neck in the tiny curtained booth of the PICU, I had an image of a swarm of friends, family, and neighbors rallying to our aid. But as I considered it more during our stay, I saw in greater detail the contours of this support we were enjoying.

As I thought about each person or couple who helped us, or wrote, or called, I noticed these weren't simple bilateral relationships. In almost every case, there was an *institution* that linked us. Again, this wasn't how we thought about our friends generally—they were just our friends.

But whenever I described to others the help we got, I found myself speaking of *the couple from our parish*, or *the family from our pool*. Some help came from parents at the same boys' school where our oldest sons go. Others were my college classmates. Others were my work colleagues at the *Examiner* or the American Enterprise Institute. Parents of the kids I had coached in baseball helped. The woman who sent the Corner Bakery feast is in my wife's book club and attends the same Virginia parish as my wife's parents. The GrubHub gift card, again, came from an organization whose board I had sat on.

Our dense and broad network of friends, which had become a short-term safety net, wasn't merely a network of friends. It was a network of organizations, companies, churches, schools, and clubs. The hubs that bound us to these friends are what we call "institutions of civil society." Sociologists might say that during those five days, we were drawing on our deep reserves of "social capital."

My favorite moment to reflect came on Sunday, as I was sprinting down Georgia Avenue with a blue-lipped lethargic Eve in a jogging stroller. Katie had gone to a late-morning Mass at our parish with our oldest daughter. When she finally looked at her phone and ran out of Mass to meet me at the urgent care center, she turned to Lucy and said, "Go sit with Dorrie," pointing to the mother of an old school friend. "She'll give you a ride home after Mass. If not, someone else will."

Katie simply knew that we could count on our parish—on the people in that community—to help. That knowledge, the certainty that someone can help you when you need it, was always there, but we hadn't noticed it until we needed it. Like the health insurance that paid most of the bill, the "insurance" of the social networks had provided great peace of mind without ever rising to the front of our consciousness.

In short, we always took for granted the social capital we possessed, and the dense, expansive networks of civil society in which we were entangled. Why? Because this was how we both grew up.

If you belong to a church, you've probably experienced something like it, on either the giving end or the receiving end, or both.

Alternatively, if you are college educated and married, even if you don't belong to a church, you probably have many ties to civil society institutions—swim clubs, PTAs, workplaces, book clubs—that provide this sort of infrastructure of friends and associates.

Dense social networks may not seem remarkable to you, the reader, for the same reason water doesn't seem remarkable to a fish. "[N]etworking power is like the air we breathe—so pervasive it's easy to miss," author J. D. Vance wrote when he finished law school and joined the elite.[1]

Vance *noticed* the networks, though, when he was at law school. It was a shocking realization for him that personal connections, typically through institutions of civil society, were central to the success of the elites. Growing up in a broken family in a working-class suburb, Vance hadn't had those networks. It wasn't so much that people in working-class towns had less powerful connections; it was that every family was less connected—to anyone. His Middletown, Ohio, was a place of alienation.

Hillbilly Elegy, Vance's memoir, became a bestseller in 2016 because it offered insight into a part of the country that the educated and affluent had missed—the dark, broken places in working-class Middle America. What generated the interest in working-class white Middle America?

Donald Trump.

So yes, as a book about the death of the American Dream, this is also a book about how Donald Trump became president of the United States. But Trump isn't the subject of the book. How he has governed, how he has tweeted, and how his mind works are far beyond the reaches of this book.

Rather than a book about Trump, this is a book about Trump *voters*. More specifically, it's about Trump's core supporters, who voted for him in the Republican primaries in 2016. The Republicans' nomination of Trump is best understood as a referendum on whether America is currently great, or in need of great making again. If you wondered how places like Michigan and Wisconsin could swing so rapidly from Trump to his opposition in 2016 and 2018, it's because the 2016 election wasn't about the man or his party. It was a referendum on whether or not the American Dream was still alive.

The election told us something about America that we didn't see, and for that reason, we use the election map as a path that we follow on our journey through the country's cities and towns, past and present.

This isn't a book about Trump. It's certainly not a book about Hillary Clinton. Only indirectly do Trump's policies and proposals play a role here, because what Trump has done as president is largely immaterial to this story. What candidate Trump said is mostly immaterial, except for his central message: The American Dream is dead.

Everything Trump said during the campaign elicited an angry retort from many quarters, including the media. On his claim that the American Dream was dead, a thousand commentators came up with refutations that proved nothing except the shallowness of our understanding of the good life.

They'd point to the stock market. They'd point out the decent wages of Trump's core voters. They'd point out the historical privilege enjoyed by these old white Christian men. All of these points were supposed to pierce any claims to sympathy and invalidate any gripes by the people who immediately and strongly embraced Trump and his dire diagnosis.

The materialistic view of the American Dream, however, misses the point. The worst analyses assume that *wealth* or the *opportunity* for wealth is the American Dream. Slightly better, some analyses see wealth as the necessary precondition of other goods, like intact families or strong public schools.

But maybe the things we think *accompany* the American Dream are the things that really *are* the American Dream. What if the T-ball game, the standing-room-only high school Christmas concert, the parish potluck, and decorating the community hall for a wedding— what if those activities are not the dressings around the American Dream, but what if they *are* the American Dream?

In this book, I'm going to take you to the parts of America where the Dream is clearly alive, as well as the places where the Dream seems dead. To really learn from this tour through time and place, you, the reader, may need to abandon your understanding of how to measure the good life. We will look at many numbers, regarding marriage, suicide, income, employment, and so on. But those numbers are epiphenomena—they are ripples out from what matters.

Hopefully, like any good tour, this book will open your eyes to things not only far, but also near. If I succeed, things will look different when our trip is done, when you return home and look around.

So we will study the American Dream in the coming chapters—where it's alive and where it's dead. (And I use the word *where* intentionally.) This study turns out to be a study of place, of social capital, of civil society, of community, and of church. The things you may take for granted—the things that washed over me, my wife, and our baby Eve in that ICU—they are the material of this book because they are the material of the good life.

Alienated
America

CHAPTER 1

It Takes a Village

Where the American Dream Lives

S adly, the American Dream is dead."

After rambling, off script, for most of his fifty-minute speech to announce his presidential candidacy in June 2015, Donald Trump had returned to his written remarks for the final section. He delivered these somber words slowly, pausing for emphasis.

"Sadly. . . the American Dream is dead," he enunciated, pausing again.

In the cavernous lobby of Trump Tower, an eager supporter filled that pregnant silence. "Bring it back!" she shouted.

Sure enough, that was Trump's promise and the final line, the bottom line, of his candidacy: "But if I get elected president, I will bring it back bigger and better and stronger than ever before, and we will make America great again!"

This became his motto. Make America Great Again. The premise of that motto—the American Dream is dead—carried the day in state after state, and it drew crowds at rallies in places like Lowell, Massachusetts; Beaumont, Texas; Mobile, Alabama ("We're running on fumes. There's nothing here. . . ."); and Springfield, Illinois.

"These rally towns," the *Washington Post* reported in an early effort to decode Trump's meaning, "lag behind the country and their home states on a number of measures. Their median household incomes are lower, and they often have lower rates of homeownership or residents with college degrees."[1]

On April 26, 2016, my own state of Maryland, along with four other states, voted for Trump, putting him on the doorstep of the Republican nomination. "Every single place I go is a disaster," Trump said in his victory remarks that night.

Trump obviously didn't go where I had gone that morning: to Chevy Chase Village Hall, off Connecticut Avenue, just outside Washington, D.C.

When I arrived at Village Hall, which is the polling place for the village, I found a parking spot between a BMW and a Porsche SUV. That was unsurprising. Chevy Chase Village is the wealthiest municipality in the D.C. region, which is probably the highest-income region in the country. The mean household income in the Village of Chevy Chase is $420,000.[2] Only about 2 percent of America makes that much.

Chris Matthews and George F. Will are just two of the well-known residents of the village. Ambassadors, lawyers, bankers, and lobbyists populate the beautiful massive homes off Connecticut Avenue, almost all of which are worth more than $1 million. The median home costs $1.52 million.[3]

Chevy Chase Village isn't merely wealthy in material things. To the extent we can measure the good life, Chevy Chase has it. About 95 percent of Chevy Chase's families had two parents at home in 2015. The Village Hall hosts a monthly speaker series, which kicked off in April 2017 with a talk by documentary filmmaker Tamara Gold. CIA veteran David Duberman was slated for the next month.

A committee of volunteers throws regular parties for the whole village. Saint Patrick's Day included a "Father/Daughter Pipe/Harpist Team and True Scottish Piper," according to the *Crier*, the village's own newsletter. Children and toddlers can take ballet and musical theater classes at Village Hall. Adults can take Tai Chi.

Almost exactly one year after the primary, I returned, to observe the village's annual meeting.

"Oh, Mrs. O'Connor!" the village's chief of police, John Fitzgerald, shouted across the parking lot, with a flirting tone. "I didn't recognize you in that new car." Mrs. O'Connor blushed and smiled. She chairs the village's Committee for Seniors.

Having its own village police force is impressive enough, considering the population of two thousand. Fitzgerald knows how extraordinary this is. "This community is really, really good to work in," Fitzgerald, a big Irish cop of the type I'm used to from New York, said at the annual meeting. "Small is good."

When he discussed the force's most recent initiative—a camera on Grafton Street to bust folks using it as a cut-through to Wisconsin Avenue—Chief Fitzgerald described it as "right near Mr. Marsh's house." The evening seemed like a scene out of Thornton Wilder's *Our Town.*

The community is engaged. At the village meeting, there were presentations by the volunteer members or chairmen and chairwomen of the Community Relations Committee, the Ethics Commission, the Financial Review Committee, the Public Safety Committee, the Traffic Committee, the Local Advisory Panel to the Historic Preservation Commission, the Western Grove Park Friends Group, the Environment and Energy Committee, the Parks and Greenspaces Committee, plus Mrs. O'Connor for the seniors committee.

A village of two thousand people stocking ten committees with a handful of volunteers each is extraordinary. There are other details. The coffee-and-desserts reception before the annual meeting featured seasonal flower arrangements provided by the village's Garden Club.

The Community Relations Committee organized a parents' night out where they brought in neighborhood teenagers to babysit in the charming Village Hall, so that the adults could enjoy a dinner at the restaurants within walking distance. Betty O'Connor's seniors committee brings in innovative experts to help the village's elderly who are struggling physically or with dementia.

Walk down Grove Street on a Monday evening, and you will see kids from a handful of families mixing together to ride their bikes and scooters, and dribble their basketballs and soccer balls down the brick sidewalks. Parents hanging out front keep an occasional eye on the neighborhood kids.

Chevy Chase is "the Village" Hillary Clinton said it *took* to raise a family.

And it's no surprise Hillary Clinton *took* the village.

At one of the village's impressive homes, a politically connected financier, who is also the son of a former top diplomat, hosted a fundraiser for Hillary Clinton in November 2015. The couple hosting the event raised enough to qualify as "Hillblazers"—Clinton's name for those who raised over $100,000. But so did a dozen other Chevy Chase residents.[4]

The day I was there for the 2016 primary, Hillary raked in 85 percent of the primary vote. She would a few months later also dominate the general election at this polling place, beating Donald Trump by 56 points. This tells us that wealthy, white Chevy Chase is very liberal. But a closer look tells us something more specific.

Compare Hillary's 56-point margin with 2012 when Obama defeated Mitt Romney by 31 points. There is something about Chevy Chase that makes it like Trump so much less than it likes Romney.

Chevy Chase's aversion to Trump appears much more clearly when we set aside the general election, which is a choice between a Republican and a Democrat. We need to focus instead on the Republican primary.

Trump performed dismally among Republican primary voters in the Village of Chevy Chase. John Kasich, the moderate of the three-man field, overwhelmingly won the village with 64 percent (compared with his 23 percent statewide). Donald Trump scored only 16 percent in the village (compared with his massive 54 percent statewide).

Chevy Chase's wealth is extreme, but the phenomenon in play here—wealthy, highly educated people in affluent communities eschewing Donald Trump and his proclamation that the American Dream is dead—is common. Chevy Chase is in Montgomery County, Maryland, which is the third-most-educated county in the nation, measured by advanced degrees—31.6 percent of adults over twenty-five have a graduate or professional degree.[5] (Nationally the rate is less than 12 percent.) The rest of the top four—Arlington and Alexandria in Virginia, and the District of Columbia (functionally a county for our purposes)—are among Trump's thirty-five worst counties in America.

You can spot the suburbs chock-full of advanced degrees and six-figure salaries by looking at a primary election map for counties that voted for John Kasich or Marco Rubio.

If we begin at the beginning of the nominating contests, in Iowa, Rubio won Polk County (home to prosperous Des Moines) and two adjacent counties, Story and Dallas, while Trump finished third in that trio of counties. Story County is home to Iowa State University. College towns across the country are also part of that Rubio-Kasich Country.

In Michigan, Kasich won Washtenaw County (home to the University of Michigan) and Kalamazoo County (home to Bell's Brewery and Western Michigan University). While Trump won every county in Pennsylvania's primary, Kasich's strongest showing wasn't his birthplace in Western Pennsylvania but the wealthy and highly educated "collar counties" around Philadelphia: Montgomery, Delaware, and Chester.

It's easy to see this pattern as a simple matter of ideology: Kasich was running as the moderate candidate, and colleges and rich people are more moderate. But during the primaries, Trump, by most measures, was less conservative than Kasich. Trump was more open to taxing the rich, wanted higher spending, was less enamored of free trade, and was more enthusiastic about a government role in health care.

The best explanation of why these pockets of elites rejected Trump is found in Trump's own words. He was selling a sense of decline and a desperate need to turn things around. In Kasich Country, though—in college towns and prosperous suburbs—people believed the American Dream was alive. These people also believed America was Great already, while much of the electorate didn't.

This isn't a universal rule, and it doesn't apply as well to the general election, when voters were picking between Trump and Hillary. But, as a general rule, you can use Trump's electoral strength in the early Republican primaries as a proxy for pessimism.

Trump Country, by this definition, is the places where hope is low and where the good life appears out of reach. So the flip side is this: Where Trump bombed—especially in the GOP primaries, but also compared with Romney in 2012—are the places where you can sniff out confidence, optimism, hope, and, if you'll pardon the treacle, the American Dream.

This story is far more important than political analysis. If we come to understand what makes Trump Country *Trump Country*, we can better understand the plight of the working class and the current economic and cultural splitting of this country. More important, discerning what made some of the country immune to Trump, aside from standard partisan allegiances, will show us where lie hope, mobility, and optimism.

What makes some places thrive, but others collapse?

This is a huge question. It's probably the central question of American society today, in which it is increasingly true that where you start (geographically and socioeconomically) determines where you end up. It's a question about growing inequality, stubborn pockets of immobility, and the cultural coming-apart we are suffering. Trump's shocking wins of the Republican primary and the general election were the most visible symptoms of this problem. If we start our search for the American Dream in Hillary's Village, the Village of Chevy Chase, it's tempting to come to a materialistic conclusion: People with money have hope, and the American Dream is alive and well in wealthy neighborhoods.

But a closer look at the primary map reveals other pockets of Trump opposition (in the early days)—another model of the good life. There's a different sort of village out there.

The Other Village

Oostburg couldn't be more different from Chevy Chase.

While Chevy Chase borders the District of Columbia, the Village of Oostburg sprouted up in the farm fields of Wisconsin. It's an outlying suburb of Sheboygan, Wisconsin—which is itself not exactly a booming metropolis.

The median home in Oostburg is worth $148,000, meaning you could buy ten homes in Oostburg for the price of one in Chevy Chase.[6] Oostburg is not poor: The average household earns $58,000, which is slightly above the national average. Even that slight advantage in household income has a clear—and salient—demographic explanation: Oostburg is a family town.

As a rule, different types of households nationwide have very different median incomes. Married-family households on average have higher incomes than non-married or nonfamily households. Oostburg is much denser with married-family households than the rest of the country is (two-thirds of all households in Oostburg compared with less than 50 percent nationwide), and that difference explains Oostburg's advantage over the national median.[7]

In other words, Oostburg's wealth is literally its family strength. And if you ask Oostburgers, they'll say their family strength is really community strength.

A few weeks before that Maryland primary, I spent a couple of days in Oostburg to cover the Wisconsin primaries. Just as I would visit Chevy Chase because of what made it stand out—its wealth—I picked Oostburg because of what made *it* stand out: its Dutchness.

Forty-five percent of Oostburg claims Dutch heritage according to the census. Another 42 percent are German. "Oostburg" is Dutch for East-town. Dutch settlers came here in the 1840s, and the signs of the Netherlands, such as tulips and miniature windmills, are everywhere. "If you ain't Dutch, you ain't much," was a phrase I first heard at the lunch counter of Judi's Place, the family-owned diner.

On Sunday morning at Judi's, I saw the truest manifestation of the town's Dutch heritage, and it wasn't the diner cuisine: Dozens of families streamed in to dine with their neighbors after service at one of the four Reformed churches in the village.

While there's no speaker series highlighting famous residents, the community's strength is unquestionable. Neighbors all greet each other at Judi's. Customers of the diner prepared and delivered frozen meals to the waitress, who was scheduled to have surgery the next day.

One man—a mechanic named Dan at the local farm—complained to me about the recent Christmas concert at the public school. He

couldn't get a seat in the gym for the concert, because all of his neighbors, even those with no school-age children, were taking up the
seats. One neighbor shrugged at Dan's plight of having no seat. "We
gotta come see our kids," the neighbor said. Again, the neighbor had
no children singing that day, but Oostburgers consider the kids of
Oostburg "our kids."

It takes a village, and Oostburg fits the bill of that village. But this
isn't Hillary's type of village politically. Trump won 80 to 13 in
November. Back in 2014, one blogger suggested Oostburg was the
most conservative town in Wisconsin.[8]

But just as in Chevy Chase, Oostburg's Republicans had no use for
Donald Trump in the primary election. Trump, who dominated most
of Wisconsin's rural areas, scored only 15 percent in the Republican
primary in this village. That's a familiar percentage—it's only one
point off from his total in Chevy Chase.

What made Oostburg so immune to Trump's appeal? It's inadequate
to say that Christian conservatives rejected this twice-divorced recently pro-choice New York playboy. In South Carolina, a few weeks
earlier, Trump won the evangelical vote with the same percentage (33
percent) that he won the rest of the state, according to exit polls.

Oostburg wasn't a mere outlier, either. If you wanted to predict
which rural, Christian counties would buck the Trump train when
they had a choice among Republicans like Cruz and Rubio and Kasich,
you could have done a lot worse than looking at a county's Dutch
population.

The country's Dutchest county, Sioux County, Iowa, was Trump's
worst county in the caucuses. The country's Dutchest region, western
Michigan, was a major hole in Trump's Great Lakes dominance in the
spring primaries.

It wasn't merely the Dutch who offered a conservative, religious
resistance to Trump in the primaries, though.

If any state embodied conservative resistance to Donald Trump, it
was Utah. In the general election, Trump didn't even get 50 percent
in the country's most Republican state. The state's Republican junior
senator, Mike Lee, refused to endorse Trump, and the state's GOP
governor was very late to do so—and later withdrew his endorsement.

And in Utah's caucuses, Donald Trump garnered only 14 percent, just about the same fraction he got in Oostburg and Chevy Chase.

Utah is the most religious state in the country by almost any measure. It also boasts strong families, a strong economy, and a strong safety net. No state has as much economic mobility—the ability to earn more than your parents—as Utah, according to researcher Raj Chetty.[9] The American Dream is alive and well there.

There's a pattern here, even if it's not immediately obvious.

In the 2016 Republican primaries and caucuses, across more than three thousand counties in the United States, only about 1 percent of counties gave Donald Trump less than 20 percent of the vote. We listed three of them above—Arlington, Alexandria, and Montgomery Counties—the most educated counties in the country. The rest, among counties with at least twenty thousand in population, are all, with one exception, exceptionally Mormon (at least 47 percent Mormon) or exceptionally Dutch (at least 25 percent Dutch).[10]

So you can boil the anti-Trump places in the early primaries down to two categories: (1) the highly educated elites and (2) the tight-knit religious communities. These look like two different (maybe even very different) types of places. But in a crucial sense, they're one type of place.

Here's the common thread between the Oostburgs and the Chevy Chases, and among analogues around the country:

Both villages have strong institutions of civil society—local governments, churches, country clubs, garden clubs, good public schools, and, in Oostburg's case, Judi's Place. Those community institutions constitute the infrastructure that is necessary to support families. And the institutions in turn are supported by families. Strong families are the precondition for the good life, and for mobility—the dream, grounded in realistic hope, that no matter your starting point, you can succeed and your children can do even better.

Trump Country

We began in the Villages of Chevy Chase and Oostburg because they were the exception. Trump dominated the Republican primaries across the country, winning the nomination fairly easily. He won the general election without a majority or even a plurality, sure, but 46 percent of the electorate is not shabby. He also showed strength in places where past Republican candidates had been weak, which is why he carried Ohio easily, and also won Pennsylvania, Wisconsin, and Michigan.

What Hillary Clinton thought was her "firewall" proved to be Trump Country.

I say Trump *Country* intentionally.

Sometimes when we talk about elections, we talk about demographics: the Soccer Mom Vote, the Hispanic Vote, the Youth Vote, or other ways of describing people by personal traits. If we imagine all Americans lined up in alphabetical order, or age order, and then sortable into these traits of race, age, sex, income, ideology, wealth, and so on, we commit a fatal abstraction. To understand the phenomenon of alienation and coming apart, we need to do more than consider *who* these people are. We need to consider *where* they are.

Geography, more than we typically assume, is destiny.

Employment is far worse in rural counties, but not only in rural counties. Most of *Hillbilly Elegy's* tale of alienation took place in the Ohio suburb of Middletown. Death rates, especially death by suicide and overdose, correlated with Trump's best counties (again his strong primary showings and his increases over the typical Republican). Educational attainment is lower in Trump Country. More people are on unemployment. More people are on disability.

These economic indicators are devastating, and crucial. But more telling are the social indicators. More men have dropped out of the workforce. Marriage rates are lower. Illegitimacy is higher. Divorce is higher.

Trump did better in the primaries among people who didn't go to church, polls show. "Trump trailed Ted Cruz by 15 points among Republicans who attended religious services every week," Peter Beinart reported. "But he led Cruz by a whopping 27 points among those who did not."

When data show that the white working class was Trump's base, it's easy to see the phrase "white working class" as a simple statement of race and income. It's more important, though, as a description of a social class—even a way of life. "White working-class Americans of all ages," writes Emma Green in the *Atlantic*, citing research by the Public Religion Research Institute and the *Atlantic*, "were much less likely than their college-educated peers to participate in sports teams, book clubs, or neighborhood associations—55 percent vs. 31 percent said they seldom or never participated in those kinds of activities."[11]

This had political salience. That PRRI poll, taken in mid-primaries, when Ted Cruz was the last viable challenger, found Trump leading among GOP voters 37 to 31. But among GOP voters who were "civically disengaged," Trump led 50 to 24.

Oostburg voted Cruz and Chevy Chase voted Kasich. Within the context of Republicans, churchgoing white Christians are conservative while wealthy, highly educated white suburbanites are moderates. You could see these two things as opposites, but the stories of Kasich Country and Cruz Country are the same story: People enmeshed in strong communities rejected Trump in the early primaries while people alienated, abandoned, lacking social ties and community rushed to him immediately.

Trump's best large county in the Iowa caucuses, Pottawattamie, had the weakest civil society—churches, neighborhood groups, volunteering, voting—of any large county in Iowa, and is known instead for its neon-lighted casinos erected to bring in out-of-state gamblers. His best small county is notable mostly for church closures and the shuttering of its largest employer in early 2016. It also ranks at the bottom of the state in widely used measures of civil society.

His other best places in those early primaries—places like Buchanan County, Virginia; and Fayette County, Pennsylvania—looked similarly *vacant*.

Everyone trying to explain Trump's rise early on noted that he had "tapped into a deep sense of frustration." That phrase became a cliché, but it was true. Articulating that frustration precisely and explaining its causes were a lot harder. Almost every politician posited that the frustration happened to reflect the very criticism that same politician already had of current affairs: war, national debt, insufficient safety net, overgenerous safety net, bank profits, et cetera.

After the election, conservative intellectual Yuval Levin put his finger on it best. "At the root of the most significant problems America faces at home is the weakening of our core institutions—family and community, church and school, business and labor associations, civic and fraternal organizations."[12]

To explain Trump's core supporters, many commentators pointed to the factories that were closing, but they should have been pointing to the churches that were closing.

Trump was one symptom, which traveled together with the other symptoms of working-class woe—the deaths, the dropping out of the workforce, the poverty, the illegitimacy. *Idleness* is the word scholar Nick Eberstadt used to describe the central problem of the working class. Charles Murray documented the collapse of certain virtues in white working-class America. It's easy to see these judgments as attacks. "Idleness," after all, is often counted as a root of many sins.

But if we see the problem as primarily a dissolution of civil society, a collapse of community, then it becomes clear that "idleness," if you want to call it that, can be understood not as a sin but as an *affliction*. These people have been deprived of meaningful things to do.

In places like Chevy Chase or Oostburg, people are *given* things to do. Any longtime member of a robust religious congregation has laughed and warned someone, "Oh, don't go talk to Sally Davis unless you want to be given some ministry to run." If you belong to a small neighborhood swimming pool, you probably can spot the look in the eye of the board member when he's coming over to ask for volunteers.

Our bosses, our wives, our husbands, our neighbors, and our kids' swim coaches rope us into stuff. Those of us tangled up in thick webs of civil society show industriousness not mostly because we are self-starters. Our industriousness is thrust upon us.

Strong communities function not only as safety nets and sources of knowledge and wisdom, but also as the grounds on which people can exercise their social and political muscles. These are where we find our purpose.

If we want to say that parts of America like Fayette, Pottawattamie, and Buchanan Counties are low on virtue, we need to recall that virtue is not some inherent inner state. Virtue is a habit. As a habit, it requires action. And most human actions that are tied up with virtue

are human *inter*actions. Many virtues, if not most, are developed socially. Anne Case and Angus Deaton, trying to figure out the causes
of a disturbing rise in middle-aged deaths, granted that an erosion of
virtues is likely part of it, but they added, "Virtue is easier to maintain in a supportive environment."[13]

Someone lacking the proper social settings is as handicapped on
virtues as an athlete without access to proper training facilities,
coaching, or even opponents. In desiccated communities, men and women
lack these opportunities. A sociologist might say such communities
are poor in terms of *social capital*.

Sociologist Robert Putnam defines *social capital* as "social networks
and the associated norms of reciprocity and trustworthiness." Places
poor in social capital are places with fewer and weaker networks and
thus less trust.

This dissolution of civil society leaves people alienated. Robert
Nisbet, author of *The Quest for Community*, defined *alienation* this
way: "The state of mind that can find a social order remote, incompre-
hensible, or fraudulent; beyond real hope or desire; inviting apathy,
boredom, or even hostility." The alienated individual "not only does
not feel a part of the social order; he has lost interest in being a part
of it."[14]

Alienation is the disease of working-class America. Its most important accompaniment is family collapse. Strong families are the
necessary condition of the good life, of economic mobility, and of the
American Dream. The story of Election 2016, the story of the working-
class struggle in America, the story of rising suicides and crumbling
families, and the story of growing inequality and falling economic
mobility, is properly understood as the story of the dissolution of civil
society.

Why do so many people believe the American Dream is dead? I
think the answer is this: because strong communities have crumbled,
and much of America has been left abandoned, without the web of
human connections and institutions that make the good life possible.
More of America is a wasteland of alienation. Less of America is the
"village."

Can this change?

America has more Chevy Chases today than it did a generation ago, but that's because wealthy people are clustering more. Making more Chevy Chases is a zero-sum game: It means drawing the skilled, the active, the educated, the leaders out of other communities and concentrating them in places where normal folk can't afford a house. There is also a clear limit on how many pockets of elites America can have, because by definition, the elites are few.

But remember the second village. There could, conceivably, be more Oostburgs. The raw material is more renewable there, and arguably it used to be more plentiful and could be again. It's a sense of duty to one's neighbors—a duty that includes a sense of duty to one's family. It's a sense of both being looked after and being needed. It's a sense of a common, higher purpose. It's shared, resilient mediating institutions. And frankly, in America at least, that common purpose is a common faith, and those mediating institutions are really the church.

Seek the *shalom* of the city to which I have carried you into exile.
Pray to the Lord for it, for in its *shalom* will be your *shalom*.

—JEREMIAH 29:7

The Hebrew word *shalom* is typically understood as "peace" and often gets translated here as "prosperity." These two divergent translations show the breadth of meaning of this word. "Welfare" is another common translation in this passage.

This word's meaning is broad, because the good it tries to convey is broad. It could be translated as "flourishing" or "well-being."

Jeremiah, in this letter to the exiles, relays from God a striking causal statement. God says that an individual's flourishing relies on something very worldly: the city. Only if the city flourishes can you flourish. If the city doesn't flourish, you cannot flourish.

CHAPTER 2

Progress at a Price

The Changing American Dream, 1955-2018

The Ohio River starts in Pittsburgh where two smaller rivers meet. The Allegheny flows in from coal country off to the northeast. The Monongahela ambles up from West Virginia. That woody and hilly region south of Pittsburgh is called the Mon Valley, and it once had a humming economy that earned the envy of other regions.

The Pittsburgh Steel Company in 1901 chose a spot forty miles up-river from Pittsburgh, on the Monongahela, to erect a steel mill. The mill covered a two-mile stretch of Monongahela's banks.[1] Monessen had been a sleepy farm town a few years before, but wealthy investors (including future U.S. senator and U.S. attorney general Philander C. Knox) saw its potential, given the river, the rail line, and the nearby coal that would power the plant. A tin mill had popped up a few years before the steel plant, followed by a hoop mill.

Pittsburgh Steel, the sort of scrappy upstart that populates tales of the American Dream, bought the land. Pittsburgh Steel was one of a handful of independent steel companies owned by prominent local citizens, which collectively frustrated U.S. Steel's ambitions to control the whole industry and thus set prices.

Within a year, the mill employed 3,000 people. Those 3,000 Pennsylvanians made many steel products, but most of all they made nails.

The inventor of the chain-link fence, J. Walter Page, also built a factory in Monessen soon after. These factories, making nails and wire, *made* the local economy. The Pittsburgh Steel plant expanded during World War I, and for decades it continued to hum. Monessen's population exploded from 2,200 people in 1900 to more than 11,000 a decade later. Then it kept climbing.

Pittsburgh Steel became the dominant factory in the Mon Valley, and the company survived the Great Depression. The tanks and planes that saved Europe were made in the Mon and Allegheny Valleys, and this was good for Monessen. The end of the war wasn't the end of happy days for the plant. A new company president, Avery Adams, took over in 1950 and modernized the mill; this led to record profits of $7.5 million in 1955.

Times were good. They were good enough that this very point in time and place, the Mon Valley in 1955, is a common image of the American Dream.

The Golden Age

The U.S. economy grew at a mind-bending 11.9 percent rate in the first quarter of 1955. It would grow at 7.1 percent over the course of the whole year.

A decade after World War II, the future looked bright—and it was. Economic mobility is at the heart of the American Dream, and mobility was very real back then. A kid graduating from high school in 1958 (and thus born in 1940) had a 90 percent chance of earning more money than his parents.[2]

Up and down the income scale, the economy was robust. Blue-collar workers made up about one-third of the workforce, and three-fourths of them enjoyed membership in unions.[3] Businesses, booming, had bought peace with Big Labor. The result was reliable labor, reliable pay, and good retirement.

The old folks back then were propped up by Social Security, funded by 8.6 workers for every retiree. Able-bodied men were expected to work, and almost all of them did. The unemployment rate in July 1955 was 4.0 percent. If a household was headed by adults in their thirties or forties, odds were overwhelming (above 80 percent) that at least one adult worked forty hours a week[4]—this was true even for families whose head didn't go to college.

Good breadwinner jobs for white-collar and blue-collar men allowed 80 percent of wives with young children to stay at home.[5]

America was fairly equal, economically, and inequality was shrinking. The average household was within striking distance of the top 10 percent of households, with income about 33 percent lower (these days, the shortfall is about 60 percent).[6]

That relative equality extended beyond the economic and into the social realm.

Marriage was the norm. Nearly 90 percent of all adults were married by age thirty in the mid-1950s. This norm applied roughly equally to both white-collar adults and working-class adults.[7] Almost all babies were born to married couples. Ninety percent of all first births occurred after the parents' marriage (about one in nine of those infants was conceived before the marriage).[8]

Wealthy Americans were a bit more likely to go to church than middle-class and poorer Americans, but that difference was shrinking. Religion was on the rise. "Ever since the nation's founding," religious historian Phillip Hammond would note, "a higher and higher proportion of Americans have affiliated with a church or synagogue—right through the 1950s."

"Churches and synagogues were packed," sociologist Robert Putnam would write decades later, "as more Americans worshiped together than only a few decades earlier, perhaps more than ever in American history."[9]

American towns have always had a right side of the tracks and a wrong side, but when you looked at the big picture in the 1950s, the data suggest that the rich and poor were fairly likely to live side by side.[10]

"Most people can be trusted," a vast majority of Americans agreed. About two-thirds of Americans agreed with that idea right after the war, and that number would rise to three-fourths by the mid-1960s.[11]

Civil society was robust and climbing. For instance, half of all

families had a parent in the PTA in 1959. Sociologists Daniel Bell and
Virginia Held would write during the 1960s: "There is more participation than ever before in America . . . and more opportunity for the
active interested person to express his political and social concerns."[12]
Kiwanis Clubs, bowling leagues, American Legion, labor unions, and
local athletic associations were all booming.

The American Dream was alive and well for the type of guy who
worked in a steel mill in the Mon Valley. But times, of course, were
changing.

Men Who Make Nails

The year 1955, it would turn out, was the peak year for Monessen's
steel mill. For one thing, that was when Europe was finally getting
back on its feet. When we Americans think of the time line of World
War II, we think: Pearl Harbor; war abroad and austerity at home;
then Victory! Happy Days Are Here Again!

That's because the war was fought not here but *over there*. Europe
was devastated by the war—physically wrecked and bombed to rubble
in London, Berlin, and other places. Politically upended. The body
count was even higher. A decade after the war ended, the continent
was finally recovering in the mid-1950s.

One result of Europe's resurgence: Foreign steel mills in the late
1950s would sell an average of 1.3 million tons of products in the
United States. The nail makers of Monessen had competition.

Then on April 29, 1959, a Canadian icebreaker called the *d'Iberville*
made a historic trip, passing through the newly completed Saint
Lawrence Seaway. The seaway was a joint U.S.-Canadian project that
opened the Great Lakes up to massive ships from the Atlantic Ocean.

It was a huge breakthrough for transatlantic trade. It would make
the world richer by greasing the skids of global trade.

However, the Saint Lawrence Seaway also diminished the Monongahela's status as a tributary of the Ohio, which is in turn a tributary
of the Mississippi River; it wasn't as crucial as it once was. Imports of
steel-mill products tripled from 1958 to 1959. For the first time, the

United States imported more steel-mill products than it exported. By 1965, ten million tons of steel-mill products were entering the United States annually, more than ten times the imports during Monessen's golden year just a decade earlier. Imports accounted for about 10 percent of all U.S. steel use.

"Off-shore producers had literally invaded the U.S. market," one history of the Monessen plant put it, "selling their wares at prices twenty to thirty percent below those of American firms."[13] The European plants were newer and more efficient. Also, they paid much lower wages. This allowed them to sell their steel more cheaply. One of the most commonly imported steel products was the humble nail—the heart of the Pittsburgh Steel plant in Monessen. In June 1966, the company announced that it would phase out production of nails. Six years later, the entire rod and wire division—once the core of the steel mill that was the core of Monessen—was gone.

Killing this division proved a shrewd move for the company. The steel mill came out sounder, and so the town benefited. It was the sort of modernization and adaptation that comes with capitalism.

As competition grew fiercer, Pittsburgh Steel sought economies of scale. In 1968 the company bought up Wheeling Steel, which produced flat-rolled steel at its plants on the Ohio River. This combination proved wise, and the Wheeling-Pittsburgh steel company was solid. Steel demand went up in the 1970s, reversing its slow fall since the *d'Iberville*'s voyage. In the early 1970s, prices jumped about 20 percent and would stay high for years.

In 1969, up north in Ohio, a different river lined with steel mills had made the news. Floating in the Cuyahoga, near the Republic Steel mill in Cleveland, a pile of oily junk caught fire on a June Sunday. The river fire was extinguished in about half an hour.

When *Time* magazine covered the fire a month later, the smallness of the blaze presented a problem: there were no photos of it. So instead, *Time* ran a picture from a much bigger fire on the same river seventeen years earlier. The pictured inferno, with towers of black smoke, caught America's attention and helped drive the environmental movement into full gear. The following year, the first Earth Day occurred. Two years later, Congress passed the Clean Water Act.

More environmental regulations came and helped clean rivers like the Cuyahoga and the Monongahela.

Progress, as always, came at a cost. The regulations that protected the rivers also cut into profits of the Wheeling-Pittsburgh mill.

At the same time, advances in steel production were allowing smaller mills to pop up. American manufacturers loved the glut of steel, both from these domestic mini-mills and from burgeoning international trade. Steel prices fell steadily through the late 1970s.

The Wheeling-Pittsburgh steel company responded by cutting a few thousand jobs in Monessen, reducing the workforce from 18,000 in 1972 to 13,500 in 1978.

New management looked at the challenges and changes the way good businessmen always do. They pledged to modernize. The layoffs throughout the 1970s presented the same challenge to the men of the Mon Valley: In this modern economy, they would have to adapt.

Workers had to adapt, too. Adaptation included moving beyond the idea of the lone breadwinner with a good union manufacturing job. Maybe the Mrs. would be the big earner. The world was changing, after all, and the Pittsburgh region wasn't going to be left behind. That's evident if you visit the town today.

Pittsburgh and Paris

"I was elected to represent the citizens of Pittsburgh, not Paris," President Trump said in the summer of 2017. It was a brilliant rhetorical flourish to justify his decision to withdraw the United States from the Paris climate accords, a deal he said served the rest of the world more than the United States. Invoking Pittsburgh invoked U.S. manufacturing, and coal country in particular.

Pittsburgh is the stereotypical blue-collar, rust-belt town. The football team is called the Steelers, after all. A federally funded history of the Monongahela, Allegheny, and Ohio Valleys in western Pennsylvania is called "rivers of steel." Political reporters and sportswriters are prone to call the city "gritty."

Trump's pitting Pittsburgh against Paris was an alliterative echo of his campaign theme, that he was standing up for the working man and would bring back the industrial glory of the golden age.

Critics immediately noted the problem: Pittsburgh proper didn't vote for Trump, and Pittsburgh's economy isn't a steel-dependent depression case.

Pittsburgh's economy in 2017 was coming out of a decade of growth. The per capita gross domestic product had jumped 18.1 percent from 2006 to 2016—the U.S. economy had increased only 4.4 percent over that same period. As a result, Pittsburgh went from a per capita GDP that was far below the nation as a whole to one that was larger in 2016. In other words, Pittsburgh by 2016 was above average in economic productivity.

Pittsburgh has a dynamic economy, with new industries entering the city, filling the voids left decades ago by the collapse of the steel industry. Manufacturing was no longer central—only about 7,300 Pittsburghers worked in manufacturing during the 2012 economic census of the city.[14] By comparison, there were more than twice as many retail jobs in the city, and nearly five times as many finance jobs. There were about nine times as many health-sector workers in Pittsburgh in 2012 as there were manufacturing workers. One 2017 news story said renewable energy employs more people in Pittsburgh than steel does.[15]

And Pittsburgh wasn't Trump Country. About 75 percent of voters inside city limits voted for Hillary Clinton. Pittsburgh mayor Bill Peduto, a Democrat, had some fun with these facts, pointing out that Trump was trounced in Pittsburgh, and declaring that his city stood with Paris over Trump. Later that week, Peduto cowrote a *New York Times* op-ed with Paris mayor Anne Hidalgo.

"As the sun sets each evening on the Allegheny River," the mayors wrote, "Pittsburgh's Rachel Carson Bridge lights up with 27,000 multi-colored bulbs. This nightly display downtown in the City of Bridges is powered entirely by 16 wind turbines attached to the arches of the bridge. It's just one example of how a city once famous for its steel mills has emerged as a trailblazer in environmental innovation."[16]

The changes the U.S. economy experienced have upended Pittsburgh, but they haven't left the city flat on its back. The city and its workers have adapted, and, as Mayor Peduto tells it, progressed.

What Peduto called progress, of course, Trump called decline.

This debate, between Trump's tale of decline and Peduto's story of adaptation and progress, is the debate over how to understand the country's changes since 1955. It was arguably the central debate of the 2016 election. And sometimes it seemed that different sides were looking at two different countries.

Changes

"I'm tired of getting shafted and not making good money."

Bald, avuncular, and foulmouthed, Jeff Mason is a burly guy from Pittsburgh. I met him outside a Trump rally where he laid out a common idea of the American Dream: "I'm hoping for a future for my kids. I think the key—the secret—to life is for your kids to do better than you, and I don't want my kids to go down the path that I go down."

Mason's path included a stint as a repo man in Pittsburgh: He towed cars whose owners had defaulted on their loans. This was during the Great Recession of 2008–2009, and so plenty of people were missing car payments. Mason had found income in others' economic woe. He told me that his conscience made him quit. Outside of capitalizing on the credit crisis, he found "there was no jobs" in the Pittsburgh area.

Mason packed up his family and moved down to South Carolina, where he spent six months searching for a job. When we met, in January 2016, he was working six days a week behind the wheel of a delivery truck, bringing people their groceries. Mason told me he was making less than $14 an hour to support his family.

"What happened to the twenty-dollar-an-hour jobs?" he asked. "They're gone."

Mason blamed China and immigration. "Close the borders. Send 'em back home," Mason proposed. "Let's get jobs here first."

Across the country, you can hear the same complaints from working men and women—or formerly working men and women. "Free trade and NAFTA [North American Free Trade Agreement] are the worst things that have happened to the working man," Tracy Pritchard told me outside a General Electric plant in Indiana in 2005.

This was Trump's account. "We're losing our jobs to everybody," Trump would say. "To places like China. Vietnam is the new hot one—they're taking our jobs. Mexico always."[17]

So in 2016, Trump came to Western Pennsylvania and visited Monessen, where the old steel mill's memory still looms. Trump said, "Globalization has made the financial elite who donate to politicians very wealthy. But it has left millions of our workers with nothing but poverty and heartache."

Andrew Duda Sr., who used to make nails, agreed. He worked at the Pittsburgh Steel plant for decades, including through its death throes. "When Trump talks about the trade deals, he's a hundred percent right," Duda told me in Vargo's Newsstand in Fayette City just around the river's bend from where the mill used to be. "That NAFTA—that was the worst thing."

But just as with Trump's story of Pittsburgh, the claims that trade and immigration are destructive crash pretty hard into some economic facts. Yes, immigrants and free trade have changed the U.S. economy, but nearly every economist agrees that these things have provided a net gain to the country.

"The presence of all immigrant workers (legal and illegal) in the labor market makes the U.S. economy (GDP) an estimated 11 percent larger ($1.6 trillion) each year," Harvard's George Borjas, a leading immigration scholar, wrote in a 2013 study.[18] On one level, that's obvious: More immigration means a bigger population, and a bigger population will produce more goods and services, which is what GDP measures. Immigrants come here, and they work; thus, more stuff is getting done or made.

Employers pay almost that same $1.6 trillion to immigrants in the form of wages and benefits, Borjas finds. But on net, immigrants produce more than they take in. Borjas calculates an "immigration surplus," defined as "the benefit accruing to the native-born population, including both workers, owners of firms, and other users of the services provided by immigrants." That surplus is an impressive $35 billion a year. By this math, all the people who were already in the country are richer in aggregate by $35 billion per year, or 0.2 percent, because of immigrants.

Regarding international trade, the gain is even cleaner. Perhaps the closest thing to a consensus on policy among economists is that free trade benefits all nations involved. "If economists ruled the world," wrote Nobel Prize–winning economist Paul Krugman, "there would be no need for a World Trade Organization. The economist's case for free trade is essentially a unilateral case—that is, it says that a country serves its own interests by pursuing free trade regardless of what other countries may do."[19]

Greater international trade means more exports for the United States, plus cheaper goods for the United States. For one thing, this means middle-class families can better afford what they need, and maybe have something left over for a vacation or a splurge. Also, it means U.S. manufacturers get cheaper inputs. If General Motors can buy Chinese steel, this brings down the price GM has to pay to manufacture a car. This translates into more cars, higher pay, and cheaper cars.

The U.S. economy was $2.1 trillion larger in 2016 thanks to the expansion of global trade since 1950, economists writing for the Peterson Institute for International Economics estimated in 2017.[20] That translates to more than $7,000 per person in 2016. "Disproportionate gains probably accrue to poorer households," the economists wrote, undermining Trump's populist take on trade.

The 1960s and 1970s saw the U.S. economy open up to many more immigrants and much more international trade. The 2000s and early 2010s saw even more. And in those years, while there have been ups and downs, the economy has flourished.

Economic Progress

The stock market is the most visible thermometer of our economy. The market's falls characterized both the Great Depression and the Great Recession, and its relentless climb marked the booms of the Reagan and Clinton years. Since March 2009, most of the stock market's movement has been upward.

Since the peak of the financial crisis in March 2009, it's been nearly a decade of up. The Dow doubled in Obama's first term, surpassed the 2007 record highs in early 2013, and then kept climbing.

The market hasn't merely *recovered* from the financial crisis; it is climbing faster than ever, and this was true during the 2016 election. When Trump announced his candidacy, the Dow was within 1 percent of an all-time high. The day before Trump accepted the nomination, the Dow had hit a new all-time high of 18,595. A massive market rally in Trump's first months in office brought the Dow past 20,000 for the first time. In Trump's first year, the Dow hit 26,000.

Interest rates and mortgage rates have been historically low, making home ownership—often sold as the American Dream—more accessible to more people. Americans are nearly twice as likely to own their home as to rent.[21]

Consumer confidence, a key economic indicator, generally rose from its depths just after the credit crisis and by 2016 had returned to the normal post–World War II levels.[22]

Most important—and most contradictory of the complaints from the Jeff Masons and Donald Trumps of the world—has been the job market, especially since 2014. The unemployment rate dropped below 4 percent in 2018. That's lower than about 90 percent of the time since 1955.

So why all the grousing?

Yes, it was good to be a steelworker in the Mon Valley in 1955. Things changed after that. From thirty thousand feet, that change looks like the typical sort of adaptation that happens in modern life and in all of capitalism. When you look at Pittsburgh today—as it really is, and not as Trump pictures it—it's easy to conclude that the American Dream is doing just fine.

Trump's appeal, of course, was his assertion of the opposite reality—his lamentation that the American Dream was dead. Where did that claim come from, and why did it resonate? Was it mere fiction? Did it tap into some legitimate fear or anxiety?

Critics of Trump and of his supporters had an explanation for the attitudes held by guys like Jeff Mason and Andrew Duda. And it wasn't a flattering one.

CHAPTER 3

"They've Chosen Not to Keep Up"

Is it Economics or Culture?

I f you look at the map of the United States," Hillary Clinton told a Mumbai audience in 2018, "there's all that red in the middle where Trump won. I win the coast, I win, you know, Illinois and Minnesota, places like that."

What did "places like that" mean?

"I won the places that represent two-thirds of America's gross domestic product," Clinton explained. "So I won the places that are optimistic, diverse, dynamic, moving forward. And his whole campaign, 'Make America Great Again,' was looking backwards."

Then she characterized the Trump message that she says won over those voters in the unproductive middle of the country: "You know, you didn't like black people getting rights, you don't like women getting jobs, you don't want to see that Indian American succeeding more than you are, whatever your problem is, I am going to solve it."[1]

While it got headlines and evoked outrage, Hillary's wasn't an original analysis. It was a fairly standard argument from 2015 on. The productive people backed her, she explained, and her opponents' supporters were swayed by arguments stoking cultural resentment. *Times were changing for the better*, in other words, *and some guys who couldn't keep up didn't like it.*

"Many of these people haven't been left behind," liberal journalist Sean Illing put it; "they've chosen not to keep up. But the sense of victimization appears to overwhelm everything else."[2]

There was a deeper criticism embedded in this one.

ECONOMIC ANXIETY DIDN'T MAKE PEOPLE VOTE FOR TRUMP, RACISM DID was the blunt headline at the liberal magazine the *Nation* in May 2017. The writers had analyzed the American National Election Studies survey of four thousand voters. "[W]e found little evidence to suggest individual economic distress benefited Trump," the two wrote.[3]

"It wasn't the economy, but racism and xenophobia, that explains Trump's rise," liberal website Vox.com explained.[4]

Citing data that individuals "who reported being in fair or poor financial shape were 1.7 times more likely to support Clinton," the liberal writer said, "This finding rebukes the common sentiment that poor white Americans came out in droves to put Trump over the top in 2016."

One typical headline read, IT WAS THE RACISM, STUPID: WHITE WORKING-CLASS "ECONOMIC ANXIETY" IS A ZOMBIE IDEA THAT NEEDS TO DIE. The article pointed out that "the typical Trump supporter comes from a household that earns $72,000 a year—significantly above the national average."[5]

Complaints about immigration were really complaints about dark-skinned foreigners, this line of argument went—*the economic dimension was a cover story. Complaints about jobs going overseas were racially charged excuses of people who couldn't adapt or wouldn't move. It wasn't the economic nationalism that appealed to these people, it was the rank bigotry. And what they were objecting to was really progress.*

Should the United States have left the Saint Lawrence River—and thus the Great Lakes—unnavigable for larger ships? Should steel companies have been prohibited from modernizing, so the Pittsburgh-Wheeling plant in Monessen could have kept it 1955 forever? Should America have not helped Europe's economy recover, so that steel competition would have stayed at pre-1955 levels?

Nostalgia

It was in early January 2016, outside the basketball arena at Winthrop University in Rock Hill, South Carolina, that I met Kent Armstrong. Armstrong wore a red MAKE AMERICA GREAT AGAIN hat and scarf while waiting in line for a Trump rally. Armstrong didn't need Trump to convince him the American Dream was dead.

Armstrong told me of a moment a few years ago, on a public golf course, when he struck up a conversation with a peer who was working as a park ranger. "He said to me, 'If you lived in the sixties, you've probably seen this country the best it will ever be.'"

Armstrong wasn't sure back then, but by 2016 he was convinced. He didn't study socioeconomic data. He was arguing from his heart. "We had, I guess, a more God-fearing country," was his explanation.

A few yards ahead of Armstrong in line at the rally were Bob Garrett Sr. and Bob Garrett Jr. Both Bobs had specific complaints about the economy and immigration, but Bob Sr. at one point turned to the past and said simply, "I liked it better then. It was better to be an American."

It's easy to accuse Armstrong and Garrett of nostalgia. "People say 'back in my day, [culture/this city/society] was better,'" Josh Barro, a socially liberal thirtysomething New York–based commentator, tweeted around the same time, "but they really mean 'back in my day, I was younger and thinner.'"[6]

If these laments about a lost Golden Era are mere nostalgia, then "Make America Great Again" is nothing but an airy dream. At best it's "Make Me Young and Thin Again."

The data in the previous chapter bolster Armstrong's and Garrett's argument, though. Economic equality, employment, wages, family strength, marriage, religion—all those numbers were better in the 1950s and 1960s.

There are plenty of people, however, who can't look back at 1955 or 1960 as the good old days. Professional-minded women, for one, are far better off today. In 1960, less than 35 percent of women were in

the workforce. Now, *most* women are working or seeking work—
nearly 60 percent.

The average woman earned about two-thirds as much as the average
man in 1979 (as far back as the data go), and by the 2010s, that portion
hit 90 percent.[7]

Nearly any corner of society that used to be men-only is now open
to women. For one visible example: In 1955, the U.S. Senate had only
one woman, and only nine women had ever served in that chamber,
almost all appointed to fill out their late husbands' terms. In 2018,
twenty-two women served in the Senate.

Meanwhile, women have gone from unwelcome at many colleges
and rare at many others to dominant at both college and grad
school. A majority of U.S. grad students in 2017 were women.[8]
More money, more education, and more occupations open to them
mean more autonomy for women.

And the most obvious retort to the "golden days" view of 1955
is the plight of African Americans. Segregation was still the law of
the land back then, and discrimination was far more open and ram-
pant than it is now. The KKK planted fifteen sticks of dynamite at
the Sixteenth Street Baptist Church in Alabama in September 1963,
killing four. Blacks were told to settle for segregation and inequality,
and to sit quietly at the back of the bus or suffer this sort of terror
in response.

While racism and racial inequality persist, attitudes have improved
immensely, and most (though not all) of the facts on the ground have
improved in black America as well.

Similar stories can be told for other minority groups and immigrants. The period from 1960 to today has not been the tale of decline
Garrett or Armstrong would tell, but it has instead been a bumpy,
slow, and incomplete march to equality of opportunity. Here was a
telling poll finding: While there's plenty of reason to believe men
still have it easier than women, a majority of women disagreed with
that notion in a recent Pew poll—59 percent of women say either (a)
women have it easier, or (b) there is no difference.[9]

So the view of 1955 as a Golden Age might be true for the white,
non-college-educated Christian male. What has happened since then

could be seen as the opening of the American Dream to other sorts of people.

Individualism and Solidarity

One way to view the progress since 1955 is as the advance of individualism. But oddly enough, it's also a time of increasing centralization. These two ideas sound contradictory, but they have both been at the heart of the cultural changes for sixty-plus years.[10]

Rising individualism may be the easiest to see. People like to describe the 1950s as a decade of conformity. Some of that "conformity" was really the virtues of the era, such as more income equality and more intact families. But the most common "conformity" critique of the 1950s, which is surely not all wrong, is that individual choice was repressed by overbearing cultural expectations and even by the law.

Increased access to education, money, and career options for women and racial minorities meant increased *autonomy*. It meant they had more control over what they did with their lives. For women, that might or might not include marriage. With or without marriage, it might or might not include children. And with or without marriage or kids, life might or might not include a career and full-time job.

Thanks to changing public morality, American culture now accepts and embraces all sorts. Gay men and women become congressmen, senators, governors, and television anchors. A divorcée or a single mother is not scorned or shamed as she may have been in 1955. (Heck, a thrice-married man open about his infidelity has become president.)

Cultural openness to difference is evident in things small as well as big. For instance, dyeing one's hair purple or getting tattoos has gone from radical to clichéd to not even noteworthy.

Technology has also turbocharged individualism. Instead of a couple of television networks that everybody watched, we have hundreds of channels on television, and infinite "channels" on the Internet. Social media, meanwhile, enables people to find groups that share their eclectic interests.

In economics, there's an analogous story. Regulation has generally receded since the 1960s, and innovation has meant a million different business models and business ideas.

But at the same time as all this centrifugal motion, the progress since 1955 has involved centripetal force. Most important, the civil rights movement happened because the federal government stepped up and took power from states, localities, and even local businessmen. There was a centralized decision that we wouldn't allow segregation, and a strong central government enforced that decision.

The Great Society included some efforts to juice local institutions, but its biggest impact was in centralizing the safety net. Medicare and Medicaid were the most obvious examples of this. These new programs helped make sure fewer people died because of poverty.

And the same media technology that has helped people choose their own narrow silo has also resulted in an increasingly centralized focus in news and public affairs. From Maine to Los Angeles, those who follow government and the news are following the same news about the same figures. Politics are more nationalized.

These seemingly conflicting trends of centralization and individualism have worked to keep people out of poverty, expand individual autonomy, and boost equality of opportunity. As with all changes, along with winners, there are also losers.

The Protected Provincials

In the 1950s, the white male American was protected from competition. Some of the barriers were explicit. Some were less formal. Some were codified in law, and some were simply the consequence of economic reality. One barrier until 1959 was the unnavigability of the Saint Lawrence Seaway. The many barriers obstructed competition by African Americans, women, immigrants, would-be immigrants, and factory workers in China, among others. It's probably not a coincidence that the 1950s, the peak decade in American manufacturing jobs by some measures, was the decade when Europe was still recovering from World War II and thus unable to compete as fiercely against the United States.

And this protection didn't end in 1955 or even in 1960 or 1970. Discrimination, protectionism, restrictions on immigration, and natural frictions persist to this day. The barriers have eroded plenty, though, in recent decades, freeing up competition.

One of the most consequential dams to break was the one keeping women from competing fully in the workforce. More opportunity for women, minorities, foreigners, and immigrants meant a harder time for white male Americans.

In this light, Hillary's harsh critique of Trump Country has some merit. Asserting that America was once great can be seen as looking back at lost protection and privilege.

While Trump's success caused plenty of agitation among liberals (and later depression), you couldn't help noticing an undercurrent of triumphalism—a belief that those "on the right side of history" would inevitably win and maybe were already winning. Hillary bragged that she won the economically productive, "forward-looking" places—the *places of the future*. The implication was that Trump represented a last gasp of a dying regime that was falling to social progress and equality, and that the complaining white males were lamenting only their lost privilege.

"Yes, the world has changed," journalist Sean Illing acknowledged in an interview with an author studying the rural working class. "[I]t's always changing. And I understand the sense of loss some people feel because of that, but at some point, we have to acknowledge that culture evolves and stop trying to unwind the historical clock."

Illing asserted that the suffering parts of the world are weighed down by "nostalgia for a bygone world or a world that probably never really existed in the first place."[11]

"America is now two countries," Michelle Goldberg, a smart millennial liberal, wrote in her debut *New York Times* column in 2017, "eyeing each other across a chasm of distrust and contempt. One is urban, diverse and outward-looking. This is the America that's growing. The other is white, provincial and culturally revanchist."[12]

The slightly sneering phrase "provincial and culturally revanchist" is evocative. Both adjectives are geographically rooted. "Provincial" literally means *from the provinces*, that is, from the countryside—*not* from the city. It's the opposite of *urbane*. *Revanchist* is a word going back to the Franco-Prussian War in the 1870s. The revanchists were the Frenchmen dead set on reclaiming the territory of Alsace-Lorraine from the Germans who had conquered it. With the accusation "culturally revanchist," Goldberg is saying that aging Middle America wants to take back the parts of the culture that the Left has seized. *Progressives have won the culture wars*, that is, *and some dead-enders in the working class are just bitter that they've lost*.

"Badly educated men in rich countries have not adapted well to trade, technology or feminism," a writer at the *Economist* put it.[13] "Badly educated" is quite a tell there. It sounds like blame. Either these guys slacked off, or their teachers or parents were *bad*.

"In almost all societies a lot of men enjoy unwarranted advantages simply because of their sex," the *Economist* article stated. "Much has been done over the past 50 years to put this injustice right." That righting of male dominance is bad news for working-class men who haven't adapted to a more meritocratic era and therefore "lack the resources of training, of imagination and of opportunity to adapt to the new demands. As a result, they miss out on a lot, both in economic terms and in personal ones."

It sounds like the story of a spoiled rich kid who is stripped of his privilege and cannot hack it in a world as well as those of grittier upbringing. But the "spoiled" kid in this story isn't the soft-handed prep-school and college kid raised by a lawyer and a doctor. That kid is doing fine in twenty-first-century America. The "spoiled kid" in this way of seeing things is Jeff Mason, Andrew Duda Jr., or any of millions of white men who thought they'd be fine with only a high school degree and a willingness to put in eight-hour days at the factory.

Efficiency

"Fifty thousand factories across America have shut their doors" since 2000, Trump said in Monessen. His 2016 speech there praised the importance of manufacturing and deplored the devastation of its disappearance.[14] The thing is, manufacturing in the United States has changed, but it is actually doing quite well.

The National Association of Manufacturers in 2016 published the "Top 20 Facts about Manufacturing." NAM bragged that "manufacturers contributed \$2.18 trillion to the U.S. economy in 2016," and that this is about 11.6 percent of the economy. Sure enough, going back to the 1970s, manufacturing has consistently accounted for about 11 to 13 percent of U.S. gross domestic product.[15] In general, America manufactures more stuff every year, keeping up with the overall growth of the economy. NAM points out that "over the past 25 years, U.S.-manufactured goods exports have quadrupled."

So why the complaints about disappearing factory jobs?

NAM explains that, too: "Manufacturers have experienced tremendous growth over the past couple of decades, making them more 'lean' and helping them become more competitive globally. Output per hour for all workers in the manufacturing sector has increased by more than 2.5 times since 1987. . . . [U]nit labor costs in the manufacturing sector have fallen 8.4 percent since the end of the Great Recession, with even larger declines for durable goods firms."[16]

"Labor productivity" is a good thing. But productivity, as a mathematical point, means fewer workers are needed to make the same amount of goods. The equation is

$$Productivity = \frac{Stuff\ Made}{Man\text{-}Hours}$$

So increasing productivity means, in part, holding down the denominator on the bottom right of that equation. Since manufacturing *product* (stuff made) has been a steady portion of the economy for decades, and manufacturing *productivity* has grown steadily, that means manufacturing man-hours are plummeting.

More than one in four American workers toiled in manufacturing in 1970, according to the U.S. Bureau of Labor Statistics,[17] and that number has fallen every single year, during economic growth and economic recession. It reached about 10 percent in the recession year of 2009 and has flattened out since then, just below 10 percent.

We are making more stuff with fewer people.

Automation is central to this. Factory jobs have tended to be low-skilled jobs. The first time I entered a factory and watched the General Electric employees assemble components of a refrigerator, I was shocked at how simple and repetitive their work was. A conveyor belt brought a partially assembled evaporator to a worker who was sitting next to a bin of brackets. The worker picked up a bracket, used a corded driver to screw the bracket onto the evaporator, and then put the assembly back down on the conveyor belt, which carried it along to the next guy, who would conduct an equally mundane task.

I was surprised, watching this in 2005, that these jobs weren't done by machines but were instead done by unionized, $24-an-hour American workers. Today these jobs are gone. GE closed its fridge factory in Bloomington in August 2016. Most of those refrigerator jobs moved to Mexico, but this isn't representative.

The primary killer of U.S. factory jobs isn't China or Mexico but robots. Again, the United States is increasing, not decreasing, how much we manufacture every year. It's just that machines and robots empower fewer workers to make more stuff. "Had we kept 2000-levels of productivity and applied them to 2010-levels of production," economists at Ball State University's Center for Business and Economic Research stated in 2015, "we would have required 20.9 million manufacturing workers. Instead, we employed only 12.1 million."[18]

"Automation has transformed the American factory, rendering millions of low-skilled jobs redundant," trade scholar Mireya Solís said in 2016. "Fast-spreading technologies like robotics and 3D printing will exacerbate this trend."[19]

Think of how much better iPhones have gotten in a decade. A similar improvement has occurred in the quality of industrial robotics. Then think of how much cheaper a television or DVD player has gotten. A similar drop in price has happened in factory machines. Using welding as an example, the Boston Consulting Group wrote in 2015 that "an investment of $100,000 today buys a robotics system that is capable of performing more than twice as much work as a robotics system costing the same amount a decade ago."[20]

This is tough to compete with. "A human welder today earns around $25 per hour (including benefits)," the Boston Consulting Group paper stated, "while the equivalent operating cost per hour for a robot is around $8."

Robots are a harder "problem" to address than foreign competition. If you brought the factories home, they wouldn't be filled with Tracy Pritchards and Andrew Dudas and Jeff Masons. They would be filled with robots.

The Wheat and the Chaff

There's more to this tale of increased efficiency making low-skilled men redundant.

The Great Recession provided a terrible and terribly interesting lesson, and economist Tyler Cowen spelled it out in his 2013 book *Average Is Over*. If you recall that economic downturn, the stock-market crash happened at the end of 2008. It was only then that companies began their most aggressive downsizing. The last three quarters of 2009 were the three quarters when unemployment rose the fastest.

In this ugly nine-month stretch, something else increased a lot: "average per-labor-hour productivity." This number, measuring how much value workers produced per hour, climbed, jumping by 5 to 8 percent each of those three quarters. "It is an average," Cowen explains, "which means that if the lesser workers are fired, the number will go up even when total output is going down."[21]

This was an awkward dynamic—more people than ever were losing their jobs, and businesses were becoming more efficient. Cowen calls this "fairly direct numerical evidence that the laid-off workers weren't worth as much as we thought." In other words, lots of Americans were employed only through the inefficiency of American employers. When hard times hit, employers slimmed down to only those who were actually worth it—"firing workers who weren't producing much value," as Cowen puts it.[22]

Such gains of efficiency weren't always possible in the past, because data and measurement tools weren't as available. Modern technology—on the factory floor and in office computer networks—helps employers determine who is most productive and who is least productive.

Cowen's book suggests that much of the growing inequality in America today is from such increased economic efficiency. Technology has allowed highly skilled people to leverage their skill more, and it has made that superior productivity more visible.

Put another way, the American Dream of yesteryear was partly the product of inefficiency due to ignorance. The rough economic equality of 1955 (among white men) was partly due to employers' inability to distinguish the truly productive from the merely productive-seeming. Many people were employed in tasks employers overvalued or were, unbeknownst to anyone, doing their jobs badly.

The death of the American Dream, by this account, is an increase in efficiency that is good news for the productive workers now pulling in their fair share, and for the economy as a whole, which benefits from efficiency gains. But this is bad news for those who—whether through natural inability, bad work habits, or landing in the wrong field—are less valuable to employers than was previously believed.

The Hillary Clinton tale is that those less-valuable guys live in fly-over country and voted for Trump to bring back the American Dream of excelling while mediocre.

"Too Easy for Smart People to Meet One Another"

There's a parallel story of efficiency on the social front that is very relevant.

Before the era of modern transportation, more people would live their lives close to where they were born. This resulted in what an economist may see as inefficient sorting: With a small number of jobs in every town being drawn from a small pool with diverse skills and personalities, you were apt to get an eclectic mix. The second-smartest kid at the local high school might end up running the drugstore. The smartest girl might be a second-grade teacher.

Who doesn't love a brilliant schoolteacher? Who wouldn't want to sit at the soda-fountain counter chatting with the bright local guy? But the economist might say: *These skills are being allocated inefficiently. These people could be leveraging their intelligence into more productive activities.*

Charles Murray described the early twentieth century as "an age when the majority of parents in the top five centiles of cognitive ability," that is, most of the highest-IQ men and women, "worked as farmers, shopkeepers, blue-collar workers, and housewives."[23] That's mostly because 90 percent of *all* workers were in low-level jobs or worked on farms,[24] but also because there weren't means to pair people precisely with a job for the skill set.

The twenty-first century has seen what you could wryly call a more "orderly sorting." Transportation (highways, safer cars, cheaper airfare), communication, information technology, standardized testing, and other technological tools have all made it easier, as Cowen's book points out, to identify and *sort* the most skilled.

"Today," Murray writes, "the exceptionally qualified have been so efficiently drawn into the ranks of the upper-middle class, and . . . they are so often married to people with the same ability and background." Murray sees this sorting as creating an "ominous" situation.

But from the narrow perspective of economic efficiency, it has to be seen as a gain. Murray frames it that way at one point in *Coming Apart*: "When America got serious about identifying cognitive talent, shipping the talented to colleges and the most talented to the best colleges," Murray writes, "it also augmented the nation's efficiency in tapping its human capital by some unknowable but large amount."[25]

More poignantly, many consider this "ominous" sorting as social progress. Libertarian commentator Virginia Postrel, for instance, mocked Murray's concern here: "His real worry is that it's gotten way too easy for smart people to meet one another."[26]

This is just one small example of cultural changes lamented by some as turns away from the "American Dream" but celebrated by others as social progress.

The End of the Breadwinners

So it's a rough time for blue-collar men. The economy has shifted the advantage from an older conception of a "man's job" to more "knowledge workers." In this realm, the average male loses the biological advantage he enjoyed over the average woman when physical labor was at a higher premium.

Decreasing the demand for male labor also decreased the demand for male companionship, it seems. With women more able to support themselves, and men less able to earn enough to keep a household, marriage has fallen.

The *Economist* magazine explained, "Women who enjoy much greater economic autonomy than their grandmothers did can afford to be correspondingly pickier about spouses, and they are not thrilled by husbands who are just another mouth to feed."[27]

There's more going on here than the economics. Again, from the *Economist*:

> *The pill, which was approved in America [in 1960], allowed women to regulate their fertility. It used to be common for brainy women to drop out of college when they became pregnant. Now they can time their babies to fit with their careers. The ability to defer children is one of the reasons why 23% of married American women with children now out-earn their husbands, up from 4% in 1960. Few women in rich countries now need a man's support to raise a family. (They might want it, but they don't need it.)*

Men were becoming unneeded in the household and the workforce. There's data on this. Economists, through some simple math, can measure how far a week of earnings goes for a blue-collar guy. They find that working-class wages fell dramatically after 1972, to about two-thirds of their former high in the 1990s. This pay is still lower today than it was in 1972.

Elizabeth Warren, now a U.S. senator, studied this phenomenon. When she was still a scholar, Warren put it this way: "Starting in about 1970 a fully employed male's wages completely flattened out, and in fact, a fully employed male today, on average, median, earns about $800 less than his dad earned a generation ago."[28]

The causality here is pretty well established by careful studies. For instance, economists Daron Acemoglu and David Autor from the Massachusetts Institute of Technology used World War II and the wartime surge of women into the workplace to look at long-term effects on wages.

Some states sent a higher portion of their men to war, and thus pulled more women into the workforce. More women working *during* the war, the economists found, translated into more women working *after* the war, as well.

And so comparing states, the economists were able to put a number on how women in the workforce affected pay. They found that "greater female labor supply also reduces male wages. A 10 percent increase in relative female labor supply typically lowers male earnings by 3–5 percent."[29]

Is this legitimate cause for male complaints? Well, men still earn more than women and so the complaint would be that *some* of their privilege has been eroded. Hardly compelling stuff.

And it's not all men whose wages have suffered. More educated men didn't take a hit to their pay as women entered the workforce. The pay cuts hit the men who didn't get with the program and start educating themselves—the men who, as the liberal journalist puts it, have "chosen not to keep up."

Wings and Resentment at Smitty's

"The economy is *bad*, bad," Frank at Smitty's tells me. "Everyone is on welfare. There's just no jobs around here. What jobs there are don't pay. You're lucky if you get ten dollars an hour."

Smitty's is a roadside bar in Uniontown, Pennsylvania, the county seat of Fayette County, in the heart of the Mon Valley. While planning election-season travels, I chose Fayette County because it looked like prime Trump Country. (I chose Smitty's because of its renowned chicken wings, which live up to the hype.)

Fayette County had the highest unemployment in the state, 8.2 percent in 2016, and rising.[30]

Fayette County's median household income was $38,789, compared with the statewide median of $53,115. Only one in seven Fayette County residents finished college (half the rate of the rest of the state).[31]

Almost any number you can find about Fayette County tells a dire story. Uniontown had a median household income of $26,000, half the national median. Only 40.5 percent of the population over sixteen was working, compared with the national rate of 58 percent.

Fayette County was a tie in the 2008 election, with both Obama and John McCain getting 49 percent.[32] In contrast, Trump would win it by 30 points a month after my visit.[33]

This former steel town was the flyover country Hillary was talking about, which looked backward, contributed little to the economy, and never adapted to change. The last big layoffs for Fayette County workers came in 2013 when First Energy in neighboring Greene County shut down a coal-fired power plant.[34] While local Republican politicians would put the blame squarely on Obama's environmental regulations ("Obama's war on coal"), the fact is that capitalism and modern technology bore most of the blame: Fracking had made natural gas so much cheaper that burning coal for electricity was inefficient.

Cleaner air. Cheaper electricity. *Progress.* Except for the workers of Fayette County.

Dave, sitting two stools down from Frank, embodies Frank's characterization of the economy and Hillary's characterization of rural Trump voters. Dave doesn't work, and he's not even in the workforce, because he's on disability. "If I could work, I would," he says. His back is too bad, though. "I got three blown disks," he says, after recounting the surgeries he's undergone since the late 1990s.

Higher disability claims are another typical trait of former industrial places.[35] In theory, disability benefits shouldn't vary significantly with unemployment rates—either you're too disabled to work or you aren't. In reality, there are a million shades of gray. If good high-paying jobs exist, a guy with a bad back might toil through with the pain. If there are no good jobs, though, and unemployment benefits are about to run out, a guy with real pain might seek a note from a doctor in order not to go hungry. Also, on real humans, unemployment takes a psychic toll, and in turn a physical toll. Being out of work and seeing no good jobs anywhere around you can make a bad back worse.

Adaptation would require someone in Uniontown to launch a new business probably in a new industry. Or the people of Fayette County would have to get up and move. There are good jobs an hour north in Pittsburgh, and good public schools in the suburbs around the city.

But Dave stayed in Uniontown because his elderly mother, who is retired, is in Uniontown. He lives with her, not just to help her out but also because he has no better option. "I take care of my mom," he tells me over a vodka tonic at Smitty's. "If it weren't for that, I'd be out on the street."

The politics at Smitty's are what you'd expect. Everyone at the bar is voting for Trump. "Guns" is the first reason Dave, Frank, and the other patrons give. And, sure enough, they complain about how things have changed. They point to mass immigration, complaining not so much about the immigrants who work but about the immigrants they see as free riders who come here and get on welfare. Talk of welfare brings out comments and stories from everyone.

The guys at the bar all share secondhand stories of undeserving recipients of government aid—the woman they heard about who bought steak with her food stamps, or the druggies they know who are buying pills with their unemployment benefits. Welfare and single moms are the bogeymen, on this early Tuesday afternoon in this bar of working-class white retirees and labor-force dropouts.

Sitting there, I wonder if the political and cultural views in this bar are just the cultural resentment of people who have seen life get a little bit harder as some of their privilege was stripped from them. So after a while, I decide to prod. I ask Dave, *If your back hurts too much for you to work, how can you sit at this barstool for hours?*

"I'm numb right now," he says, staring straight at me, "because my son just died."

Death in the Valley

They had found the body that morning, and Dave was self-medicating today in the nearly windowless country bar. Dave hadn't been to Smitty's in a while. "I haven't drank in five years," he says. Frank and the bartender confirm this. As we speak, Dave has a few. Nobody says it that afternoon, but when Dave is gone, everyone speculates on whether it was a heroin overdose.

"Heroin and pills," one customer says from the video poker machine at Smitty's, "that's all Fayette County is. It's a shame you can't even walk down the street without seeing a needle." A couple eating in the nearby booth pipe up to say they saw needles at the school bus stop where they drop off their kids.

Fayette County, with a shockingly high 43 overdose deaths per 100,000 population in 2016, wasn't even in the top 10 in the state.[36] The top overdose counties were coal counties—Fulton, Cambria, Beaver, and Armstrong. These places dug up the coal that powered the mills on the banks of the Monongahela. These are also lands where industry left, and left behind ruins—carnage. If you were studying Pennsylvania and Ohio in the 2016 election, you could have predicted a county's swing to Trump by looking at its rate of overdose deaths.

When the steel plant shut down, Monessen, Fayette City, Uniontown, and the rest of the Mon Valley didn't just incur a decrease in the number of jobs or a shift to the service sector. The collapse of the coal industry didn't merely set a slightly lower economic equilibrium in Cambria County. Economic forces didn't merely result in lower wages and a different workplace for low-skilled workers. If free trade and modernization helped kill Pittsburgh Steel, and if an expanded national workforce helped drive down wages in the Mon Valley, then these changes left a scar far deeper than an unemployment rate.

Something happened here that certainly isn't progress. Given the body count, it also can't flippantly be written off as *the price* of progress. And it sure can't be fully explained by economics. Lower wages and fewer jobs aren't killing people. Dave's son was employed, Smitty's patrons tell me. He was working in construction, driving a bulldozer, and getting trained on the bigger machines.

You can't look at Fayette County and say the problems aren't cultural. You also cannot walk into Fayette County and tell the people to "choose" not to be left behind, to get better educated, to adapt, and to stop being so backward. Something deeper is broken.

CHAPTER 4

American Decay

Broken Places, Broken People

A reas like this," said the clerk of Vargo's Newsstand in Fayette City, eighteen miles from Uniontown, "there's never gonna be anything here."

"Just drive down through the river roads," said Andrew Duda Jr., sitting across the counter, "from here through Monessen—it's all shut down."

"All shut down" is the bluntest and truest way to describe the Mon Valley as a whole. The area is bleeding people. The tiny town of Fayette City had a population of 2,000 in 1920. By 2010, Fayette City had fewer than 600 people.[1] The figure was probably even lower when I sat at Vargo's in 2016. Vargo's was practically the only business still operating on a rotting, rusting Main Street in a ghost town five miles upriver from the corpse of a steel plant.

Fayette City is not a city. It's barely even a town. It's a *former town*.

Fine old buildings crumble, empty, giving off unmistakable whiffs of faded glory and former beauty. Main Street includes a Fayette City community center whose windows are broken. The sign hanging out front is rotting. All of Main Street is.

So those numbers on Fayette City, Uniontown, and Fayette County that I had researched before visiting—the state's highest unemployment

rate, the dirt-floor median wages, the absence of college education—
they couldn't tell the whole story. If the numbers were the whole
story, then the Hillary critique would be true: Those who haven't
gotten a modern education are suffering under the changes that are
benefiting all those willing to get with the times.

The story of Fayette County starts with the steel mill, but it doesn't
end there.

The Pittsburgh-Wheeling steel plant that *made* Monessen and
helped make the Mon Valley so lively had entered bankruptcy in
1985.[2] Thanks to modernization and burgeoning international trade,
prices of steel fell, and the old factory couldn't keep up. One by one,
the company, under instructions from creditors, shut down certain
operations. On June 28, 1986, the furnaces at Monessen went cold.[3]
And in March 1987, the plant closed down for good. Except for brief,
minor spurts, it would never reopen.

The idle factory loomed over this stretch of the Monongahela for
nearly a decade before its rusty skeleton was torn down. Losing the
factory should have meant the workers of the Mon Valley had to
slide into new jobs, maybe in the service sector. Since steel would be
cheaper throughout the country, there would be greater "consumer
surplus," meaning businesses and individuals would have more
disposable money after buying their cars, refrigerators, fences, nails.
That disposable income would go to purchasing services, and thus
rope the former steelworkers back into the workforce.

But things didn't work that way.

The China Effect

I was lucky to find Andrew Duda in Fayette City, because he was
a real-life former steelworker. The steel mill's memory still hung
over this part of Fayette County, but the jobs had been gone for a
full generation—a fact that made Monessen an odd place for Trump's
speech on the evils of free trade.

It was partially free trade with Europe that killed this factory.
But in later years, even more employers in Fayette County, in the Mon

Valley, and around the country would collapse under the weight of something far bigger than the *d'Iberville* passing through the Saint Lawrence Seaway.

It was China.

"China's rise is really a kind of a world historical event," MIT economist David Autor told National Public Radio in 2016.[4] "This is the largest country in the world. It has caused a wholesale substantial contraction of U.S. manufacturing employment."

Autor, together with coauthors David Dorn and Gordon Hanson, has studied the relationship between China's manufacturing boom and the plight of workers in manufacturing-reliant areas in the period from 1991 to 2008. In 1991, an overwhelming majority of U.S. manufacturing imports came from wealthy countries. Only about 9 percent of manufacturing imports that year came from low-income countries, the scholars reported.

China got its act together starting in the 1990s. From 1991 to 2007, U.S. imports from China grew by a factor of ten. That was good news for American consumers, who got much cheaper sneakers, coffee mugs, and electronics. It was bad news, however, for local economies forced to compete with China.

What made Autor, Dorn, and Hanson's work so revealing was that instead of merely studying the effect of China on the entire U.S. economy, or on certain industries or demographics, these economists studied *places*. They parsed the data for each of the 741 "Commuting Zones" into which the U.S. government has divided the entire national population. These zones include urban, rural, and suburban areas. The populations of these zones vary, as do the geographical sizes. The idea of mapping a Commuting Zone is to delineate a local economy. Monessen, for instance, is part of the same zone as Pittsburgh.

The scholars went out and calculated how exposed a local economy was to Chinese competition. How much of a local economy's workforce was employed making things that could, down the line, be imported from China? (The economy in the Pittsburgh area wasn't that harmed by China, because, frankly, the steel industry had already been demolished before 1990.) Orlando's economy is mostly dependent on tourism, and so it is not much exposed to China trade. Washington,

D.C., depends on government and tourism, making it also one of the least exposed Commuting Zones. (Companies aren't yet outsourcing their revolving-door lobbyist jobs to Guangdong Province.)

Autor's study doesn't undermine the idea that America's economy, as a whole, benefits from freer trade. But by looking at local economies, it does unearth problems the economic models may not have predicted. The U.S. workers who were outcompeted by cheap Chinese labor didn't simply take pay cuts. "Rather than modestly reducing wage levels among low-skill workers nationally," Autor and crew wrote in a 2016 update to their study, "these shocks catalyze significant falls in employment rates within trade-impacted local labor markets."

In other words, China's rise did hurt many parts of the country by lowering wages and killing jobs. Higher unemployment rates, though, didn't reflect all the harm, and this is the key. People in these areas were more likely to simply drop out of the workforce. They also were more likely to draw disability benefits from Social Security. That is, low-skilled manufacturing workers didn't just see their wages fall; many of them became men who counted themselves as unfit to work.

So the factory workers didn't all slide into lower-paying service jobs. They landed on their butts. Autor's measure of "trade exposure" predicted not only a fall in manufacturing jobs but a rise in unemployment overall, including a fall in nonmanufacturing jobs, probably as the businesses *serving* the factory and factory workers and their communities—all the businesses that used to dot Main Street in Fayette City, Pennsylvania—lost paying customers.

Factories that compete with China aren't scattered equally about the United States like molecules of gas that expand to equally fill a chamber. They are concentrated in various regions. The trade pressures in the 1970s and 1980s applied disproportionately in the Mon Valley. The trade pressures of China hit a few parts of the United States extra hard.

An overview of the United States as a whole shows a country benefiting from free trade. But when we look at *places*, as Autor and his colleagues did, we see how uneven the effects have been. One problem: It turns out that lots of people aren't happy to pick up and move to chase jobs. As Autor wrote in 2013, "mobility responses to labor demand shocks across U.S. cities and states are slow and incomplete." That's economist-speak for *people often stay in their hometown even if there's some job in some new industry waiting for them off somewhere new.* "Mobility is lowest for noncollege workers," the scholars found, and manufacturing workers are extra likely to be noncollege workers. The guys who lose their factory jobs to trade don't tend to move.[5]

This is a hard fact that an economist may not always consider when speaking about the costs and benefits of economic dynamism: When a factory leaves, it takes many things with it, but it often leaves people behind. *Homo economicus*, the fictional person who populates economic models, would move out of Fayette County when his factory shuts down and gravitate toward where the balance of labor supply and labor demand was resulting in higher wages. Real people don't always get up and go. While most of Fayette County has emptied out, thousands have remained, like the three men at Vargo's on Fayette City's Main Street, or the clientele of Smitty's Bar and Restaurant in Uniontown.

Again, China didn't kill the Pittsburgh-Wheeling plant. It was killed by other external factors like European steel and modernization. China also didn't kill the Mon Valley coal plant in 2015. Mostly fracking did. But the China Shock just happens to be the shock Autor studied. His findings apply more broadly: When an external shock introduces new efficiencies and thus kills the older, less efficient employer, it can wreck more than prices and wages. It can wreck lives.

American Carnage

"For typical American male workers," economists Jeff Madrick and Nikolaos Papanikolaou wrote in 2008, "there has been no general rise in wages since the late 1960s, with only short periods of modest improvement. In other words, the typical male today earns less than the typical male did in 1969." Another way of putting it: "A typical son in his thirties makes less today than his father did thirty years ago, after inflation."[6]

This is just one economic measure showing stagnation, and it's a big one. The average dude is making less than his dad did. That's almost perfectly antithetical to the common understanding of the American Dream.

Americans born after 1950 were the first generation in our country's history "in which at every stage of adult life, they have less income and less net wealth than people their age ten years before," economist Phillip Longman wrote.[7]

This is even starker for less-educated men. "For males between 25 and 44 with only a high school diploma," Madrick and Papanikolaou write, "median wages and salaries incomes today are below their level in 1969."

That's just money. The key here is that the bad story runs deeper than that.

Life spans in America plateaued in 2015. From 2015 to 2016, the life expectancy of an American ticked down by a percentage point or two.[8] That bucked the long trend of climbing life expectancy. It was the first time in decades that Americans had seen a downtick.

Dig further and you find this upsetting fact: More middle-aged Americans (particularly white Americans) are dying now than in recent decades.[9] Economists Anne Case and Angus Deaton published a paper in August 2015 reporting that they found "a marked increase in the all-cause mortality of middle-aged white non-Hispanic men and women in the United States between 1999 and 2013."

White Americans still live longer than black Americans, and they are less likely than blacks to die young. But while the trends for blacks have been improving, trends for whites are worsening. "This change reversed decades of progress in mortality and was unique to the United States," Case and Deaton wrote. "[N]o other rich country saw a similar turnaround. The midlife mortality reversal was confined to white non-Hispanics.

"[H]ealth progress in America essentially ceased in 2012," Case and Deaton wrote.[10]

War, a meteor strike, or a plague could be expected to cause a major downturn in life span. The causes here are more haunting. "This increase for whites was largely accounted for by increasing death rates from drug and alcohol poisonings, suicide, and chronic liver diseases and cirrhosis."

In other words, more white men were drinking themselves to death, overdosing, and killing themselves. These are "deaths of despair." Such deaths rose by more than half from 2000 to 2014.[11]

Deaths of despair rose in all segments of the population, but most significantly among white Americans who have no college degree. This jumped out at researchers, because that population allowed for a cleaner comparison internationally. Among white adults in their early fifties, the United States back in 1990 had far fewer "deaths of despair" compared with such people in European countries. Since then, some countries in Europe have seen an improvement, and some have worsened a bit, but all have converged on about 40 deaths of despair per 100,000 in that age range. White America has climbed steadily for more than twenty-five years to 80 per 100,000—twice as bad as Europe.[12]

Politicians from Jeb Bush to Donald Trump in the 2016 race took notice of the opioid epidemic plaguing much of the country. And it wasn't a made-up issue. "[M]ore Americans died from drug overdoses (largely but not wholly opioid abuse) than from either traffic fatalities or guns," the federal Drug Enforcement Agency reported in late 2015.[13]

Another barometer of economic and physical ill health in America is the number of people taking Social Security Disability Insurance payments. And that number has generally climbed over recent decades. In 2002, 5.5 million people were taking SSDI payments. In 2016, that number had climbed to 8.8 million.[14]

It's a grim picture. When you look more closely at the days and nights of these middle-aged white men, it gets grimmer.

Men without Work

While the unemployment rate went below 4 percent in 2018, there was a darker story hiding behind the math and out of sight for many of America's elites. First, any close observer of labor markets has to be rattled by how recently unemployment was in the double digits (late 2009) or as high as 8 percent (2013).[15] But there's more buried in that data.

Calculating the unemployment rate involves a lot of work for the U.S. Bureau of Labor Statistics, but in the end, the math is simple division: Divide the number of people unemployed by the number of people in the labor force.

$$\text{Unemployment Rate} = \frac{\textit{Unemployed People}}{\textit{People in the Labor Force}}$$

But "unemployed" doesn't include everyone not working, and "labor force" doesn't include the whole U.S. population. Your twelve-year-old doesn't count as unemployed, regardless of how lazy he is, because he's not in the labor force—so he doesn't appear in either the numerator or the denominator of that division problem.

Neither is Grandpa part of the labor force if he is retired, nor your niece who is at school full-time seeking her master's degree. You don't enter into the unemployment calculation if you are neither working nor seeking work. So the labor force is, as the BLS puts it, the *sum of those working and those seeking work*. You might assume that that's equal to the number of adults minus retirees, stay-at-home moms, full-time students, and the severely disabled. But that's not quite right.

America has a growing class of working-age adults—mostly men—who are not in the labor force, not in school, and not raising children to allow a spouse to bring home the bacon. By all appearances, these men have dropped out.

How many dropouts are there, and how does today's number compare with the past? Among men in the prime years of working (ages twenty-five to fifty-four), only about 3.4 percent—one in thirty—were neither working nor looking for work back in 1964. By 2015, even after six years of recovery from the Great Recession, that number stood at 11.8 percent. More than one in ten[16] American men were out of the workforce.

This isn't a constantly rotating pool of men. Nick Eberstadt, my colleague at AEI and author of *Men without Work*, writes that "fully two-thirds of those prime-age males who were out of the labor force for any part of 2014 were out of it for the entire year."[17] Recall, 2014 wasn't a down year. The economy grew at its fastest rate since the recession. We were speeding away from the wreckage of 2008 and 2009, and these millions of men were simply not on board.

What do they do all day? It's not pretty. Consulting time-use surveys, Eberstadt finds that dropouts from the workforce don't do "much in the way of child care or help for others in the home either, despite the abundance of time on their hands. Their routine, instead, typically centers on watching—watching TV, DVDs, Internet, handheld devices, etc.—and for an average of 2,000 hours a year, as if it were a full-time job."[18]

Men dropping out of the labor force may be the most important negative economic indicator—worse than low wages, poor health, lack of wealth, or low educational attainment. Those other maladies are all symptoms of this deeper problem, fruits of this bitter seed.

Lack of work (or even lack of an effort to work) is close to the root here. In this cluster of factors lies the cause of the poverty, and it is what makes the poverty persist—over a lifetime and down the generations. Lack of work is also the root of the deaths of despair, as men face a life without purpose or means.

It's easy to look with disdain at men who have dropped out of the labor force. Americans aren't supposed to give up on work. When things get tough, we're supposed to work harder. Just surrendering and picking up a video game controller may seem inconceivable.

We owe it to these men to figure out who they are. That will also help us untangle the contradiction before us: How is the U.S. economy so good yet so bedeviling? And who are the labor-force dropouts?

These aren't spoiled men of leisure. America is not suffering from a plague of wealthy dilettantes frittering away inheritances and passing their days idly. Disproportionately, they are working-class men. "In 2010, 92 percent of male college graduates and 80 percent of female college graduates were in the labor force," Harvard researcher George Borjas wrote, "as compared to only 74 and 48 percent of male and female high school dropouts, respectively."[19]

The unmarried or divorced are also more likely than their married counterparts to be in this class of men outside the labor force.

It's a dark life. "Prime age men who are out of the labor force," economist Alan Krueger wrote in late 2016, "report that they experience notably low levels of emotional well-being throughout their days and that they derive relatively little meaning from their daily activities."[20]

It's not limited to emotional suffering. The health problems highlighted above are concentrated among the dropouts, the men of prime working age who are neither working nor looking for work. Of this population, almost half take pain medication on a daily basis, mostly prescription medications, Krueger wrote.[21] A clear majority (57 percent) of nonworking males were collecting disability payments in 2013, Eberstadt reported.[22]

This looks like the "American carnage" Donald Trump lamented in his inaugural address. Trump and many commentators say it was Trump's ability to speak to this carnage that landed him in the White House.

This is where some other commentators and politicians jump in to object. The "carnage" is a myth, they say, and the voters who lined up behind Trump and the men who groused about the economy at Smitty's had no real material privations to complain about. They were simply upset by cultural change—*progress*.

It turns out there are numbers on this, and they tell a story that does mess up the "economic anxiety" account of Trump and working-class white woe, but it also complicates the "cultural resentment" story offered by Hillary Clinton and friends.

Broken Places

Recall the assertions that economics had nothing to do with Trump's win: "Economic anxiety didn't make people vote for Trump, racism did," and "It wasn't the economy, but racism and xenophobia, that explains Trump's rise."

Comparing Trump voters in the general election with Hillary voters is not terribly useful. That's often just looking at the difference between Republican voters and Democratic voters. Throughout this book, when possible, we try to look at Trump's core supporters. One way to find these is to find the people who voted for both Barack Obama and Donald Trump. Another is to look at who supported Trump early in the primaries. Looking there, you'll find the same argument. Nate Silver, the renowned data journalist, headlined a piece during the primary season: THE MYTHOLOGY OF TRUMP'S "WORK-ING CLASS" SUPPORT.[23] Trump's supporters, he calculated from exit polls, had incomes of $72,000—well above the average voter's, an income equal to those of Cruz's voters, and higher than those of Sanders's or Clinton's voters.

Other data advanced the contrary idea that economic anxiety gave us Trump. First, there's Hillary Clinton's brag, grounded in data dug up by the liberal Brookings Institution, that she won the counties with the most economic productivity and lost the counties producing the least.[24]

Nate Silver's colleague Ben Casselman, a statistician, found that "the evidence suggests that anxiety did play a key role in Trump's victory." In places where jobs were more vulnerable to outsourcing or foreign competition, Casselman found, Trump did better than Romney had. Where fewer men had college degrees, Trump did better than Romney had. "Trump significantly outperformed Romney in counties where residents had lower credit scores and in counties where more men have stopped working."[25]

Casselman wrote, "The list goes on: More subprime loans? More Trump support. More residents receiving disability payments? More Trump support. Lower earnings among full-time workers? More Trump support."

And the poverty and suffering weren't merely economic. You could have predicted the Rust Belt counties that would flip in 2016—counties Obama won in 2012 that Trump won in 2016—by looking at overdose deaths[26] or countywide measures of poor physical health.[27]

So how do we reconcile these two different story lines—the one that found "little evidence to suggest individual economic distress benefited Trump" with the one that found that struggling places gave the election to Trump?

This isn't merely a matter of studying two different data sets, or of biased journalists massaging numbers. It's a matter of different people asking two similar but different questions.

The studies finding little or no correlation between economic woe and Trump support tended to be polls. The studies finding an economic cause of Trumpism tended to examine election results and look at which counties moved toward Trump. What does that mean? Studies of *individuals* found Trump supporters doing just fine. Studies of *places* found Trump doing well where people were doing poorly.

In other words, it wasn't that economically struggling *individuals* tacked to Trump; it was that voters in struggling or vulnerable *places* shifted toward Trump.

This is crucial. Trump did well among *individuals* who seemed to be doing okay except that they lived in *places* that were very much not okay. Studying people by demographic data on a chart tells you only so much. Studying people in the context of where they are—as members of communities—is necessary if we want to understand our country.

"The Land of Opportunity"

Increasingly, place matters in America. "The land of opportunity" is how we describe America as a country, but it's becoming more accurate to say that America possesses some "lands of opportunity" and many lands of hopelessness.

The wealthiest and most educated Americans are clustering together into more compact, more homogeneous places (like Chevy Chase), thus leaving the less educated, less skilled, and poorer Americans in their own, also more homogeneous, communities.

That is, America is geographically segregating by class more than before. "During the late twentieth century," researchers Douglas Massey, Jonathan Rothwell, and Thurston Domina wrote in a 2009 paper, "the well-educated and the affluent increasingly segregated themselves off from the rest of American society."[28]

This physical, spatial "coming apart" was at the heart of Charles

Murray's 2012 *Coming Apart*. Murray identified a handful of neighbor-hoods, demarcated by a few hundred zip codes, and called them SuperZIPs. Murray's research zoomed in on the elites and confirmed an increased clustering of the rich and educated in elite neighborhoods.

And there have been measurable consequences.

If we consider the country as a whole, the economic story of the past decade has generally been this: A sturdy economy got shaky in late 2007, collapsed in late 2008, bottomed out in 2009, and has slowly climbed back up, eventually recovering fully (at different points in time for different measures). The slow pace of employment recovery has been particularly frustrating for observers.

But separating the rural economy from the economy of America's cities tells a more nuanced story. Through 2008 and 2009, employment in metropolitan areas and in nonmetro areas fell by similar amounts, about 5 percent and 6 percent, respectively,[29] according to data from the federal government. The employment picture turned the corner in the fourth quarter of 2009 in both parts of the country and began a climb. But the similarities end there.

By mid-2013, metro-area employment had returned to its pre-crisis levels. Non-metro employment never has. There was no job growth in these rural areas in 2013 and 2014. As of mid-2016, the non-metro employment index was still about 3 percent lower than it had been when 2008 began. And labor-force dropouts are more common in non-metro areas than in metro areas.

The economic recovery since 2009 has occurred mostly in big metro areas, skipping rural America.[30] Twenty counties accounted for half of all new businesses in the four years after 2009.

"Economic prosperity is concentrated in America's elite ZIP Codes, but economic stability outside of those communities is rapidly deteri-orating," the political analysis site Axios concluded after reviewing a study that broke the economy down by location.[31]

"Most of today's distressed communities have seen zero net gains in employment and business establishment since 2000," the Axios report found. "In fact, more than half have seen net *losses* on both fronts."

Different places have different types of jobs. In some places, there are more highly skilled jobs. In some places, the jobs are easier to ship overseas, or become automated. Rural counties have a much thinner stock of high-skilled jobs. "These are thin economies," economist Mark Zandi said of rural areas. "Other than the hospital or local government, there isn't a whole lot going on."[32]

"This is about big-county, cosmopolitan metropolitan areas pitted against small-population rural counties and some small metros," Brookings Institution Fellow Mark Muro said. "It is absolutely clear that the economic story has been much more difficult in that second group of non-big-metro counties."[33]

The more important inequality story is not unequal wealth or income, but unequal opportunity and hope. And if you travel across the country and crunch the numbers, you see how unevenly these are scattered.

Returning to Harvard's Raj Chetty (and we will explore his work in more depth in later chapters), a key finding of his was that "intergenerational mobility varies substantially across areas within the U.S."[34] In other words, your odds of doing better than your parents seem to depend in part on where you live. Chetty and his coauthors said the "land of opportunity" moniker for the United States might need to be modified: "The U.S. is better described as a collection of societies, some of which are 'lands of opportunity' with high rates of mobility across generations, and others in which few children escape poverty.

"For example," Chetty wrote in this 2014 paper, "the probability that a child reaches the top quintile of the national income distribution starting from a family in the bottom quintile is 4.4% in Charlotte but 12.9% in San Jose." Translated: Poor kids are very unlikely to grow up to be rich adults, but in some places, their odds are nearly three times better than in other places.

"Places themselves have causal impacts on kids' outcomes," sociologist Melissa Kearney said when examining the data in March 2016. This is the piece that we too often miss when we abstract away from the fact that humans exist in communities—in *places*.

The unequal geographic distribution of opportunity helps explain the 2016 election in so many ways. "Make America Great Again" sounded odd to many of us not only because so many of us were living successful, happy lives, but because we were surrounded mostly by thriving families and communities. From the perch of these thriving communities, it seems that whether or not to be left behind really is a matter of choice.

The result is a sort of geographic determinism. Even the death data from Case and Deaton have a geographic divide. White middle-aged mortality was growing by 1 percent a year in sparsely populated counties, but the death rate for middle-aged whites wasn't growing in any counties of more than one million.

Above we discussed how the worsening of life expectancy is concentrated in certain demographics (middle-aged whites). The problem is also focused on certain places, according to a 2017 study published in the *Journal of the American Medical Association* (*JAMA*).[35]

The average American can expect to live 79.1 years, the study found. But that life expectancy varied massively by geography. The worst counties had a life expectancy of about 66, while in a few counties, the expected life span was 87 years. That's a wide gap. The worst counties were mainly Indian reservations in South Dakota, poor black counties along the Mississippi, and some Appalachian counties in West Virginia and Kentucky.

There have always been geographic differences in life expectancy in the United States. What this *JAMA* study found was that the inequality had grown from 1980 to 2014. Life expectancy lengthened significantly in the mid-Atlantic, the Northeast, and central Colorado. Meanwhile, lives didn't get longer or they got shorter in the Bible Belt.

There's a particularly gory political story on this note.

Right after the Iowa caucuses, one statistician found a strong and dark correlation: "In some Iowa counties compared to others, middle-aged white people are twice as likely to die," *Washington Post* reporter Jeff Guo wrote a few days after the caucuses. "These are the same counties where Trump was more likely to succeed."[36]

This wasn't just an Iowa thing. A few weeks later, after the bevy of primaries called Super Tuesday, Guo looked at the numbers in the nine states with county-level data. "In every state except Massachusetts, the counties with high rates of white mortality were the same counties that turned out to vote for Trump."[37]

So a map of those deaths of despair had an echo in the map of the 2016 election: Trump outperformed Mitt Romney the most in the counties with the most suicides, overdoses, and alcohol-related deaths. This was especially true in the industrial Midwest: Trump outperformed Romney by 8 points in the counties with the lowest rate of these deaths but outperformed him by a full 16 points in the counties with the highest rate of suicides, overdoses, and alcohol-related deaths.[38]

Getting outside one's bubble, and breaking down by geography the numbers above, we see that the dividing lines between the Two Americas aren't merely lines on a spreadsheet but are also lines on a map. And the differences among places aren't merely differences of income, wealth, or education. They are differences of health, hope, and opportunity.

TRUMP'S CORE VOTERS—THE MEN like Kent Armstrong and both Bob Garretts who backed him in the early primaries, or the voters in Pennsylvania, Ohio, Michigan, and Wisconsin who came to the GOP only because of Trump—were voting that the American Dream is dead. But it turns out they weren't necessarily the ones falling into poverty, dropping out of the workforce, or going on disability. They were the *neighbors* of those people.

The vote that the American Dream was dead was a cry of "My community is crumbling." Polls show this. Trump voters were more likely than Clinton voters to place cultural worries over economic worries. What defined the pessimistic, less hopeful voters wasn't their individual well-being as much as the well-being of the place where they lived.

In this light, it becomes absurd to argue over whether Trump voters and angry blue-collar Americans are upset about economics or culture. They're inextricable. It also looks absurd to wave off these people as backward-looking folks who refuse to adapt, because some of their objections to social changes deserve to be taken seriously.

ב

Seek the *shalom* of the city to which I have carried you into exile.
Pray to the Lord for it, for in its *shalom* will be your *shalom*.

Jeremiah is conveying an order from the Lord. He is telling the exiled Israelites what they are to do.

The Jewish holy books are filled with instructions on how to please God. Many of them are about prayer. Others are about personal conduct. This is an order to be civic-minded and to look on the local level.

The Hebrew *ir*, for "city," conveys a sense of localness, of small scale. This local city is where the solutions will be. If we care about human flourishing (*shalom*), then we need to care about the local and to attend to it.

CHAPTER 5

"I Don't"

The Dissolution of the Family

The most profound social change in America over the past two generations has been the retreat from marriage.

The household with a married mom and dad living with their children—the norm two generations ago—becomes less and less common each decade. In many parts of the country, the child raised by both her biological parents is a rarity.

The facts aren't up for dispute. America used to have a societal norm of marriage. A person was expected to get married before having kids (even if the nuptials occurred when baby number one was on the way). Back then, being a grown-up usually meant having kids.

It would be hyperbole to say *marriage* is dead. But it's not debatable that the mid-century *norm of marriage* is now dead. There is a fierce debate over who killed it, how, and why.

The suspects in this murder mystery are many.

Maybe the norm of marriage was killed by cultural forces. This thesis finds a home among both cultural liberals and cultural conservatives. There are some liberals who say marriage-as-the-norm was a system of patriarchal oppression, and we have thankfully moved beyond it. Conservatives say cultural elites and the sexual revolution killed marriage.

Others finger material deprivation. Growing inequality has made it economically impossible for many people to start a family. Slow economic growth has dampened marriage, and so perhaps a sluggish economy is to blame.

This murder mystery, like any good mystery, will have some plot twists. The investigation will take us to a seedy bar in North Dakota, and a back-alley meeting with a guy named Joe in Indiana. And the crime will turn out to be more complicated than the simple explanations would allow.

"I Don't"

The Brady Bunch debuted in 1969, featuring a family that was at once untraditional (the children were all from Mom's and Dad's previous marriages) and also incredibly normal: school-age children living at home with a married mom and dad. In 1970, the U.S. Census Bureau determined a house filled with married parents and their children under eighteen years constituted 40 percent of all households. By 2012 that number had fallen to 20 percent.[1]

In 1960, 72 percent of all adults were married. By 2016, it was only half.[2] In 1965, 17 percent of adults aged twenty-one to thirty-five were never married. In 2017, the never-married number was 57 percent.[3]

These are only two data points, but a massive pile of data confirms it and seems to prove the common conservative lament: Since the 1960s, family in America is crumbling. Marriage is less common, single mothers are more common, and fractured households are increasingly normal to see.

More and more children are raised outside marriage. About 40 percent of all children born in 2016 were born out of wedlock (which marks a slight improvement).[4]

A related trend is childless women. In 1976 about one in three women of childbearing age was childless (35 percent). In 2016, nearly half were (49 percent).[5] Most of this is a consequence of delayed motherhood—women in their twenties aren't having babies as much. Even so, women in their thirties and early forties are also far more likely to be "child-free" (as one liberal writer phrased it) than they were in 1976.

These trends aren't really up for debate. Women are working more, marrying less, having babies less, and having babies out of wedlock more.

So what?

Progress?

In this investigation, the first question is what to make of the murder. If the pre-1960s norm of marriage was killed, was this justifiable homicide?

For some, it's a story of liberating women from social expectations and economic need. "I don't need to push a baby out of my vagina to be a real woman," one feminist author wrote at the liberal *Huffington Post* in 2014. "Why add another mouth to an overpopulated planet for an ego-driven biological imperative I don't feel?"[6]

The data in earlier chapters suggest that possibly marriage is retreating because changing economics have liberated women from marriage. The more money women can make, the less they rely on a husband for reliable sustenance. The more career opportunities they have, the more they seek meaning outside family formation.

If women react to increasing pay equity by getting married less, that suggests that our mothers and grandmothers in days of yore were getting married out of financial dependence.

"The 'decline' of marriage isn't a problem," argued liberal blogger Matt Yglesias in 2015. Instead, it represented liberalization of women. "In places where women have very few economic opportunities, they can't afford to be too choosy about marriage partners. Where women are more empowered, they become choosier."[7]

A sizable minority of America thinks this way: About one in six Americans said marriage is an outdated institution, in one 2017 poll.[8]

A liberal baby-boomer woman from San Francisco, Arlie Russell Hochschild dedicated years of her life to creating an ethnography of white conservatives in Louisiana. The fitting title is *Strangers in Their Own Land*. She put in a great effort to capture how these people—so different from her in experience and in worldview—saw the world and the times. She encountered among conservative men the lament, as she put it, "These days a woman didn't need a man for financial support, for procreation, even for the status of being married."[9]

So maybe marriage was never really a great bargain, and women had been choosing it out of desperation. So we all ought to cheer these developments, right?

The timing of the retreat from marriage lends more ammo to those who see the shift as a matter of liberating women. Marriage's decline in America roughly tracks the uptake of the birth control pill in America.

Shortly after the Pill hit the market, there was a small decline in marriage. The full-force retreat began after 1970 when the Public Health Service Act provided federally funded birth control for low-income women. Marriage has continued to fall over the years, as contraception use has climbed, thanks to the Pill's becoming more affordable and having fewer side effects.

We should say fewer *medical* side effects. The cultural effects seem vast.

The separation of sex from marriage "was driven in part by birth control," sociologist Mark Regnerus wrote in 2017. "Its widespread adoption by women in recent decades not only boosted their educational and economic fortunes but also reduced their dependence on men. As the risk of pregnancy radically declined, sex shed many of the social and personal costs that once encouraged women to wait."[10]

According to the "liberation" argument, the death of the norm of marriage is the fading of an outdated social order in which men held outsize power and traditional values irrationally constrained true human flourishing.

Where Marriage Is Dead

Any good murder investigation considers *where* the killing occurred. The location helps us sniff out the perpetrator and whether the motive was liberation of women.

When we think of the drop-off in marriage, in large part driven by women getting married later, it's easy to chalk it up to upper-middle-class women going to college and choosing a career over family. A conservative-minded reader might see the data above about women eschewing or delaying marriage and think of Lena Dunham or of the feminist intellectuals of the 1960s and '70s who liked the mantra, "A woman needs a man like a fish needs a bicycle."

This is a common and tempting picture to draw. Reading the *Huffington Post* and Vox.com and recalling *Ms.* magazine from decades past, we have all seen liberal elites pooh-poohing marriage as a backward institution. Looking at Hollywood stars, we see a cavalier attitude toward marriage—as if they're simply *above* this pedestrian idea of lifelong commitment. Heck, you probably know a French couple, or a Park Slope couple, who are living together and having their second child but have said that they don't feel the need to get married.

It's easy to see these trends and conclude that they are what is killing the norm of marriage.

But that's not what the numbers tell us. The above assumption I call the Lena Dunham Fallacy: the tendency to attribute to decadent elites social phenomena really located among the working class.

The norm of marriage is dead not among our elites but among our working class. It's not the Wesleyan alumnae living in Greenwich, Connecticut, who are killing the norm as much as it is the working-class men and women living in Middle America.

"[W]hen it comes to the family, America really has become two nations," scholar Kay Hymowitz wrote in her 2006 book *Marriage and Caste in America.* "The old-fashioned married-couple-with-children model is doing quite well among college-educated women. It is primarily among lower-income women with only high school education that it is in poor health."[11]

"The most educated women are the most likely to be married," was the blunt assessment of Brookings Institution scholars in 2016.[12]

Marriage has dropped across the board, but it has dropped more for the working class.

College-educated women are surely getting married later than they were two generations ago, but that accounts for a tiny portion in the drop-off of marriage. "In the affluent neighborhoods where many college-educated Americans live," researchers Brad Wilcox and Andrew Cherlin found, "marriage is alive and well and stable families are the rule."[13]

The gap is growing. In 1990, about two-thirds of all adults over 25 were married, with only a slight advantage (6 percentage points) for the higher educated. By 2017, only half of those who never went to college were married, and the gap between the highly educated and the less educated had more than doubled.[14]

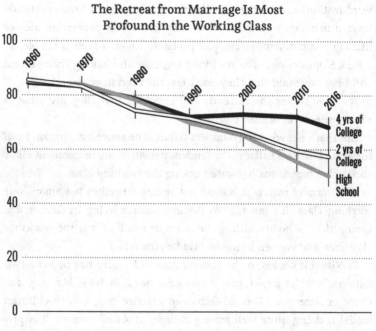

The Retreat from Marriage Is Most Profound in the Working Class

Percentage of women married at age 40
Source: IPUMS

This undermines the assertion that the death of marriage represents liberation. If marriage were a bum deal foisted on women who lacked opportunity, you'd expect the most liberated women—those with college degrees, decent incomes, and good prospects—to be the ones shedding marriage. They're not. The elite women are practicing what social conservatives have long preached: getting married, having kids with their husband (in that order), and raising the kids actively. Pop culture may not reflect that fact, but the numbers show it. And these elites live within bubbles where traditional families are the norm. These bubbles are not representative of the country as a whole.

"The majority," wrote columnist Megan McArdle, reviewing trends in marriage and family formation, "are the people without a four-year degree, for whom late marriage has combined with early parenthood to produce a crisis in family structure. The fragile, often fatherless family that used to be associated with the deepest urban poverty is increasingly becoming the norm for everyone except the educated: urban and rural, black and white, Northern and Southern."[15]

Women who don't attend college are more likely to give birth outside marriage than in marriage—58 percent of all babies born to noncollege women are born out of wedlock. That's a big increase from the early 1980s. Among those with some college but no degree, single mother-hood has risen from 13 percent to 44 percent in those three decades.

The numbers are far lower among women with college degrees: one in twenty in the early 1980s rising to one in ten in 2009–13.

Statistically, then, the women going through childbirth and the other moments of life unmarried are not the liberated, educated, and wealthy but the ones who have *fewer* choices—for whom no good marriage is within reach.

Married with Children

We've established that marriage is dying mostly among working-class women, undermining the idea that empowerment of women is behind its demise. If you're still unconvinced that there's anything to mourn here, the economic data might sway you.

In short, married people are much less likely to be poor.

This is why scholars like Isabel Sawhill of the Brookings Institution see marriage as an antipoverty measure. "Work and Marriage: The Way to End Poverty and Welfare," was the title of a paper she produced in 2003.[16]

Some commentators say this is nothing special, just a matter of accounting plus the fact that a half gallon of milk costs less than twice a quart of milk. "Marriage's potency as an anti-poverty tool," liberal blogger Yglesias asserted in his article arguing that the retreat from marriage isn't a problem, "is largely a mechanical result of how poverty is defined in the United States, paired with the existence of basic household economies of scale."[17]

That is, the official poverty line for a couple is *not* twice the poverty line for an individual. So two people just *below* the poverty line could move in together and technically be out of poverty. That's not an accounting fiction, though. It really is cheaper to live as a pair. These economies of scale shouldn't be waved away as trifles. In the case of marriage as opposed to temporary shacking up, this pooling of resources allows for the real creation of wealth, and thus stability, for the long haul.

But there's a bigger effect here: Marriage is good for the kids.

A leading scholar on social and economic mobility is Melissa Kearney. She works at the University of Maryland and the Brookings Institution, both left-leaning institutions. Just on the economic front, Kearney found a lot more to recommend marriage than Yglesias did. Kearney begins with the "marriage premium for children."

About 8 percent of children born to married parents end up in poverty as adults, while about 27 percent of children born to unmarried parents do.[18] Children born to unmarried parents are more than twice as likely to have no high school degree by age twenty and less than half as likely to earn a decent income (defined as four times the poverty level). These are neither mere economies of scale nor some moralistic idea of "the right way to do things." There's tons of hard data showing that kids who grow up in intact families do better as adults.

"[Y]ouths who grow up with both biological parents earn more income, work more hours each week and are more likely to be married themselves as adults, compared to children raised in single-parent families," social scientists Robert Lerman, Joseph Price, and Brad Wilcox found in a 2017 study. "Many of these differences continue to be statistically significant even after we control for family income experienced as an adolescent."[19]

That last line, about controlling for family income, suggests that family structure contains some sort of causal factor, aside from wealth. In other words, given two kids from two families of the same income, the one from the intact family is more likely in the long run to do better workwise and family-wise.

These researchers even put a price tag on the traditional family relationship: Children of intact families earn at least $4,700 more per year than their peers from other families.

The social science is remarkably uniform in its conclusions on this matter. A child will see the best outcomes in childhood and adulthood if she is raised by both of her biological parents with those parents being married. Childhood aggression and hyperactivity, for instance, are lowest in married-parent households. Murray, in *Coming Apart*, lists and cites other traits for which married biological parents can expect the best results: less "delinquency in adolescence, criminality as adults, illness and injury in childhood, early mortality, sexual decision making in adolescence, school problems and dropping out, [poor] emotional health," to name a few.[20]

Hope for the Future

Married parents help ensure better outcomes for children, all of the data show. But the most convincing answer to the *So what?* question isn't about the children of single mothers. It's about *all* children, and the American Dream itself.

Jeff Mason—the foulmouthed former repo man from Pittsburgh we met outside the Trump rally—put it concisely: "I'm hoping for a future for my kids. I think the key—the secret—to life is for your kids to do better than you, and I don't want my kids to go down the path that I go down."

The best dollars-and-cents measure of the American Dream is economic mobility. The data on this are mixed. On the whole, it looks like economic mobility is not changing a lot. Maybe it's flat; maybe it's a bit down.

But as always, aggregate data can hide currents occurring below the surface. On immobility, it turns out, plenty is happening beneath those placid top lines. Economist Raj Chetty from Stanford and Harvard conducted an amazing study into mobility and opportunity in this decade. He saw major differences from place to place. Mobility is high in some places and cratering in others. This takes us straight to the heart of the story Donald Trump told in the 2016 election, that the American Dream is dead, or that it is being hoarded by the elites.

There are many ways to measure economic mobility. Rather than studying simply *relative* mobility, which measures a person's ability to get ahead of his fellow man, to climb from one quintile to another, Chetty also examines *absolute* mobility: a person's ability to earn more than his or her parents did.

All sorts of factors contribute to mobility, Chetty found, but one factor mattered more than any other: neighborhood family stability.[21]

That is, the best way to predict whether a child might end up better off than his parents is to look at his neighborhood and ask if most of the kids in his neighborhood were raised by single mothers or by two parents. In the communities with intact families, the American Dream was alive and well. In the communities where the single mom was the norm, economic mobility was absent.

Look after the well-being of the city, as the book of Jeremiah says, *for its well-being is your well-being.*

So the death of marriage has gone hand in hand with—and perhaps has helped cause—the desiccation of economic opportunity in much of the country. It's impossible, looking at the data, to see the decline in marriage and still suggest it's "not a problem."

The Marriage Premium

The death of marriage is a working-class phenomenon, we've learned. We've also seen that it harms children.

As we try to sniff out the culprit—who has killed working-class marriage?—a third piece of evidence provides a clue: Unmarried men do worse, by all sorts of measures, economic and social, than married men.

This takes us into the perilous land of cause and effect—correlation and causation. Sociologists try to avoid asserting causation, because often they are able to establish only which phenomena *happen together*, while the question of *what caused what* is beyond their reach. But figuring out the bigger mystery of what happened to the American Dream compels us to sniff out the cause and effect in play in the working-class retreat from marriage.

Maybe marriage is the path to wealth and health. Or maybe, to put it harshly, men who are bad at life are also bad at getting married. Economist Tyler Cowen believes this latter explanation is partly true: America, like any society, has many *bad men*. The cultural and economic changes of recent decades mean fewer women feel forced to marry these *bad men*.

But even if that's true in many cases, it may not be the main explanation. So let's dig deeper.

Men who are married make a lot more money than men of the same age who are not married. This is a separate phenomenon from the ones discussed earlier. It's not merely that poorer men get married less—it's that unmarried men are poorer.

This isn't simply because married men are older, or because married men tend to be more educated, or for any demographic reason, according to a study by Wilcox and Lerman in 2014. All else being equal, *married men make more money*.

The correlation between marriage and better pay survives when researchers control for all sorts of factors. Take two men of the same age, the same level of education, the same race, in the same region of the country—and the married man makes more. A lot more.

"[M]en enjoy a marriage premium of at least $15,900 per year in their individual income compared to their single peers," Wilcox and Lerman wrote in 2014. This finding has been replicated again and again and is widely accepted in social science circles.

How to sort out causes and effects here? When I e-mailed Wilcox about his work on the marriage premium in 2017, he pointed me to an intriguing study of the topic, using identical twins. This study, by economists Kate Antonovics and Robert Town, concurred with the consensus that the marriage premium was real, finding that married men make about 19 percent more than unmarried men.[22]

But they wanted to investigate the possibility that some men who are naturally more productive and reliable also get married more. That is, maybe "born workers" are also "born husbands." The twin study destroyed that hypothesis. When one identical twin was married and another was not, the married one made 27 percent more than his brother—a *larger* marriage premium than normal. Their conclusion: "No. . . . Not all the good men are married. Rather, our results suggest that marriage causes men's wages to rise."

That last line bears repeating: "marriage causes men's wages to rise."

So your genes don't determine your wages and marriageability, but that doesn't mean these traits aren't passed down through the generations. Recall that people who were raised in intact families also made more and were more likely to go to college and finish it, thus making themselves in turn more likely to get married. The vicious and virtuous circles are visible here.

Being a family man is good for your prospects, and better prospects make it easier to be a family man. Your children will do better if you get married and actively raise them, and having a good income makes it more likely you will stay in your children's lives.

But we can't get ahead of ourselves here. While Antonovics and Town think marriage *causes* higher wages, the reverse explanation is still plausible: Perhaps men with more money find it easier to get married.

The China Effect

If it turns out that marriage causes wealth, then we can't accuse poverty of killing marriage, since poverty or wealth would be a *consequence* of marital status rather than its *cause*. Poverty can say, "I showed up on the scene *after* the murder!"

But there's evidence for the opposite explanation: that poverty deters marriage because tough economic situations make marriage and family formation harder. In other words, perhaps working-class economic woe has killed the norm of marriage among the working class. This argument often goes together with the suggestion that marriage can be restored with either (a) a better redistribution of wealth or (b) broad economic growth.

MIT economist Autor, who found that the decline in marriage was mostly among working-class women, gave some ammunition to this materialistic explanation. In a 2016 study with his partners, David Dorn of the University of Zurich and Gordon Hanson of the University of California–San Diego, Autor argued that the erosion of low-skilled jobs, particularly in manufacturing, is behind the erosion of marriage.[23]

"[M]anufacturing jobs are a fulcrum on which traditional work and family arrangements rest," Autor wrote.

First, there's the basic economics. When a local economy finds itself facing more foreign competition—for instance, when the nail-makers of the Mon Valley see a flood of foreign nails from China—"it also increases the share of young men in a local labor market who earn less than women of the same age, race and education."

Thanks to all the changes from 1955 to today, working-class men have seen not only their earning power decline but also their marriageability. When manufacturing jobs erode, Autor found, male incarceration, death, and homelessness go up, and many men move out of the old factory towns. Few things make a man "unmarriageable" like being dead, being in prison, or having moved away.

Even short of these extreme outcomes, the intermediate steps—being drunk, high, a criminal, or an itinerant—all make a man less attractive to a potential bride, less interested in marriage, and less physically available to get married.

Why focus on the "marriageability" of men? Why not simply say that *it's harder to start a family when economic situations are poor*? Because marriage—even in our relatively egalitarian times—is thoroughly asymmetrical. Autor and his coauthors found "asymmetric marriage-market impacts that depend upon the source of the shock: adverse shocks to labor demand in male-intensive industries reduce the prevalence of marriage among young women, whereas analogous shocks to female labor demand significantly raise the prevalence of marriage."[24]

Translated: It's *male* unemployment that undermines marriage.

A factory shutting down (or needing to scale back or cut wages) makes men less marriageable for many reasons. These woes also drive down childbirth, the data suggest, but not as much as they drive down marriage. That means more out-of-wedlock babies.

This account makes historical sense. Marriage was a norm in the 1950s and 1960s, when good factory jobs were plentiful. The norm has been dead since the late 1960s because working-class men can't find steady, high-paying jobs.

Here's one possibility suggested by Autor's analysis, and by many related studies: that "shrinking the pool of marriageable low-education men has eroded the incentive for men to maintain committed relationships, curtailed women's gains from marriage, and strengthened men's bargaining position vis-à-vis casual sex, out-of-wedlock childbirth, and noncustodial parenting."

Autor has established that bad economics is causally connected to marriage's erosion. To prove that bad economics is *the* culprit, we would have to prove that *if not for* the economic woe, marriage *would not have* fallen among the working class. In other words, we have two possible suspects here—(1) low wages and (2) membership in the working class (that is, low educational attainment). We need to get these two suspects in different rooms.

One way to accomplish this is to get low-skilled men more money. How to do that?

Go west, young man.

"Don't Go to DK's"

The girls at the front desk couldn't get me a room, but they did give me advice:

"Don't go to DK's."

The Holiday Inn where they worked was booked solid. It always was. They handed me a preprinted list with the names and phone numbers of every other hotel, motel, and boardinghouse in Williston, the North Dakota town that had become the hub of the fracking boom, and thus was bursting at the seams with people seeking work.

As one hotel after another told me over the phone, "No vacancy," I struck up a conversation with the Holiday Inn girls. (And they were *girls*, high schoolers, because every adult in Williston already had a job that paid more than a Holiday Inn front desk slot.) I asked where I could go to meet and interview the locals. I wanted to see how this extraordinary oil boom in the middle of nowhere had created a brand-new civilization on this frontier. They named a few family restaurants that might still be open, and one bar or two.

"But don't go to DK's," one girl said.

"Yeah," the other said. "Don't go to DK's. There's always fights there."

So I went to DK's.

There were—to the detriment of this book but the relief of my wife—no fights at DK's that night. The barmaid explained that fights are only on payday. That's when the young men feel too rich, drink too much, and eventually get violent. "Usually it's about girls," Chris Duell told me over a Budweiser. Chris, unlike most of the clientele, was middle-aged. In dire straits a few years back, he left Michigan and came to Williston, where he launched a drinking-water distributorship. He told me his business made a million dollars the year before.

As oil prices climbed around 2010, and fracking technology was perfected, Williston, which sat above the deep shale saturated with oil, became a magnet for the industry. Oil companies like Halliburton and their countless subcontractors like Penkota Wireline needed labor, and modest Williston couldn't provide it. Demand outpaced supply, and so wages went up, which drew in men from the region and soon from the whole country.

At DK's I met one young man who had traveled by bus from California with his dad to find a job—and he did, at $18 an hour. One hippie, who told me he had once been arrested for driving a semitruck full of marijuana from Mexico into California, came to Williston and landed a job administering drug tests for job applicants.

The DK's population, even on this non-payday, was overwhelmingly male. And loaded. "Everyone in here has a wad," Kel, a patron of DK's and a beneficiary of the fracking boom, told me.

With transplants from around the country landing in this small town, Williston seemed like a social experiment while I was there. Economists Melissa Kearney and Riley Wilson of the University of Maryland realized that fracking towns like Williston in Texas and Pennsylvania really *could be* an experiment in the relationship between men's earnings and marriage: If marriage has fallen alongside working-class men's wages, and if married men are paid more, will boosting the wages of blue-collar men also boost marriage? If it did, this would strengthen the case that income determines marriageability, thus fingering economics as the murderer of marriage.

So what did they find? "[I]n response to local-area fracking production, both marital and non-marital births increase and there is no evidence of an increase in marriage rates."[25]

That is, the men flashing their wads at DK's had something to fight for—as the mini–baby boom demonstrated—but the presence of wealthy men didn't cause a rush to the wedding altar.

"We find no evidence to support the proposition that as the economic prospects of less educated men improve," Kearney and Riley wrote, "couples are more likely to marry before having children."

While Autor's study suggested that the disappearance of good blue-collar jobs *reduced* blue-collar marriage, Kearney's findings indicated that the appearance of lucrative blue-collar jobs *didn't increase* blue-collar marriage.

The *Washington Post*'s *Wonkblog* covered this study under the headline WOMEN JUST AREN'T THAT INTO THE "MARRIAGEABLE MALE" ANYMORE, ECONOMISTS SAY.[26] This headline told us more about the *Washington Post*'s "wonks" than it did about men, marriage, and income. The writers defined "marriageable male" as a male with a high income. Call it the gold digger understanding of marriage; this materialistic, purely dollars-and-cents definition of "marriageable" isn't useful, especially after Kearney's fracking study undermined it.

Pro-business or pro-free-market conservatives have argued that economic policies that unleash job creation will boost family formation. Fracking in Williston was that jobs program, but it didn't work on the family front. Liberals argue that aggressive cash redistribution and a more robust safety net are the answer. But if a job and money didn't make men more marriageable or more marriage-minded, why would a welfare check do the trick?

In other words, economic woe has shown up at the murder scene of marriage, but Williston shows that economics can, in rare cases, be separated from marriage's health. There's another culprit here.

The Joe Adams Effect

To review the evidence: When factories die, marriage does, too. When good-paying jobs pop up, though, marriage does not necessarily come back. Married men make more money, but making more money doesn't get you married. Marriageability seems to pass from generation to generation, but it isn't genetic.

This requires more investigation. And while DK's and the nightlife of Williston are so much fun, we need to head to a factory town like those in Autor's study. Specifically, we'll head to an Indiana strip mall and visit an office space behind a pawnshop, where I spoke with a guy named Joe who made refrigerators.

Joe Adams's job, from which he was being laid off when we spoke in 2005, was called "low-skilled" for a reason. Joe and his colleagues assembling GE refrigerators in Bloomington were doing simple tasks—ones for which it seems you or I could be trained in a morning. While I was shocked when I first saw the simplicity of the labor, this was widely known among the working class of Monroe County.

Joe was vice president of Local 2249 of the International Brotherhood of Electrical Workers, and as we chatted in the union's office on the backside of a strip mall, he thought back to when he first sought factory work, out of high school.

"They told me I couldn't get a factory job without factory experience. That didn't make sense. What's the experience you need?" This wasn't rocket science. It wasn't carpentry. But after he finally cracked in, Joe learned that there was something of a skill to the job, something employers needed their workers to have: "Are you gonna be here, on time, every day? Are you experienced with the mundane? Can you stand to do the same thing again and again?"

GE didn't need workers with training in machinery, refrigeration, or really anything. It needed a man who would show up on time, wait till the whistle to take lunch, call in when he wasn't going to show up, tolerate hours of the unpleasant, and largely do as he was told.

I was a single twenty-six-year-old guy when Joe and I had this conversation, and so I didn't see then what I see now: These skills of the unskilled factory job are the skills of marriage and fatherhood. Being a good husband doesn't require an advanced degree in psychology, and you don't need a college education for it. Basically every dad and every husband has learned "on the job" the specific job skills—cooking breakfast, changing diapers, actually *listening* to other humans. The prerequisites, what you need coming into the job, are some basic skills, which are probably best called "virtues": Are you passably reliable, honest, and patient? Can you delay gratification? Do you see the value in self-sacrifice? Are you willing to give decades of your life to one partner?

Good factory jobs *rewarded* and *cultivated* these virtues. The guy who graduated from high school and worked on the factory floor was getting, in some important ways, the same training as the guy going to law school or the guy at the white-collar job: habituation to the "skills" of being a family man.

As these low-skilled but reliable jobs have become scarcer since the 1960s, it's not surprising if these virtues become rarer. Put one way, a world with fewer reliable jobs means a world with fewer marriageable men. If you think about work as one of many training grounds for life skills, men deprived of a reliable factory job have been denied the chance to exercise these muscles of delayed gratification, self-mastery, patience, communication, and reliability.

For college-educated men, high-skilled jobs still exist in today's economy, and those jobs often demand and cultivate these same virtues. For the man who was or *would have been* a factory worker, though, there aren't the salaried jobs of the elites or the reliable factory jobs of the past. There is instead irregular and even unreliable work—contractor jobs, occasional gigs. These are the sorts of jobs that don't reward or cultivate reliability or commitment, in large part because they don't *offer* reliability or commitment in return. They reflect more an on-again, off-again relationship of convenience than a marriage, and perhaps they cultivate other habits: detachment, the default stance of constantly looking for a better deal, and a survival instinct that elevates self-preservation over loyalty.

The working class has fewer reliable jobs these days, and so the fall in marriage probably reflects, among other things, that fewer working-class men have been given the chance to develop the virtues and the income that make them marriageable. There are fewer eco-systems amenable to the growth of these virtues.

And again causality goes both ways, creating a vicious circle.

Families and Communities

The Joe Adams theory of marriage's decline jibes perfectly with the data above. As Autor shows, losing factory jobs reduces the number of marriageable men. As the twin study suggests, there's no innate trait of the marriageable man that makes him better at all aspects of life.

We still have not nailed down the killer, though. When it's hard to distinguish cause from effect—when you don't know whether the economic woe causes the family breakdown or vice versa—it's a good idea to always consider a third option: that both phenomena are the effects of a shared cause.

Put another way, economics keeps showing up at the murder scene of marriage, but maybe economics is just a *fellow traveler* of the real killer. To study this possibility, we need to go back to DK's in Williston, and we need to come armed with Raj Chetty's research.

One premise of Chetty's study was built into the methodology and was imprinted plainly in the title: "*Where* Is the Land of Opportunity?" The subtitle is "The Geography of Intergenerational Mobility in the United States."[27]

In English: *Where* a kid grows up determines his chances of climbing the ladder.

"The U.S. is better described as a collection of societies," Chetty wrote, "some of which are 'lands of opportunity' with high rates of mobility across generations, and others in which few children escape poverty."

This is the same phenomenon we encountered in the previous chapters: Economic strength, family strength, the American Dream, are all local. "The main lesson of our analysis," Chetty and his colleagues wrote, "is that intergenerational mobility is a local problem." *Place* still matters, in some ways more than ever.

This isn't a small hypothesis. Chetty and colleagues set out to ask what allows some poor people upward mobility but denies that opportunity to others. The answer was *where the poor person lives*. "[P]laces themselves have causal impacts on kids' outcomes," is how Kearney aptly put it.[28]

"Intergenerational mobility varies substantially across areas within the U.S.," is how Chetty phrases it. The Charlotte area, where I met Jeff Mason, has the least mobility. The chance of climbing from the bottom quintile as a child to the top quintile as an adult is 4.4 percent there. In places like Silicon Valley and Salt Lake City, it's nearly three times as high.[29]

"Why do some areas of the U.S. exhibit much higher rates of upward mobility than others?" Chetty asks.

One factor: income segregation, specifically the "isolation of low-income families." Poor people whose neighbors are all poor are less likely to see their children climb out of poverty.

Here's a stronger and more interesting correlation: Places with more civic activity, regardless of income, have more upward mobility. Chetty calculated an area's "social capital" score using a variety of factors including participation in community organizations. He found a very strong correlation here: the more civic activity, the more upward mobility. Specifically, going to church makes a difference. "Religiosity is very strongly positively correlated with upward mobility," Chetty found.

The single strongest factor, though, was "the fraction of children living in single-parent households." If you grow up in a neighborhood full of broken families, your chances of climbing the ladder are slim. If you grow up amid intact families, the American Dream is alive and well.

Perhaps this was a family-level matter? Maybe it's a simple thing: Children raised by single moms have less economic opportunity. But

Chetty's data undermined that conclusion. Even aside from an individual's family situation, the family structures in the local area mattered the most.[30]

In other words, the single most important factor in the upward mobility of a child is the strength of families in the community.

Broken families and economic woe go together. Crucially, though, they go together *on the community level*. When an aberration separates these two factors—when a fracking boom at a remote shale field brings tons of rootless money into good-paying jobs in a Wild West town—we see the role of community even more clearly.

The Mancamp

After the pumpjacks and the parade of trucks (whose drivers easily made six figures per year), the first sign that you were approaching Williston was the mancamps. Mancamps are sprawling warrens of modern trailers allowing oil companies to house hundreds of men in a large barren field. Each man had his own small modern room, usually with his own flat-screen television, and a bathroom he shared with a couple of other guys.

One mancamp I visited had a big (also temporary) building that served as the common room, and it was what a student union might look like if college had only dudes in their twenties: carpeted rooms full of recliners and big couches, Ping-Pong tables, air hockey, and massive TVs. Plus, of course, an all-you-can-eat hot buffet including burgers and fries running most of the day.

All the cheeseburgers, NFL Network, video games, and idle entertainment a young man could want were available, free of charge, in the mancamp. If he wanted to go out and spend his wad, there was always DK's, which featured the further attractions of women and beer. This all happened hundreds or thousands of miles from home. I met a couple of guys who were homesick for wife and kids, but who came out to make good money for a few months until economic prospects recovered back home. I met a few more at DK's who were running away from home and responsibility, or a painful past.

This land of cash and basic pleasures was not a complete human community. Mancamps were no place to raise a kid. The work schedule often involved eleven days on, with long hours, followed by three days off. This was a place to come and simply trade your labor for cash and whatever comforts the oil companies could provide to keep you in the barren plains of western North Dakota. They made everything as easy as possible. There was no set mealtime. You didn't have to get yourself to work, because the bus took you from the mancamp to the job site. And your time off work was entirely your own.

Much of that time—an extraordinary portion, if you believe the reporting and firsthand accounts—was spent at strip clubs. The fracking boom brought a second strip club to Williston, and women came from miles around to make thousands of dollars a night.[31]

This was no community.

So Williston created something of a natural experiment, isolating the two variables—money and community—that often go together. It turns out that if you remove the community, the money doesn't bring the family formation.

We've found the killer: The erosion of community is what killed the norm of marriage in the working class.

Community strength and social capital are the roots of the good life. Community and steady jobs both offer men the *work* of being a good employee and a family man—the Joe Adams Factor. Family strength and economic well-being are the fruits.

Autor's study showed that the disappearance of jobs in a place led to a retreat from marriage in that place. This is true, but it skips a step: The factory closing in Monessen destroyed Monessen *as a community*. It wiped out the institutions of civil society. Community serves as a support structure for families. In a place that no longer had community, family became too difficult.

The working-class retreat from marriage is the fallout of the working-class loss of community.

This reveals the truth behind the old understanding of virtue. Virtue is a habit, as Aristotle explains. Habits require practice. Being a worker and being a member of a community both count as practice. When you don't have regular employment, and you don't have a cohesive community, you don't have the practice. The result is men who find the skills of economy and family harder to come by.

Strong communities make family rearing more possible. This is glaringly true to anyone who's ever tried to raise a family. Community, which can seem merely a *nice* thing to have when you're a singleton in your twenties, becomes *necessary* when you take on the difficult and crucial work of marriage and child rearing.

Communities also set expectations that a couple will get married before they have a baby, or at least soon afterward. They provide support structures, delivering meals to new moms and providing adult company for parents who otherwise spend their time with children, who can be maddening and who do not always provide the most intellectually stimulating conversation.

The norms promoted and supported by strong communities—finishing high school, getting married, and having babies, in that order—keep people out of poverty.

This all gets at divergent understandings of the nature of marriage. Many people these days talk of marriage as a bilateral contract that reflects the couple's love for each other. After all, wedding vows can sound like that. But this modern view of marriage is too narrow. There's a good reason the wedding ceremony, and not merely the reception, is performed in front of a large community of friends. Marriage is a covenant not just between the bride and groom, but between both and a community—and in turn between the community and the couple. Marriage, by this understanding, exists not just between two people, but *within a community*.

"One source of the growing marriage gap in America," the National Marriage Project at the University of Virginia wrote in a study in 2010, "may be the growing disengagement of Middle Americans from civil society over the last 40 years." Marriage, that is, was collapsing among the same people who were seeing a collapse in civic engagement. The report, helmed by Brad Wilcox, concluded, "The eroded power and presence of churches, unions, veterans' organizations, and athletic groups in the lives of Middle Americans has likely undercut many of the habits of the heart that would otherwise sustain strong marriages and families."[32]

The disappearance of reliable jobs and the erosion of local community may look like two different things that happen in the same places. In a crucial way, though, they are the same thing. Cohesive communities and a regular workplace are both institutions of civil society. Institutions of civil society provide material resources, such as pay and a support structure, but they also provide more abstract resources such as a sense of security and a sense of purpose. If pay and family stability go together, it's because both depend on the same thing: social capital.

Fewer reliable jobs, less marriage, and less civil society are all manifestations of the same phenomenon: Life for the working class is becoming deinstitutionalized.

This view of the nexus of family structure and economics—the "it takes a village" framework—ties together all the findings in this chapter. Working-class people are getting married less and are earning less. Behind both of these phenomena is weaker community. It's not a question of genes—that some men are just naturally better at marriage and earning than others—but instead a question of *environment*. Some places have less social capital and fewer strong families, which in turn makes it harder for the people in those places to make good money or build families.

From all the data above, this is plausible, but still a hypothesis. Digging deeper into this hypothesis, by examining the collapse of communities, makes it hard to deny.

CHAPTER 6

Bowling Alone

The Dissolution of Civil Society

"The American Dream" as a phrase connotes that there is something exceptional and particular to the United States. It's something other countries don't have, at least in the way we have it. The American Dream involves a story that we tell about ourselves, and that we believe makes us special.

One special story we tell, particularly regarding our immigrants, is the story of social mobility. In school, we read our Jane Austen and George Eliot and roll our eyes at how stultified and regimented is the empire from which we broke. In America, more than anywhere else, you can become what you want to become regardless of where you started out.

It's easy to fall into materialistic thinking here, and to view this mobility as a purely economic phenomenon. That would be a mistake. You cannot understand the American Dream and American economic mobility if you look at them as matters of dollars and cents. There's another American peculiarity behind them, and Alexis de Tocqueville noted it a few hundred years ago.

"Americans of all ages, all conditions, all minds constantly unite," the Frenchman wrote in *Democracy in America*. "Not only do they have commercial and industrial associations in which all take part, but they also have a thousand other kinds: religious, moral, grave, futile, very general and very particular, immense and very small . . . . There is nothing, according to me, that deserves more to attract our regard than the intellectual and moral associations of America."[1]

These two defining characteristics of America—our "associations" and our economic and social mobility—are married.

Recall Raj Chetty, whose research found a seemingly causal link between intact families and economic mobility. His study turned up only one other local characteristic that rivaled two-parent households in boosting mobility: social capital. That is, if you measure the number of community institutions, churches, and bowling leagues, along with the amount of volunteering, the political involvement, and the amount of charitable giving, you can predict the type of place where a child born in poverty could rise up the ranks.

America is the land of opportunity *because* America is the land of civil society. The American Dream of mobility is alive to the extent that the American Dream of robust local community is alive.

The Erosion of Civil Society

The terms here may need some defining, but they shouldn't be daunting. I mean roughly the same thing when I write the common but vague term *community* as I do with the more precise but less familiar term *civil society*. One illustrative way to think of these terms is by reference to some bad advice from a character in a Robert Frost poem. The poem, "Build Soil," is a dialogue between the farmer/poet and a real farmer. When the real farmer asks for advice, the poet provides plenty, including this line:

> Don't join too many gangs. Join few if any.
> Join the United States and join the family
> But not much in between unless a college.[2]

You could think of civil society as being everything "in between"— the "gangs." Civil society is the stuff bigger than the individual or the family, but smaller than the central government. Conservative intellectual Yuval Levin writes of "the institutions and relationships that stand between the isolated individual and the national state."[3]

Social scientists use a related phrase, *social capital*. The term is intended to convey the idea of wealth, but not wealth in money or things. Social capital is wealth in relations and connections. Robert Putnam, in *Bowling Alone*, dug up an old definition of *social capital* he found workable. The phrase, from L. J. Hanifan, refers not "to real estate, or to personal property or to cold cash, but rather to that in life which tends to make these tangible substances count for most in the daily lives of a people, namely, goodwill, fellowship, mutual sympathy and social intercourse among a group of individuals and families who make up a social unit."[4]

Speaking of these things as "capital" suggests something analogous to a commercial exchange: Plugging into civil society is labor, it takes work; the wage for that labor is social capital.

These ideas are central to understanding the American Dream. Civil society and local community are the beating heart of the American Dream. A poverty of social capital defines those who believe the American Dream is dead.

This dour belief is spreading because much of America is mired in a recession of social capital that began sometime in the 1960s. The park ranger quoted by Kent Armstrong, that retiree I met at the Trump rally, was expressing this view when he said, "If you lived in the sixties, you've probably seen this country the best it will ever be."

This was the peak of civil society, Robert Putnam found in *Bowling Alone*. After that came the decline in civic involvement. Since then, fewer people have been joining clubs, parishes, or associations of any kind, and people who are still joining some institutions are joining fewer. Putnam's book title connoted the collapse of bowling leagues, once a staple of middle-class America. Their disappearance left Americans bowling by themselves.

A simple way of asking about "civil society" or "associational life" is this: *Do you do stuff with other people?* All of these terms, including the idea of *social capital*, are sociologist-speak for the matter of everyday life: connections, friendships, obligations, neighbors.

Alongside informal civil society are the formal *institutions* of civil society. Putnam charted serious drop-offs in participation in these institutions. Fewer people now attend local government or school meetings. Fewer serve as officers of some organization or serve on some local committee.[5]

Simply tracking the membership of organizations (as a fraction of the population) reveals a rise and fall over the last century. From 1900 to 1930, likely as a result of an expanding middle class and increasing education, membership in organizations grew. It then dipped during the Great Depression and rebounded with a vengeance after the war. "On average," Putnam wrote, "across all these organizations, membership rates began to plateau in 1957, peaked in the early 1960s, and began the period of sustained decline by 1969."[6]

Updating Putnam's work in 2017, Senator Mike Lee's office studied the state of "associational life." This study found similar results, and others studies confirm them.[7]

"Americans' growing isolation," French sociologist Ivaylo Petev wrote more than a decade after *Bowling Alone*, "is thus corroborated here in the case of extended networks. We see evidence for the decrease of formal and informal ties" across America.[8]

Others have found similar developments. "[A]n increasing portion of the U.S. population now experiences isolation regularly," concluded psychology professor Julianne Holt-Lunstad of Brigham Young University.[9] Her study found that "more than a quarter of the population lives alone, more than half of the population is unmarried and, since the previous census, marriage rates and the number of children per household have declined. These trends suggest that Americans are becoming less socially connected and experiencing more loneliness," said Holt-Lunstad.

People go to church less and less every year. We belong to fewer organizations than our predecessors did. We know our neighbors less than we did a generation or two ago. We vote less than we did a generation or two ago. Men have fewer jobs than they did a generation or two ago. Men are in the labor force less than they were a generation or two ago. Americans marry less than we did in 1960. We have fewer and fewer children every decade.

It all adds up to this: Americans are less attached to society, their neighbors, their communities, other humans. Lacking the environment of a strong community, more Americans lack the scaffolding to climb above their starting point. More Americans lack the support structure that they would need to build a family. More Americans lack role models, and they lack *roles*. They are displaced persons living in their home country, even in their native state or hometown. They are strangers in their own land.

Millions of Americans are alienated.

In this light, it's hard to disagree when they say the American Dream is dead. This view struck so much of the pundit class as odd because where we lived, the scaffolding was still there. There was something going on in flyover country that we had missed.

Civil Society Deserts

Back in western Pennsylvania, you may recall the divergent local economies. Both Pittsburgh and rural Fayette County had been dependent on the steel industry and on coal. Both suffered economically when foreign steel and technological innovation drove the Pittsburgh-area steel industry into the ground. Both suffered again as coal faded into irrelevance under pressure from environmental regulations and competition from cheap natural gas.

Yet Pittsburgh is doing pretty well right now, while Fayette County isn't. This makes it clear that jobs, trade, and economics aren't the whole story. There's something outside these things that Pittsburgh has that Fayette County didn't.

The answer is local community. Specifically, it's institutions of civil society. This is the core of the rural-versus-urban divide. Cities are planted far thicker with institutions of civil society, and so when a few disappear, and the money runs lower, they are more able to maintain community.

I saw this at Smitty's Bar in Uniontown, where I met Dave, whose son had died that morning, probably of an overdose.

The clientele at Smitty's liked the bar, and except for a respectful somberness around Dave, the atmosphere was cheerful. But there wasn't a lot of Uniontown pride. When talk of neighbors came up, Lisa the barmaid offered, "I don't talk to none of mine. I got one who lives behind me who I think deals drugs. I got quacks who live below me."

Dave was staying in town only because of his elderly mom, who needed his help but also provided him with a roof and a bed. "I got a loaded .22 right by my door," Dave told me. "I don't trust nobody in my apartment complex."

I asked what Uniontown kids do when they graduate from high school. "They leave," one Smitty's patron said. "Get outta town," said another. "That's about it."

One local woman at Smitty's, about twenty years old, was attending the community college. I asked her if she was planning on sticking around. She shook her head and said: "If I was rich in the mountains, I'd stay."

Fayette County, for all its economic woe, has pockets of wealth in "the mountains." In fact, Fallingwater, the famous Frank Lloyd Wright home, sits on a hillside in the Bear Run Nature Reserve about fifteen miles east of Smitty's. Because of the mountains, though, it's at least forty-five minutes' driving time. And from the average Fayette County community, the wealth of "the mountains" may as well be a world away.

The suicide numbers and the overdose numbers in counties like Fayette tell us these are not happy places. Sociologists increasingly have begun measuring *happiness* through various means. These measures aren't perfect, but they tell us something. Sure enough, poorer people are less happy, according to these studies.[10]

But the sadness here can't simply be ascribed to economic struggles. People aren't killing themselves, drinking themselves to death, and overdosing just because their bank accounts are too low.

The very economists who have charted this disturbing wave of middle-aged white death concluded as much. "Many commentators have suggested that the poor mortality outcomes can be attributed to slowly growing, stagnant, and even declining incomes," Anne Case and Angus Deaton wrote in a 2017 paper. "[W]e evaluate this possibility, but find that it cannot provide a comprehensive explanation."[11]

Later they write, "[P]urely economic accounts of suicide have consistently failed to explain the phenomenon."

A closer look at the happiness studies turns up even more evidence against the bare economic explanation, and points us toward the root cause. A quick analysis shows a stunning correlation. The states with the highest per capita suicide rate are Wyoming, Alaska, and Montana,[12] the three least densely populated states. Washington, D.C., and New Jersey have the lowest suicide rates and the highest population density. This surface analysis suggests that physical isolation is behind suicide.

But we can go deeper. Social scientist Charles Murray, in *Coming Apart*, found something interesting: The difference between the average poor person's happiness and the average upper-middle-class person's happiness could be mostly explained by two factors: marriage and "high social trust." Add on two more factors—religious observance and satisfaction with one's work—and you've explained almost the entire remainder of the happiness gap.[13]

Poor people in America, it seems, are less happy mostly because poorer people are less likely to get married and less likely to have many neighbors and friends they can trust. "There is no inherent barrier to happiness for a person with a low level of education holding a low-skill job," Murray writes.[14] Sure enough, the 1950s and 1960s had more equality when it came to marriage and neighborly trust. These have become so dramatically unequal only in recent decades.

And that helps explain the plague of deaths of despair sweeping America in recent years. It's a fruit of the disintegration of community. These deaths of despair are symptoms of alienation.

To the extent that economic circumstances determine deaths of despair, Case and Deaton write, "they work through their effects on family, on spiritual fulfillment, and on how people perceive meaning and satisfaction in their lives in a way that goes beyond material success."[15]

Alienation causes death—or at least social connection helps prevent it. This seems almost undeniable given the vast body of research on this.

"Social relationships, or the relative lack thereof, constitute a major risk factor for health," three epidemiologists at the University of Michigan found in 1988, "rivaling the effect of well-established health risk factors such as cigarette smoking, blood pressure, blood lipids, obesity and physical activity."[16]

Dozens of subsequent studies took on the same question. When gerontologists at Brigham Young University in 2010 crunched the numbers on more than 140 studies asking this question, they found that this old thesis held up. Specifically, they found small mortality effects from simple factors, such as if the person lived alone, and larger effects in studies that looked at more "complex measures of social integration."[17]

Others have found this same root cause of early death. "[T]hose who were more socially isolated were much more likely to die during a given period than their socially connected neighbors," *Boston Globe* writer Billy Baker found, "even after you corrected for age, gender, and lifestyle choices like exercising and eating right."[18]

The "decline of social capital" was a significant factor in rising American suicides, psychiatry professor Aaron Kheriaty wrote in 2017.[19] "We're not connected anymore. We live in an incredible state of isolation," Kheriaty colleague and physician Frances Hart Brog-hammer said at a conference in 2018. "We're not living in community anymore. We're living in isolation, and we don't have people to provide meaning and give hope."[20]

Death, then, is a bitter fruit of community disintegration. Broken families and the retreat from marriage are other fruits. Economic woe is present in both of these problems, but it's not the proximate cause. Alienation is.

Here, then, is the great divide in American life:

Do you belong to a strong community? Do you enjoy multiple, dense networks that provide both support and purpose? Do you consider yourself *a part* of many institutions, like a church, a club, or a cohesive neighborhood? The answer is generally *Yes* in the Oost-burgs and Salt Lake Citys, the Chevy Chases and the Madisons. It's generally *No* in the Fayette Counties, the Buchanan Counties, and the Middletowns.

The Alienated Working Class

Hillbilly Elegy became a bestseller in 2016 in part because Americans in the elite bubble were struggling to understand what they—I should really say "we"—were seeing. We had trouble believing the data from Case and Deaton about death rates rising. It was baffling to see, even as the economy improved, droves of men dropping out of the labor force. And, frankly, many of us refused to believe that we were watching Donald Trump win the presidency.

Hillbilly Elegy explains these phenomena because it tells the story of displaced persons. It's a story of a family trying to be a family without the support structure that is a community. "Social decay" is the phrase Vance uses.

Some readers on the left hated *Hillbilly Elegy*, because they read it as an assignation of blame on the working class. Because Vance didn't posit some outside villain who had ruined these communities, and he refused to settle for a bare economic explanation, he had to conclude that something was wrong in working communities. If you say the problem is endemic in the community, that can sound like blaming the community *members*—blaming poor people for being poor. But the problem wasn't *bad members of the working-class community*. It was a *lack of working-class community*.

There's a very telling correlation here, and it involves trust: People who trust their neighbors, coworkers, the police, and local businessmen more are much more likely to report being "very happy," according to data from the Social Capital Community Benchmark Survey.[21] It's not surprising when you think about it. Trust allows you to let down your guard. It makes day-to-day life easier as you leave your front door unlocked, leave your kids under the eye of the neighbor at the playground, let them run the streets. Trust is central to community. The Catch-22 is that no individual or small group of individuals can reverse a baked-in distrust.

Sure enough, the working class is half as likely to agree that "people can generally be trusted," as are white-collar Americans.[22]

The same three things we saw with the erosion of the family we see with the erosion of community: It is unequally distributed, it is concentrated in the working class, and it is geographically discrete to the point that we can see it on a map. Civil society's collapse is hitting working-class parts of America much harder than it is hitting our country's elite bubbles.

"Like financial capital and human capital," Putnam wrote in his 2015 book *Our Kids*, "social capital is distributed unevenly."[23]

Popular story lines would have you believe that the poor in America all hang together, braving material poverty through solidarity and close communities, while the rich, behind their gated mansions and plastic surgery, live isolated, barren lives. There are certainly instances of these in America (there are instances of *everything* in a country of 325 million). But they are not the norm.

"Contrary to the romanticized images of close-knit communal life among the poor, lower-class Americans today," Putnam wrote in 2015, "especially if they are nonwhite, tend to be socially isolated, even from their neighbors."[24]

The working class is less adept at networking than elites are. Vance himself, determined to climb out of the deadly swamp that was working-class, white, Middle America, looked at the chaos around him—broken families, drug abuse, disregard for school and job responsibilities—and at first decided the path out was to play by the rules. As he began to emerge, and ascended to college and then law school, he realized that the rules were a bit of a farce. "The problem is, virtually everyone who plays by those rules fails. That week of interviews showed me that successful people are playing an entirely different game. . . . They network."

Vance explains: "[N]etworks of people and institutions around us have real economic value. They connect us to the right people, ensure that we have opportunities, and impart valuable information."[25]

If this strikes you as either overstated or banal, that's likely because you, the reader, are so enmeshed in these powerful networks—communities, institutions of civil society—that you don't notice them. At Yale Law School, Vance wrote, "networking power is like the air we breathe—so pervasive it's easy to miss."[26]

Networking expert Sandra Navidi wrote a book on the tight webs of civil society in America's upper echelons, which she described as "superhubs." She contrasted them with the rootlessness in the world of Vance's childhood: "In contrast, superhubs thrive in an empowering culture," Navidi wrote in the *Daily Beast*, "where they generally receive guidance from an early age, feel very much in control of their own destiny, have confidence in themselves, a strong sense of purpose, and are given—or make—opportunities to realize their potential."[27]

Navidi's term *superhubs* could make these networks sound like some fancy new invention, but really they're the oldest thing in human civilization: communities, that is, people of shared interest or purpose coming together in formal and informal associations that will—often through intangible means—advance the interests of all involved. What's *new* is that the most skilled, most educated, and wealthiest individuals, who used to be scattered across tens of thousands of networks, are increasingly concentrated in fewer networks, thus leaving the other networks lacking in the highly successful.

This leaves downscale communities without as many guys who can get you a job, without as many examples of success, and without as many people motivated to form and cultivate networks. The result isn't really working-class networks that are less powerful and less advantageous. The result is the absence of networks among the working class.

The first step in this unfortunate process is the social and geographic clustering of elites.

What the "Bubbles" Have: Robust Civil Society

If you have a college degree, the people near you with whom you spend your time—colleagues, neighbors, fellow parishioners, fellow PTA officers, other parents involved with your kids' swim team—are far more likely than the average American to have college degrees.

This is truer today than it was a generation ago. Sociologist Douglas Massey has shown that as racial segregation has diminished, class-based segregation has increased in America. So, too, has assortive marriage: college-educated children of the college-educated marrying one another, while blue-collar boys pair up with blue-collar girls.

In terms of social capital and civil society, then, the doers, the organizers, the movers and shakers are increasingly marrying each other and moving next door to each other. And this sorting process leaves behind the environment where Vance grew up. As Navidi, the networking scholar, put it, "This network topology also manifests itself geographically . . . increasing residential segregation pushes hillbillies into high-poverty neighborhoods, which are now expanding beyond urban ghettos into suburbs."[28]

This is why Robert Sampson, a scholar who has studied neighborhoods his whole life, has concluded, "What is truly American is not so much the individual but neighborhood inequality."[29]

The working-class neighborhoods, towns, and counties as a result simply lack these networks. The institutions of civil society are absent or sclerotic. There's less work, less church, fewer civic organizations, less involvement in local government, less involvement in school boards, and simply less neighborly connection. The sorting machine has probably packed some PTAs in the country unbearably dense with type A personalities, while it has left other PTAs to wither and die. This process has left in its wake displaced, unconnected communities, which as a result are properly called not "communities" but rather bare *places*.

The importance of community may be best demonstrated by a study of one of America's most intractable problems: persistent black poverty. A civil rights movement, a war on poverty, dozens of diverse state efforts, hundreds of local efforts have failed to get America beyond the intergenerational black poverty that glares as an ugly reflection of slavery and segregation.

Raj Chetty, the Harvard economist, found one consistent (but not easy) way that black parents could secure better outcomes for their children. Chetty wrote in 2018: "The black-white gap is not immutable: black boys who move to better neighborhoods as children have significantly better outcomes."[30]

By "better neighborhoods," Chetty meant neighborhoods with lower poverty, less racial bias, and more present fathers. The kids who move to these neighborhoods, his study found, were less likely to go to jail and more likely to make decent incomes.

To be sure, the racial gap for black males on these scores persists regardless of environment. Also, you can't just tell poor black people to move to richer neighborhoods. But the data Chetty saw speak to how much of an effect a child's physical neighborhood has on his life prospects.

"Social Disintegration"

Geographic segregation may not be sufficient to destroy civil society and local community. Simple economic hardship also doesn't do the trick—again, many poor communities are shockingly strong. But in America today, poorer neighborhoods—black and white—are also generally poor in social capital. The factors that make this so are the problems we discussed in earlier chapters.

"If we pull back from a narrow focus on incomes and purchasing power," cultural historian Brink Lindsey wrote in 2017, "we see something much more troubling than economic stagnation. Outside a well-educated and comfortable elite comprising 20–25 percent of Americans, we see unmistakable signs of social collapse."

That term, *social collapse*, can be vague, so Lindsey got more specific: "We see, more precisely, social *disintegration*—the progressive unraveling of the human connections that give life structure and meaning: declining attachment to work; declining participation in community life; declining rates of marriage and two-parent child-rearing."[31]

Remember the debate over Trump's rise? *Is this cultural or economic?* At this point, that question is obviously spurious, and that dichotomy so obviously false.

The day in 1977 when Youngstown Sheet and Tube announced thousands of terminated steel jobs is known as Black Monday in that part of the Ohio River Valley. Gary Steinbeck, who was one of five thousand laid off that day, recalls how the economic collapse was a cultural collapse. "Those numbers only reflect the jobs that were lost in the plant," he told my *Washington Examiner* colleague Salena Zito. "The ripple effect was equally devastating. Grocery stores, pizza shops, gas stations, restaurants, department stores, car dealerships, barbershops all saw their business plummet and they started closing.

"No one ever calculated the cultural tragedy as part of the equation either," Steinbeck went on. "They didn't just dismantle the old mills, they dismantled the societal fabric of what made Youngstown Youngstown."[32]

When jobs leave—when the nail factory is shuttered—that's a double blow to civil society. First off, the workplace that is lost was more than a place to earn a paycheck. It was also a primary place for most people to network, to experience the benefits of community. One's colleagues, even those who aren't well connected, are a crucial network. The idle chat around the watercooler, the boring talk of fixing a leaky pipe or finding a good basketball team for Lucy or Charlie, or whose sister is unmarried and just moved back home—these often function as how-to guides for everyday life. This is true for the white-collar career man who might learn the importance of contributing to his 401(k) only when a colleague hectors him about it at the office. It's also true for the parent working solely to pay the bills who learns of a new day care from his colleagues.

When work goes away, you may assume workers now have more time to socialize or network, but statistically, that's not what happens. The unemployed end up isolated. The data come from "time-use" surveys the federal government conducts. These surveys try to measure how people spend their days, and they reveal the disconnected downscale man. Political economist Nick Eberstadt, writing on men who have dropped out of the labor force entirely (not even looking for a job), found that "the overwhelming majority of the prime-age men in this un-working army generally don't 'do civil society' (charitable work, religious activities, volunteering), or for that matter much in the way of child care or help for others in the home either, despite the abundance of time on their hands."[33] Instead, they play video games and watch TV.

The old working class had institutions that bound them together, including their jobs and their labor unions. "Their successors, by contrast," Lindsey writes, "are just an aggregation of loose, unconnected individuals, defined in the mirror of everyday life by failure and exclusion."[34]

On a more material level, when the jobs leave, so does the money that funds the other community entities. Churches run on donations from the faithful. The family restaurant can't stay open when half the local families have dialed their budget back to bare bones. The local diner that relies on men stopping in for coffee and eggs before the early shift will suffer when those steam whistles go silent.

The wedding bells go silent, too. As David Autor's studies showed, when the factory leaves, marriage drops. Family formation slows down. This shouldn't be surprising to anyone who has raised a family. Family rearing is hard, and it requires a support structure. That support structure is going to be the local community—the institutions of civil society. When local communities erode, the land is less fertile for family formation.

Of course, the causality goes the other way, too, making this a vicious circle. Intact families aren't merely a *fruit* of strong communities, they are a necessary *building block* of strong communities. With fewer intact families, there are fewer customers for the ice cream parlor or the mini-golf course in the first place, fewer attendees for Sunday service, a smaller pool from which the PTA can draw active members, and fewer role models for other families.

The result is a widespread alienation. The poverty, death, unhappiness, and other maladies of the white working class "stem to a large extent from a lack of connectivity," networking expert Navidi writes.[35]

Again, the problem isn't powerless networks. It's the *lack* of networks. "White working-class Americans of all ages were much less likely than their college-educated peers to participate in sports teams, book clubs, or neighborhood associations," Emma Green at the *Atlantic* wrote[36] after studying 2016 research from the Public Religion Research Institute.

"More and more white Americans," Green wrote, "are being pulled toward isolation, away from the thick knit of civic and religious life that has long defined American political culture."

Rural white America is beginning to look like the worst picture suburban or rural whites sometimes paint of urban black America. And the root cause is very much the same—erosion of community. Among all the efforts to battle crime in bad inner-city neighborhoods,

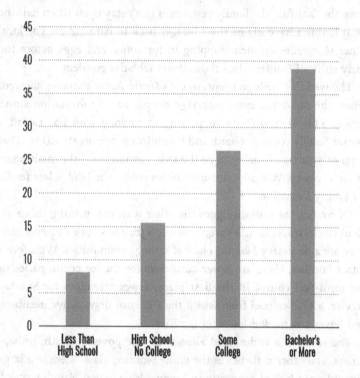

More Education Means More Volunteering
Percentage of Population That Has Volunteered in the Past Year

the most consistently effective ones have involved the creation of community groups that take steps, in the words of one researcher on crime, "designed to change the neighborhood from a dangerous, run-down, anonymous set of streets into an urban village, where the streets were clean and safe, and where people knew their neighbors and looked out for each other."[37]

And in the Mon Valley, the shadow of the rusted steel mill does not make a *place* a *community*.

"There's nothing good in the area," was the evocative way Trump voter Pam Schilling put it to a reporter in 2017. She lives in Johnstown, Pennsylvania, where her son, a laid-off coal worker, had died of a drug overdose. "I don't have anything good to say about anything in this area. It's sad."[38]

For all the movies and books following the beloved story line of elite suburbia being socially isolating, the broader demographic story is different. The elite suburbs, the Chevy Chases, are tightly intertwined. Meanwhile the Fayette Counties and Middletown, Ohios—the rural counties and the working-class suburbs—are unraveled.

And when you visit the economically struggling places in the Mon Valley, in West Virginia, in coal country, in J. D. Vance's Ohio, you find isolated individuals in places that are socially barren. You find alienated America. "We don't have anything here," barmaid Cassie told me at Smitty's. "The skating rinks closed down, and there's like two decent parks around here, the rest are all crap. . . . Friday night, you wanna do a family thing—what are you going to do? In Uniontown there's not something to do."

"In my opinion," Michael Chalmers, a newspaper publisher in West Virginia's Panhandle, told writer Margaret Talbot, "the desperation in the Panhandle, and places like it, is a *social* vacancy." Talbot went on, "Many drug addicts, he explained, are 'trying to escape the reality that this place doesn't give them anything.'"[39] This echoes Robert Nisbet's definition of alienation: individuals who not only are without community but fail to see the draw of community anymore.

Chalmers's phrase "social vacancy" is a good one. There are people around, and there are buildings. But when it comes to connecting to other humans, the place is empty. In such an environment, an intact family would be like the families on the island of the Cyclops in Homer's *Odyssey*:

> *Neither assemblies for council have they,*
> *nor appointed laws,*
> *but they dwell on the peaks of lofty mountains in hollow caves,*
> *and each one is lawgiver to his children and his wives,*
> *and they reck nothing one of another.*[40]

This isn't a natural or fitting state for the individual or the family. Hope is absent here. Thus the perception that the American Dream is dead. Thus the early and enthusiastic support for Trump.

Social Cohesion and Election 2016

Michael Barone is one of America's most seasoned and renowned political observers, so it's no surprise that he was one of the first to see this pattern in the 2016 election. The longtime author of *The Almanac of American Politics*, Barone is himself an encyclopedia of American politics. He prides himself on having visited all 435 congressional districts, and if you tell him where you're from, he'll recount the vicious county commissioner race there from 1974 and explain how the old factory anchored that community for decades.

Barone, my colleague at both the *Washington Examiner* and the American Enterprise Institute, identified early on the crucial pattern of the 2016 primaries:

"How to make sense of the electoral divisions in this year's Republican primaries and caucuses?" Barone asked in late March 2016 as Trump began to run away with the nomination. Barone noted that the old divisions didn't hold.

There's not a regional division, for example. Trump's best primary states have been Massachusetts, Mississippi and Arizona. We're not seeing the divide between evangelical Christians and others apparent in the 2008 race between Mike Huckabee and John McCain.

We're not seeing the suburbs/countryside division of 2012, when in crucial primaries Mitt Romney carried a million-plus metro areas and Rick Santorum carried almost all other counties. Trump carried metro Detroit and Chicago—Romney country last time—but lost to Ted Cruz in Raleigh-Durham and Kansas City.

How to distinguish where Trump won and where he lost? "My answer is social connectedness," Barone wrote, "or, Robert Putnam's term in *Bowling Alone*, social capital. Socially connected people have strong family ties and wide circles of friends, are active in churches and voluntary organizations and work steadily."[41]

Barone explained: "Looking over the election returns, I sense that Trump's support comes disproportionately from those with low social connectedness." The keenest observers spotted the same pattern.

In the primary campaign, running against the likes of Cruz, Rubio, Jeb, and Kasich, Trump based his campaign on the premise that America was no longer Great. Trump repeated, "The American Dream is dead." Trump proudly wore "the mantle of anger." You could take the early stages of the GOP primary as a referendum on the question: Is the American Dream dead?

This tells you what "the American Dream" means to so many people: strong community, thick networks packed with social capital, and institutions of civil society.

THE DEATH OF COMMUNITY AND THE RISE OF TRUMP was a headline in the *Atlantic* during the primaries.[42] "White Americans, especially the young and the working classes, are largely becoming detached from religious and civic institutions," writer Emma Green explained.

The more detached the voter, the more enthusiastic about Trump over the other GOP candidates, pollsters found. One survey in April 2016 found Ted Cruz trailing Donald Trump 31 to 37 among all Republican voters. But the pollster also asked questions about voters' civic involvement. The "civically disengaged"—those who didn't belong to clubs or organizations, or go to church—were Trump's base in the Republican primaries, supporting the bombastic billionaire over Cruz by a margin of 50 to 24.[43]

"How often, if at all," the Public Religion Research Institute asked voters during the 2016 primaries, "do you participate in a non-religious activity group, such as sports team, book club, PTA or neighborhood association?" Those who seldom or never participated were twice as likely to be Trump voters as to be Cruz voters.

Most Trump voters seldom or never participated in these group activities, compared with less than 30 percent of Cruz or Kasich voters who were similarly detached.[44]

Perhaps the most powerful evidence that social connectedness or social capital explained Trump's early success is a review of where he did the worst in the primaries: the Chevy Chases and Oostburgs of the country. He got about 15 percent in both of those villages. Utah, famously close-knit, was Trump's second-worst state in the primaries. Look at college towns, and you see Kasich or Rubio thrashing him. Even on the precinct level, these data show up—tucked in corners of zip codes he carried in the Maryland primary, there were Orthodox Jewish precincts that Trump lost to Ted Cruz.

The elites, the observant religious conservatives, and the college towns weren't three different categories of places. These disparate-seeming groups were a single category: places with strong communities that provided residents with a support structure and a sense of purpose. The man telling us that the American Dream was dead did worst where civil society was strongest. That is, the American Dream manifests itself on the local level and it depends on community institutions that support the family and the individual.

"To be attached to the subdivision," Edmund Burke wrote, "to love the little platoon we belong to in society, is the first principle (the germ as it were) of public affections. It is the first link in the series by which we proceed towards a love of mankind."[45] Those without a little platoon to belong to are going to suffer, too, from a diminished love of mankind. Those places where the platoons are absent are going to be places with less love and more anxiety. Alienation is a local phenomenon.

One reason it's easiest to define Trump Country by its opposite is that these social deserts are becoming the norm. A huge swath of America lacks strong civil society. In much of the country, as the election showed us, the American Dream really is dead.

The "Preservationists"

This pattern extended over the early primaries, according to one pollster's unique analysis of Trump supporters.[46]

The Democracy Fund asked thousands of adults dozens of questions. Pollster Emily Ekins then took the bucket of Trump voters and sorted them by their answers to questions on culture, economics, and politics. She detected four fairly distinct clusters (in addition to a nondescript, not very responsive cloud of voters she called the "disengaged"). While all these groups voted for Trump in November over Hillary Clinton, one group constituted Trump's core support. In the other clusters, including free marketeers and dyed-in-the-wool

Republicans, only about 50 percent said they supported Trump in the primaries over Marco Rubio, Ted Cruz, and John Kasich. Among one cluster—the group was less educated, was more concerned with immigration, wasn't particularly enthralled with free enterprise or loyal to the GOP—the early Trump support was 80 percent.

Ekins labeled this cluster of voters the "Preservationists," a term that echoes Trump's nostalgic motto, "Make America Great Again." Members of this "Preservationist" group said religion was very important to them, but among all Trump voters, they were the least likely to actually go to church. "They are the most likely group to be on Medicaid," Ekins wrote, "to report a permanent disability that prevents them from working, and to regularly smoke cigarettes. Despite watching the most TV, they are the least politically informed of the Trump groups."

Trump's core vote, in other words, was the socially abandoned voter, the person lacking strong connections to his community. As Ekins put it, the "Preservationists" who supported Trump in the primaries over sixteen other options are the voters who generally "feel powerless against moneyed interests and the politically connected and tend to distrust other people."

Among all groups that eventually voted for Trump over Hillary Clinton in November, this group was "the most likely to believe that most people look out just for themselves rather than try to help others (62 percent) and will try to take advantage if they get the chance (66 percent)," Ekins noted.

"The Preservationists don't have that community," Ekins told me. "They're isolated."

We will revisit the Preservationists in later chapters, and their relationship with religion and attitude toward immigrants, but for now it's enough to note the large body of data showing that Trump's staunchest and earliest supporters—not those who simply preferred him to Hillary, or who eventually came around to him, or who simply support him as president, but those who immediately gravitated toward him—are the *alienated*.

Those, mostly on the left, who have sniped at the white working class and declared, "There's No Such Thing as a Good Trump Voter," don't see this. Recall Michelle Goldberg, the *New York Times* columnist who sneered at the shrinking minority of the "white, provincial, and culturally revanchist." *Revanchism* is reclaiming territory some enemy has conquered. This wasn't totally wrong—the cultural Left, for instance, took over all of entertainment and academia. But there's a more important thing that's been lost and needs reclaiming. It's not the cultural institutions they've lost to the Left, but the cultural institutions they've lost to social decay.

A middle-aged man who longs for the culture he lost could be longing for *Family Ties* instead of *Transparent* on television, but he also could be reminiscing about when his town had a Little League and Memorial Day parades, and before the churches on Main Street shut down. When some Americans lament cultural changes, the media always assume this is about national cultural shifts—what the elite sensibilities consider unequivocal progress—but most important, they're lamenting cultural shifts that are more local. The elites don't think about these cultural shifts because they don't see them: The retreat from marriage and the erosion of civil society aren't happening in Chevy Chase and Princeton. They're happening in Trump Country.

Trump Country in Iowa

"Counciltucky" is the derisive name Des Moines or Omaha residents use to describe Council Bluffs, Iowa, whose denizens have a reputation as less refined than the residents of the cities to the east or west of them on I-80.

Dave Dieatrick uses the term proudly, and he introduces himself as a "Counciltuckian" as he buys me a drink at Glory Days Sports Bar and Grill on caucus night in Council Bluffs. Dieatrick is fifty-five and has lived in Council Bluffs his whole life, but he never attended a caucus until Trump ran for the GOP nomination. When Dieatrick showed up at Broadway United Methodist Church across the street for the caucus earlier that night, he saw yard signs for Marco Rubio, Ted Cruz, Ben Carson, John Kasich, Jeb Bush, and every other candidate but Trump—even a Chris Christie sign made an appearance.

When the caucus chairwoman asked for representatives of the Trump campaign, nobody stood at first. The other major candidates all had precinct captains who were recruited and briefed by statewide organizations and county-level volunteers.

Trump had dozens of supporters, but there was no organization behind them. They didn't really know each other. None were civic leaders. They weren't typically involved in politics, and they didn't really want to be. So when nobody stood to represent Trump, Dieatrick, who is naturally effusive, rose to the occasion, speaking impromptu about the need to build the wall on the southern border. Unlike the spokesmen for the other campaigns, though, Dieatrick didn't stick around after his vote—he retired immediately to Glory Days.

As the caucus chairwoman finished counting the votes inside Broadway United Methodist, the campaigns all had a handful of representatives looking on. Some were auditing the vote. Some were there to report the final tally to headquarters, and others were just neighbors chatting. Only two Trump backers remained: a couple, sitting together near the back of the church, in tattoos and matching leather jackets. They were also the only lingerers who wouldn't talk to a reporter.

Trump won the precinct easily, the precinct chairwoman announced, and the leather-clad Trump couple walked out laughing and waving off my interview request. It was like a movie where the ragtag clan of black sheep win the day. But unlike the characters in the movie, they didn't look like a team. There were no signs of cohesion. It was just that the unattached, unconnected, dispossessed—even in Council Bluffs' most urbane precinct—outnumbered the involved, optimistic, idealistic Cruz and Rubio supporters.

Trump won Pottawattamie County by 13 points. It was his best large county in Iowa, by far. Pottawattamie also distinguishes itself as a desert of civil society. In Penn State's index of social capital this county has the third-lowest score out of Iowa's ninety-nine counties.[47]

Reflecting the work of Robert Putnam in *Bowling Alone*, this Penn State "social capital index" assigns each county in America a score. It's an imperfect measure, and it would be dangerous to conclude too much about any one county's civic life simply by looking at the Penn

State number. But in general it provides a rough estimate—the more alive and connected a county is, the higher its rating.

This is the number Raj Chetty mostly leaned on in his study of economic mobility—the study that found that social capital was the number two predictor of a child's upward mobility, just behind the portion of intact families in his community.

It turns out that social capital also predicted voting in the Republican primary—again, we're talking about the primary, not the general election where voters were choosing between Trump and Hillary. We're talking about the people who instantly gravitated to Trump, who would not have voted in a GOP primary if not for Trump. The early primary results show that Trump Country is made up of the places where civil society has eroded the most. Trump's cities and towns and counties are the ones where community bonds are the weakest.

All across Iowa, the pattern jumps out: The higher a county's social capital index, the worse Donald Trump did in the Republican caucuses.

Two of Trump's worst counties were Polk and Pocahontas. They're pretty different (as far as Iowa counties go). Polk is home to Des Moines, the state capital, and according to Penn State's data, an impressive forty-seven civic organizations, thirty-two professional organizations, and seventy-three recreational organizations. Throw in the 81 percent voter turnout in 2012, and Polk was tops in the social capital score in Iowa in 2014 (the most recent data as this book is written).

It's no surprise that Polk, as a wealthy, highly educated county, voted for Marco Rubio in the caucuses. Trump finished a poor third here.

Meanwhile, Pocahontas County looks at first glance much like most Iowa counties. It's got a small town, Pocahontas, in the middle, a few tiny neighborhoods scattered throughout, and otherwise it is corn and soy. But with seventeen churches, a business and a labor association, two bowling alleys, and four public golf courses, Pocahontas was the Iowa county with the most institutions of civil society per capita. In 2014 Pocahontas was second only to Polk on the social capital score.

Like the Dutch counties we discussed in chapter 1, heavily German Pocahontas County had relatively little interest in Trump during the

February 2016 caucuses. Trump, who lost to Ted Cruz statewide by only 2.3 percentage points, was basically tied in rural Iowa, according to entrance polls. But in the very rural Pocahontas County, Trump lost to Cruz by an overwhelming 16 points.

Akin to the Dutch and the Germans in rural Iowa are the Norwegians. Winnebago County, up on the Minnesota border, is 35 percent Norwegian in ancestry. Winnebago also has the highest concentration in Iowa of evangelical Lutherans, according to the Association of Religion Data Archives (ARDA).[48] Winnebago was one of six counties in Iowa and thirty-four in the whole country where Trump got less than 20 percent.

Right next door was Hancock County, another county where Trump didn't hit 20 percent. Hancock is also heavily Norwegian and evangelical Lutheran, but also the highest-ranked county in Iowa on the score of associations per capita.

Of the twenty Iowa counties with the highest social capital index, Trump won only five (25 percent). Of the bottom twenty counties (including Pottawattamie), Trump won nine (45 percent).

The pattern held in a separate social capital index, created in 2018 by the office of Senator Mike Lee. Of the ten lowest-ranking counties, Trump won eight, losing the other two by less than a percentage point. Of the ten counties with the highest social capital score on this index, Trump won only one.

For instance, there's Fremont County, which on paper doesn't look that different from Pocahontas or the rest of Iowa. Fremont's median household income of $53,000 is perfectly average—it's almost identical to the statewide median. The county sits in the bottom left corner of the state, bordering both Nebraska and Kansas. The largest town, on the border of Page County to the east, is Shenandoah. The rest of the county is corn and soy.

If you tried to predict how Fremont County would vote, income, adults' educational attainment, or previous electoral performance wouldn't have told you much. Yet you could have predicted Fremont's love for Trump by looking at social capital.

MEMORIAL BAPTIST CHURCH CLOSES ITS DOORS IN SHEN was the headline in Shenandoah's newspaper the *Valley News*, on October 13, 2013.[49] The article quoted the pastor, Mike Brogan:

*"The church has been battling with this for quite some time," said
Brogan. "It's the way things are right now."*

*Financial issues and low attendance are two of the reasons for
the closure. It's an issue a lot of churches are dealing with, said
Brogan.*

A year later, in November 2014, the *Valley News* carried a similar
story:

*Locust Grove Methodist Church, located about 13 miles southwest
of Shenandoah, voted to begin the process of closing and abandoning
the church.*

*Pastor Buck Buckham said there just aren't the funds and members
available to keep churches afloat in these times.*[50]

Then in June 2016, the small paper would ring the same note again:

*After attending the same church for 80 years, Edith Beery is looking
for a new place to worship.*

*Sunday, June 26, will be the final service for the Norwich United
Methodist Church located east of Shenandoah on Highway 2.*[51]

By a large margin, Fremont was Donald Trump's best county in
Iowa—he pulled 42.8 percent there and won by more than 20 points.
He won every single precinct in the county. It was the only county
where that was true.[52] A couple of days later, the *Valley News* carried
the "devastating news" that the local manufacturer of car parts,
Eaton, would lay off 250 people in Shenandoah.[53]

"It's a difficult situation as a city," Gregg Connell, the executive
director of the Shenandoah Chamber of Commerce, told the *News*,
"and it's much more difficult for the families involved. We are a non-
county seat community in rural America. We don't have a college, an
interstate or a casino. We don't have any tourism."

Shenandoah, along with the rest of Fremont County, doesn't have
much of anything. Trump's best county in Iowa scored lower, by a
large margin, than any other county on the association index. Fre-

mont was also the cellar dweller on the broader social capital index—and that was *before* Norwich United Methodist shut down and before the Eaton layoffs happened.

And Trump's worst county in the state—worse than urbane, educated, wealthy Polk, and worse than German, lively Pocahontas—was Sioux County, the Dutch county in Northwest Iowa.

The Fallout

These cultural changes, under the radar of much of the readership of the *New York Times*, must not be ignored. The consequences will take much longer to fully manifest themselves, but they will be disastrous, because civil society does much more for people than fill up their social calendar or boost their count of Facebook friends.

Civil society is what makes us fully human. Only in his relations with others can man attain the good life. In pedestrian terms: Life is too hard to go it alone. But the issue is bigger than that.

Aristotle invokes Homer's Cyclops in the *Politics* when he famously asserts, "Man, by nature, is a political animal."[54] Aristotle's use of "political" shouldn't call to mind *Meet the Press* or presidential campaigns. The word needs to be understood by its root word, *polis*, often translated as "city" or "city-state." Man, by nature, is city-based, community-connected. People are not supposed to mind their own business or simply attend to their families. We are supposed to be *political*. This could make the reader envision a race of busybodies minding everyone else's business, but it has a simpler meaning: Acting out one's political nature means not merely controlling our own lives but also shaping the world around us.

It's also true that controlling our own lives and managing our own families often *require* community. Civil society provides a necessary support structure for family life, in countless ways. Young couples need older couples to provide examples and advice. A tight-knit network acts as an insurance plan of sorts: If you get sick, or injured, or lose your job, you can count on your neighbors to help out. Even on a day-to-day basis it's immensely useful to have neighbors to call on for a cup of sugar or an hour of babysitting. This insurance, even when you're not making "claims" on it, generates peace of mind and flexibility.

The second half of this same dynamic is that civil society provides a sense of purpose. Life can't be fulfilling unless you feel *needed*. When you join a club, or a parish, or enmesh yourself deeply in a tightly bound neighborhood, people start to rely on you.

When you read the tales of opioid-ravaged towns, you see that drugs often come in where people lack *purpose*. This is what Michael Chalmers, the publisher in West Virginia's Panhandle, was saying when he spoke of "social vacancy": So many individuals in these towns lack a *role* in society. Absent a role, they aren't happy-go-lucky like a working family man on vacation. They're untethered.

The fallout of this alienation is immense.

"What is lost with this decline of social capital?" psychiatry professor Aaron Kheriaty asked in his article on suicide. "Thick social networks (the real, not virtual, variety) facilitate the exchange of ideas and information, as well as norms of mutual aid and reciprocity, collective action and solidarity. These help form our identities and give our lives a strong sense of purpose and belonging."[55]

The blue-collar man whose woe is described by David Autor's studies on manufacturing areas is facing this very scourge. If he doesn't have a good job, why should the mother of his child marry him? Without a job or good prospects, without a family, without a community that relies on him, he becomes, to put it harshly, *un-needed*.

"Jointly pursuing common goals—prosaic or profound—draws people out of themselves," Senator Lee's report on associational life said, "gives them a reason to get up in the morning, and to be responsive to the needs of others."[56] On the flip side: "When people lack the meaning and purpose derived from strong bonds and routine social attachments, they are more prone to alienation and atomization."

Tocqueville put it this way:

Sentiments and ideas renew themselves, the heart is enlarged, and the human mind is developed only by the reciprocal action of men upon one another. . . . In order that men remain civilized or become so, the art of associating must be developed and perfected among them.[57]

Without strong associations that constitute civil society, these benefits are lost.

Can civil society have a downside? Of course. Sometimes we become too cliquish or conformist. The power structures of institutions create opportunities for abuse, as scandals in the Catholic church and other institutions remind us. One sociologist found that in German towns that were more tightly bound, Nazism caught on more quickly.[58] (More on civil society's dangers later.) In America today, however, we don't have to go hunting for the consequences of insufficient civil society.

The bitter irony, once again, is that the people who would benefit the most from community connection are the ones most likely to lack it. We know stories of poor villages that form tight bonds that get them through their hardship. This response has existed and still does exist in America. But generally, lower income correlates with lower education, and each with lower social capital and weaker community. Weaker community, as Chetty found, means less upward mobility.

Civil society connections "are a fundamental precondition for social mobility," Sandra Navidi, the network expert, wrote.

There are health consequences, too. Recall those early examinations of the Iowa caucuses and Super Tuesday. Trump's support correlated with middle-aged deaths. That's because Trump's support correlated with crumbled communities; and without strong community bonds, despair is more likely—and that is fatal.

CHAPTER 7

It's about Church

America's Indispensable Institution

Like every Republican nominee in recent decades, Donald Trump in 2016 overwhelmingly won the evangelical vote in the general election. Like all recent Republican nominees, Trump also won handily among white Catholics[1] on Election Day.

This tells us much more about parties than it does about Trump. Religiously observant Christians tend to vote Republican, for many reasons. For instance, observant Christians are more likely to be pro-life, and the Republican Party, regardless of the particular nominee, is generally pro-life while the Democratic Party is, as a rule, pro-choice. Many Christians see Democrats as increasingly hostile to religion, with Barack Obama condescending to Middle Americans who bitterly cling to their religion,[2] and then engaging in legal and regulatory battle against religious employers and even an order of nuns called the Little Sisters of the Poor.

More generally, Trump in November 2016 did better among old people, and old people are more likely to be religious.

So Trump's win of the Christian vote in the general election shouldn't be read as a love of Trump. In fact, his 56 percent haul among Protestants and his 50 percent among Catholics in the exit polls were both a few points below the average for 2016 Republican congressional candidates. Among those who attend church at least once a week, Trump did a bit worse than the average 2016 congressional or Senate candidate,[3] and he also did worse than Mitt Romney had.[4] Trump's record with religious voters was, in a word, complicated.

In the early primaries, for instance, different states displayed different patterns. Trump won evangelicals in South Carolina with the same percentage that he won the rest of the state. On the other hand, he lost Iowa to Ted Cruz because he lost Iowa's evangelical vote to Cruz by 12 points. Since taking office, Trump has won the love of conservative Christians, many of whom were lukewarm toward him in 2016, especially during the early primaries.

This complicated relationship between Trump and the religious vote has very interesting contours, it turns out. Why was this man, to whom religion seemed totally unimportant, doing so well among Southern white evangelicals? Why was a thrice-divorced billionaire who recently supported funding Planned Parenthood carrying Catholic exurbs of Boston so handily? And why did this same candidate bomb in Mormon Utah? Why did he do so poorly in the primaries in Oostburg, where everyone goes to Dutch Reformed churches, and then clean up in Oostburg in the general election?

Again, the most revealing data come not from the general election (when religious voters had only two choices, and the specter of Hillary Clinton hung over their heads) but from the early contests. Who gravitated immediately to Trump, and who turned to him only when the alternative was Hillary?

Pollster Emily Ekins, who detected in the electorate some distinct clusters of Trump supporters, found that the most enthusiastic, earliest cluster—largely voters who cared little about politics until Trump came along—had an odd relationship with religion: "Despite being the most likely group to say that religion is 'very important' to them," she wrote of Trump's core cluster, "they are the least likely to attend church regularly."[5]

So I called Ekins and I asked her to crunch some of her numbers for me. Looking just at the primary vote, how well did church attendance predict whether a Republican voted for Trump or for another candidate?

Pretty well, it turned out:

The more frequently a Republican reported going to church, the less likely he was to vote for Trump in the early primaries. Trump was weakest among those Republicans who go to church the most (32 percent of this group voted for him in the primaries), and did nearly twice as well (62 percent) among those who never go to church. Each step *down* in church attendance brought a step *up* in Trump support.

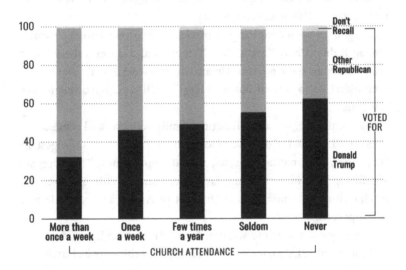

In Republican Primaries, Less Church Attendance Meant More Trump Support

This confirmed what earlier observers had noted. "Trump does best among evangelicals with one key trait," Notre Dame political science professor Geoffrey Layman noticed during the primaries: "They don't really go to church."[6]

Trump in one early poll trailed Ted Cruz by 12 points among evangelicals who go to church every week, but beat Cruz by 27 points among the less frequent attenders.[7]

When *Wall Street Journal* political reporters wanted to go to the heart of Trump Country in March 2016, they traveled to Buchanan

County. Buchanan County is in Virginia, which voted on March 1. But to give you an idea of the place, it borders West Virginia and Kentucky.

THE PLACE THAT WANTS DONALD TRUMP MOST was the headline from Buchanan County.[8] "There isn't much Jody Bostic believes in these days," the article began, zooming in on a former coal miner. While this article barely focused on religious matters, religion—or its absence—is central to the story of Appalachia. Out of 3,143 counties in America, Buchanan County ranks 3,028th in religious adherence, according to the Association of Religion Data Archives (ARDA). Only a quarter of Buchanan County professes a religion, which is half the rate of the median American county.

So again, if we see the early primaries—when voters were choosing among Rubio, Cruz, Kasich, Jeb, Trump, and a dozen others—as a referendum on the American Dream, the most pessimistic were those who didn't go to church but who largely still considered themselves religious.

Economic woe, social dysfunction, family collapse, and community erosion all characterized the places where Trump was strongest in those early nominating contests. So did empty pews. This suggests something very important and far bigger than the 2016 election: The unchurching of America is at the root of America's economic and social problems.

The woes of the white working class are best understood not by looking at the idled factories but by looking at the empty churches.

Secularizing America

America is an exceptionally religious country. There are other nations more religious than the United States, including some Christian nations. In many Catholic countries, for instance, the feast days for prominent saints are national holidays. (In the United States, by contrast, Christmas is the only Christian holiday that is also a national holiday.) But no large wealthy nation is as religious as the United States. Certainly, you won't find white Christians more dominant in any large country.

Western Europe, despite being the home of Christianity for most of the last two millennia, is currently far less Christian than the United States is. Western Europe has lower rates of attendance, lower rates of belief, and lower rates of affiliation. Many European countries have laws that are explicitly hostile to religion (the United States has some of those, and we'll discuss them in later chapters). European elites speak of "secularism" as a principle and a virtue in public life.

America is far more Christian; at the same time, non-Christian religious minorities flourish here. We are, simply put, a religious nation. But that's changing.

The Pew Research Center in 2014 found that the portion of American adults who are religiously unaffiliated jumped by 50 percent over less than a decade. Religious activity has dipped at the same time: the last few years have seen a small drop in those who report praying daily, those who believe in God, and also those who say religion is important to them.

But larger than any of these small declines was the decline in those who say they *attend* church at least monthly—in seven short years, attendance fell by a tenth, from about 40 percent in 2007 to about 36 percent in 2014.

Pew summarized its 2014 findings this way:

> *Religious commitment—as measured by respondents' self-assessments of religion's importance in their lives, frequency of prayer and religious attendance—has declined among men and women, college graduates and those with less education, married and unmarried respondents, people in every region of the country and people with various racial and ethnic backgrounds.*[9]

Compare the 2010s with the late 1960s, and the shift is more dramatic. Robert Putnam, the preeminent scholar on social capital, wrote, "[I]ndependent streams of evidence suggest that Americans have become somewhat less observant religiously over the last half century."[10]

"Church attendance decreased in the West during the twentieth century," economists Raphaël Franck and Laurence Iannaccone found in 2018, citing the International Social Survey Program, and "the decline in church attendance was particularly pronounced after the 1960s."[11]

Author Mary Eberstadt, in her 2013 book *How the West Really Lost God*, laid out the case convincingly that America and western Europe have undergone a dramatic secularization, especially since the 1960s. Attendance and professed belief were two measures. Frequency of prayer was another. Observance of church rules was another important one.

This last one shows up in personal behavior, but also in the public attitudes toward and expressions about morality and religion. Eberstadt writes that "many sophisticated people do not believe that the churches have any authority *whatsoever* to dictate constraints on individual freedom."[12]

Starting in the 1970s, the mainline white Protestant churches began fading from their preeminent position in American life. Today they are almost irrelevantly small. The Catholic church saw a huge drop-off in attendance starting in the late 1960s, and a disastrous emptying out of its seminaries at the same time. Numbers for Catholics stayed respectable only because of immigrants filling the pews at Mass, but even there, second-generation immigrants were secularizing. And the white evangelical denominations that seemed to be taking up the slack from the mainline Protestants peaked, it turns out, in the 1990s.

There are plenty of plausible explanations for *why* Americans are falling away. Maybe it's the material attractions of the modern world: We're wealthier and have cooler toys and more television channels. Maybe it's the increased availability of consequence-free sex that makes religious teachings on sexuality harder to accept. Maybe it's the failure of the Church—the Catholic church's abuse scandals, evangelicals' politicization, mainliners' lukewarmness.

While commentators like Putnam and Eberstadt (and me) find these trends foreboding, there are plenty who look at the secularization of America and cheer it as the progress of man. In this way, secularization is like the disappearance of manufacturing jobs, the retreat of marriage, and falling fertility.

But cheering on secularization is an error. On the aggregate, the Americans who are turning away from religion, particularly among the working class, are doing worse than those maintaining their connection to religion. And secularization is harming the country as a whole.

The Irreligious Suffer

While there are plenty of highly educated atheists who are doing quite well for themselves in America, the *barely religious* in general are worse off than the more devout.

Marriage and the intact family are good, even if you don't share a conservative religious view of them. Chapter 5 established thoroughly that a retreat from marriage is bad for the people and communities it affects. And healthy marriage and religious attendance are closely correlated.

"[O]n average," Brad Wilcox writes, with the data to back it up, "Americans who regularly attend services at a church, synagogue, temple or mosque are less likely to cheat on their partners; less likely to abuse them; more likely to enjoy happier marriages; and less likely to have been divorced."[13]

There's enough evidence to suspect a real causal relationship here. The General Social Survey, one of the broadest and most in-depth surveys of American culture, has data on how churchgoers behaved compared with nonchurchgoers. Wilcox studied these numbers and also controlled for income, race, education, age, gender, and region. That is, the researchers wanted to make sure they weren't finding more family-friendly behaviors among churchgoers just because churchgoers are wealthier or more educated. So, having statistical controls for these factors means you are comparing a college-educated white forty-year-old churchgoer with his college-educated white forty-year-old neighbor who *doesn't* go. You are also comparing the thirty-year-old black female churchgoer with the thirty-year-old black female who *doesn't* attend church.

With these controls in place, families that attend religious ceremonies weekly were much more likely than those who seldom or never attend to (a) eat dinner together daily (58 percent to 41 percent), (b) do household chores together weekly (71 percent to 56 percent), and (c) go out to movies, sporting events, or parks at least once a month (56 percent to 43 percent).[14]

"Churchgoing kids," Robert Putnam wrote in his 2015 book, *Our Kids*, "have better relations with their parents and other adults, have more friendships with high-performing peers, are more involved in sports and other extracurricular activities, are less prone to substance abuse (drugs, alcohol, and smoking), risky behavior. . . and delinquency."[15]

From time to time, the media will trumpet some study finding some malady among the religious—they're angrier, or stupider, or greedier. But ask almost any social scientist, Left or Right, religious or secular, and he or she will tell you with high confidence that religious people are better off socially and economically and fall into fewer negative behaviors (crime, teenage pregnancy, drug abuse, suicide) than nonreligious people. Popular culture likes to paint the dark picture of religion in America, but the actual data point the other way.

On a more fundamental level, research suggests that religious people—all else being equal—are happier than less religious people. About half of people who attend church more than once a week say they are "very happy," according to data from the General Social Survey. The number is 41 percent among those who go weekly. As attendance drops, so does happiness, down to only 25 percent among those who go once per year or less.

"[C]ulturally conservative white Americans who are disengaged from church," liberal journalist Peter Beinart wrote, leaning on social science research, "experience less economic success and more family breakdown than those who remain connected, and they grow more pessimistic and resentful."

Gallup, the pollster, has a "Well-Being Index," which measures emotional health, physical health, healthy behaviors, and more. Controlling for age, gender, race, ethnicity, region, state, and family status, the very religious scored higher on five of six measures of "Well-Being," with physical health being the only exception. In other words, Gallup found that very religious people have better lives than similarly situated nonreligious people.[16]

Interestingly, the "moderately religious" fared worse on almost every question than both the very religious and the nonreligious. So being highly religious seems correlated with happiness, but being a little bit religious does not. This is important, and we'll discuss it more later.

And to return to the first question in this book, among white Republicans, if you go to church weekly, you are 19 points more likely to say the American Dream "still holds true" than if you seldom or never attend.[17] The numbers were similar comparing white Democrats who aren't tied to organized religion.

While Christians seek their reward in the afterlife, going to church may actually postpone that blessed day: A study of 18,000 baby boomers aged fifty and older from 2004 to 2014 found that those who attended church frequently were 40 percent less likely to die in that ten-year stretch than those who never attended, even after controlling for the fact that the physically or mentally ill might be less able to attend.[18]

And on the darkest correlations, suicide, depression, and drug abuse are more likely among the irreligious. "Between 1996 and 2010," psychiatry professor Aaron Kheriaty wrote, "those who attended any religious service once a week or more were five times less likely to commit suicide."[19]

Beinart, the journalist, is a liberal. Writing in the left-leaning *Atlantic* magazine in 2017, he tried to plead with his fellow liberals to see the dangers in this secularization. Secularization, he wrote, is "making America's partisan clashes more brutal."

[I]t has contributed to the rise of both Donald Trump and the so-called alt-right movement, whose members see themselves as proponents of white nationalism. As Americans have left organized religion, they haven't stopped viewing politics as a struggle between "us" and "them." Many have come to define us and them in even more primal and irreconcilable ways.

He's right, and this deserves more discussion. For now, the suffering among the secularizing working class should be enough to convince us that the unchurching of America is a problem.

It's Not Just Christians

This book has used the words *church* and *churchgoers* in a generic sense, but everything said about Christians in America applies equally, as far as we can tell, to adherents of other religions. Religion plays the same sort of role—as a central institution of civil society—for Americans of all creeds.

An interesting survey of Muslim Americans in 2017 reflected this. Muslim Americans were worried about Donald Trump as president, and they feared that his immigration policies and his rhetoric would make life harder for them, this survey found. But here's a telling passage from the poll results: "A large majority of U.S. Muslims continue to profess faith in the American dream, with 70% saying that most people who want to get ahead can make it in America if they are willing to work hard."[20]

The striking thing: Muslim Americans were *more likely than the average American* to profess such faith in the American Dream. The simplest explanation, given what we've seen so far in this chapter: Muslim Americans believe the American Dream is alive for the same reason the people of Oostburg and of Salt Lake City believe it—their religious observance brings with it some seed of happiness and optimism.

Given the good outcomes among the religious, we need to ask, *What is the causal mechanism?*

Lessons from Ramadan

Separating causes from mere correlations in the study of religion is tough, but one group of researchers found a pretty clever method to do just that. It relies on the moon and the sun.[21]

The Muslim calendar uses lunar months, which are always 29.5 days. A lunar year (twelve full moons) is about eleven days shorter than a solar year. As a result, the Muslim calendar and the Gregorian calendar are out of sync. That means the Muslim holy season of Ramadan is at different times in different years. In 2016, for instance, Ramadan lasted from June 6 to July 5. Back in 2001, it lasted from November 16 to December 16.

Most Muslims are obliged to fast during daylight hours in Ramadan. You can see the importance of the shifting calendar, then: In the Northern Hemisphere, the hours of fasting in 2016 were much longer than they were in 2001. Come 2030, Ramadan will be in the heart of winter again, providing once more a briefer fast in the Northern Hemisphere.

Geography also makes a difference. Bangladesh, just above the Tropic of Cancer, has fairly low variation in hours of daylight from winter to summer (10:40 of daylight in late December compared with 13:36 in late July). Turkey, at the same latitude as the U.S. mid-Atlantic, has a larger variation (9:20 versus 15:00 in Ankara).

Scholars Filipe Campante and David Yanagizawa-Drott wanted to see how a longer fast affected people, and so they studied economic variations among Muslim countries across different years. They also polled Muslims on satisfaction with life. They checked the variations over time and place against non-Muslim countries in an effort to isolate the effects of longer or shorter fasting.

In a study published in the *Quarterly Journal of Economics*, they reported two things: Muslim countries saw an economic downturn in the places with—and during the years of—longer fasts (summertime Ramadan), yet they found self-reported well-being improved among Muslims in those same times and places.

The implication: Religious fasting makes people poorer but better off. We shouldn't extrapolate too much from this study, but it does have an interesting implication. If this is generalizable to other sacrifices made in the name of religion, it could suggest that communal religious observance yields happiness, even if it diminishes wealth. Because so much of our observational data find religious observance and wealth linked, this study, unlinking the two, provides a hint that communal religious observance is more closely linked to happiness than wealth is.

The Who and the Why

So America's growing irreligiosity is a problem. Only the most stubborn enemies of religion deny that.

Why and among whom is this secularization happening? The most direct and simplest way to account for the drop in religious observance in America over recent years is this: Young people are not that religious, and old people who are religious are dying.

But there are more interesting demographic patterns in the unchurching of America, which may undermine the reader's assumptions. Following the data will lead us to a revealing, if now familiar, landscape. To get on the right path, though, we need to break away from some common prejudices.

When we say the story is millennials turning away from church, it's easy to commit the same error many do when thinking about the retreat from marriage. This is the Lena Dunham Fallacy: blaming cultural shifts away from traditional norms on highly educated, wealthy, white liberals.

That wasn't the story on marriage—recall from chapter 5 how the wealthy and highly educated actually get married far more than the less wealthy and less educated; the retreat from marriage is really occurring among working-class whites.

And it's similar with church. Self-professed atheists, to be sure, are more likely to come from the ranks of the elites, so you can hold on to that stereotype with decent factual grounding. But the other half of the religiously unaffiliated demographic is the chunk of America that simply doesn't belong any religion. They don't call themselves atheists, and they probably won't preach to you about their religious disaffiliation. Pew calls them "nothing in particular."

The "nothing in particulars" are a bit *less* likely than the average American to have gone to college and to have graduated from college.[22]

The nothing-in-particulars are disproportionately male and white—the same demographic we've seen show up again and again, in discussing Trump support, suicide, and so on.

Citing a different survey the *Atlantic*'s Emma Green writes:

[T]he effects of religious disaffiliation show up prominently among members of the white working class, many of whom don't attend church very often. Religiously unaffiliated Americans are also less educated, on average, than many of their faithful peers: Less than one-third have a college or post-graduate degree, placing them below Muslims, white mainline Protestants, white Catholics, Jews, Hindus, and other groups.[23]

This will surprise the conservative who falls for the Lena Dunham Fallacy, and it will surprise the leftist who agrees with Karl Marx that religion is the opiate of the masses. American Christianity, if it is a narcotic, turns out to be a pretty high-end drug, among whites at least.

Not only Marxists drop out of religion. "The percentage of white Republicans with no religious affiliation has nearly tripled since 1990," liberal essayist Peter Beinart wrote in 2017, citing data from the Public Religion Research Institute.[24]

Sociologists Philip Schwadel, John McCarthy, and Hart Nelsen studied the relation between religious observance and income, looking specifically at Catholics and at Mass attendance. (Sunday Mass is an obligation, and skipping it is a mortal sin in Catholic teaching.) The researchers found the same sort of correlation that the above surveys found: "[L]ow-income white Catholics attend church less often than other white Catholics."[25]

There's tons of evidence to establish this same point: Poorer Americans are less likely to be active practitioners of their faiths. Robert Putnam voices this fact in a fittingly high-church way: "If you listen carefully, hymns in American houses of worship are increasingly sung in upperclass accents."[26]

The phenomena here are (a) growing irreligiosity among the white working class, and (b) the family, social, and political epiphenomena: early and enthusiastic support for Trump and endorsement of his proposition that the American Dream is dead.

There's more exploration of this landscape to do, though, because the fact of working-class irreligiosity has some interesting contours—caveats and nuances that tell us something crucial.

1.   The first caveat: There hasn't always been a meaningful correlation between religious practice and wealth. A hundred years ago, it was true—the poorer were less observant. But after World War II, interestingly, that correlation nearly vanished.

"[B]y the 1970s," Brad Wilcox writes, "social scientists had largely come to believe that the impact of social class on religion in the U.S. was no longer of much consequence in large part because the fortunes of American religion rose for both the working and middle/upper classes in the post–World War II era to the point where there were not marked class differences between these two groups."[27]

The baby boom brought with it a religious boom, and that religious boom lifted the low- and moderate-income Americans to about the same level of affiliation and observance as the wealthy. This should ring a bell: the 1950s and 1960s as something of a Golden Era for the working and middle classes, when meaningful class distinctions were smaller.

2.   There's an even more telling caveat to the wealth-religiosity correlation: It's mostly a white-people thing.

"[B]lack and Latino religiosity is less likely to be stratified by class," Wilcox reports.[28] Schwadel's study of Catholic Mass attendance found that among Hispanic Catholics, wealth doesn't predict Mass attendance. In other words, *only among whites* does poverty have a large negative effect on Mass attendance.

3.   The third caveat emerged when Wilcox ran a regression analysis—the sort of statistical exercise that aims to separate out various factors that are often connected. In this case, one problem muddling the data is that the white working class is less likely to have intact, stable, two-parent families.

Controlling for that was revealing. It turns out that much of the working class's lower participation rates can be explained by weaker family structure. According to Wilcox, growing up with divorced parents makes people less likely to go to church. So does being unmarried as an adult. These two factors explain about 40 percent of the class difference in attendance.

4.   The family factor brings us to our final clue: The white working class is less religious only by some definitions. Trump's core voters, you may recall, were more likely than the average voter to say religion was very important to them. Huge chunks of the religiously unaffiliated in Pew's surveys nevertheless describe themselves as "religious."

So how do we square this with the data on the growing irreligiosity among the white working class? Let's go back to Middletown, Ohio, and visit J. D. Vance's Mamaw. If you read *Hillbilly Elegy*, you'll recall her Christian devotion: She regularly prayed and had a spiritual outlook on life. You may also recall another trait: Generally, she *didn't go to church*.[29] Mamaw is one person, but she's the perfect totem for the working class turning away from religion. That Gallup "Well-Being" index that found the "moderately religious" the worst off? The "moderately religious" were largely people who said religion was important to them, but who only rarely *went to church*.

If you're a churchgoing, synagogue-attending, mosque-frequenting religious person, you may see it as hypocrisy that someone would say religion was very important, and then not attend services. Maybe that's fair. Maybe not. Rather than judge whether nonattendance among professed Muslims, Christians, or Jews is hypocrisy or is justifiable, it's more useful to see it as a key that will unlock the puzzle of class and religion in America: The class effect on religiosity is not so much a difference in *belief* as it is a difference in *attachment to institutions*. The key question here isn't "Are you religious?" It's "Do you go to church?"

Maybe it's best phrased, "Do you *belong* to a church?"

The study that found baby boomers 40 percent less likely to die young if they went to church? It actually found mortality was *higher* (by 4 percent) among those who said religion was "very important" to them.[30]

Let's return to the difference between poor Hispanic Catholics (who go to Mass as often as wealthier Hispanics) and poor white Catholics (who go less often than wealthier whites). What do poor Hispanic Catholics have that poor white Catholics don't? That was one of the questions that sent Schwadel and crew searching for another factor—

a factor that is often *correlated* with income, but at times can be separated from it. The key trait they found determining whether a Catholic went to Mass or not: "the existence or quantity of social ties."[31]

That is, poverty and low social connectedness tend to go together (as chapter 6 laid out), but these researchers separated these traits in an effort to determine which trait was causing what effect. Their findings suggest that wealth isn't causing or helping Catholics to attend Mass. Community ties are.

"There is little or no effect of income on church attendance for white Catholics with multiple types of organization memberships," Schwadel and colleagues concluded. In other words, being poor made you less likely to go to Mass, but not if you were enmeshed in your community. So *poverty* itself doesn't keep people out of church. Social isolation keeps people out of church.

Thus the white/Hispanic difference. Poor Hispanics were more likely to be fully enmeshed in their communities. Poor whites were more likely to be socially isolated, and *that* was what was keeping them from church.

Wilcox put this whole pattern in a larger context of the American working class: "Religious life among the moderately educated is becoming increasingly deinstitutionalized, much as working class economic and family life have become increasingly deinstitutionalized."

Here's where this chapter tells the same story as the previous one: The unchurching of the working class is a specific instance—the most important instance—of the erosion of civil society.

It's the most important part of this story even if you don't have much stake in the sacraments or sermons. First off, church is the most important part of civil society in America, in part because it is by far the biggest part.

For all the talk about bowling leagues and Kiwanis Clubs and Rotary Clubs in Robert Putnam's *Bowling Alone*, the dominant source of civic activity in America is church. "As a rough rule of thumb," Putnam wrote in that book, "our evidence shows, nearly half of all associational memberships in America are church-related, half of all personal philanthropy is religious in character, and half of all volunteering occurs in a religious context."[32]

But that understates the importance of church in American civil life, because, as Putnam documents in *Bowling Alone* and again in his 2010 book, *American Grace*, people who go to church get more involved in nonreligious activities and organizations than people who don't go.

In short, white working-class woe in America is the fruit of collapse of civil society; and in America, among the non-wealthy at least, civil society mostly means "church."

"The First of Their Political Institutions"

Discussing church as an institution of civil society might bug all sorts of people. To a believer, the church is no mere institution of civil society. It is no peer of a bowling league or a PTA. Catholics call their Church "the mystical body of Christ" and see it as different in kind from other institutions to which we may belong.

To a secular American, you may believe that religion ought to be put in its own category, separate from secular institutions. *Religion belongs in private, not out in the public square*, this mind-set holds. This view manifests itself in state laws excluding religious schools from the same standard support any other nonprofit institution could get. (Note that there are no activist groups dedicated to the Separation of the American Legion and State.)

Both classes of objection are important. Religious institutions are different in very important ways from nonreligious institutions. As a Catholic, I consider my Church to be unique among institutions on Earth in that it was instituted by Christ, given the keys to heaven, and promised that hell will not prevail against it.[33] The Rotary Club has no such powers.

Despite the crucial differences between churches and other institutions of civil society, there are important ways in which they are the same thing.

In any event, America's culture and politics cannot be considered separate from religion. "Religion, which, among Americans, never mixes directly in the government of society," Tocqueville wrote, "should therefore be considered as the first of their political institutions . . . Americans so completely confuse Christianity and freedom in their minds that it is almost impossible to have them conceive of the one without the other."[34]

Russell Kirk argued that this was always and everywhere true, that culture is always secondary to religion. "From what source did humankind's many cultures arise?" Kirk asked. "Why, from cults. A cult is a joining together for worship—that is, the attempt of people to commune with a transcendent power. It is from association in the cult, the body of worshippers, that human community grows. . . . Once people are joined in a cult, cooperation in many other things becomes possible."[35]

The shared, common life of a community finds its roots in religion.

For instance, when it comes to people serving their neighbors, churches do heavy lifting. Putnam, a decade after writing *Bowling Alone*, published an exhaustively researched follow-up called *American Grace*, along with Notre Dame government scholar David Campbell. This volume reaffirmed that church was the most important institution of civil society in America, and that it provided great benefit to its members and the broader community. "[R]eligious Americans are, in fact, more generous neighbors and more conscientious citizens than their secular counterparts."[36]

One-third of all volunteering in America is for religious organizations. Perhaps more impressively, "regular churchgoers are also much more likely to volunteer for secular causes."[37] The authors ran statistical controls, to make sure this wasn't just a factor of churchgoers being wealthier or more educated, and they found it held up: "[R]egular churchgoers are more than twice as likely to volunteer to help the needy, compared to the demographically matched Americans who rarely, if ever, attend church."[38]

Churchgoers give more, as well. The most religious 20 percent of Americans "is more than four times as generous as his or her counterpart in the least religious fifth," and that generosity spills over into secular charities, as well. If you're raising money for some good cause that has nothing to do with religion, you'll still find more open pocketbooks among churchgoers, all else being equal, than among nonchurchgoers.

Volunteering and giving could be seen as a way churches serve the wider community. But as any volunteer and many charitable givers will tell you, serving others is good for the *giver* as much as for the *receiver*. In this way, volunteering and giving are simply two easily measurable aspects of the larger and more important fact: Religious people in America—specifically, those who attend church regularly—enjoy much more social connection. Church helps churchgoers, in large part, by making them much more connected and involved with their communities, both religious and secular, both their congregation and their neighborhood association, both their "small group" and their bowling league. "Religious Americans are up to twice as active civically as secular Americans," Putnam and Campbell found.[39]

The authors concluded that it was churches, *as institutions of civil society*, that delivered this civic benefit. Putnam and Campbell wrote: "[C]ommunities of faith seem more important than faith itself," when it comes to producing this neighborliness and good citizenship.[40]

Putnam and Campbell even found that the very same person is more likely to get involved in secular community activities when he or she starts attending church and that dropping out of church usually goes along with dropping out of secular civic activities.

Crucial elements of strong communities are more common among churchgoers. Take *trust*, for instance: Americans, religious or non-religious, simply trust the religious more, Putnam and Campbell found. Also, religious people trust other people more than secular people do.[41] The religious "score significantly higher" on measures of empathy and altruism, too. Maybe this is because the Bible and the texts of other religions repeat messages of charity: "[W]hatever you did for one of the least of these brothers and sisters of mine, you did for me," Jesus explains in the Gospels.[42]

Whatever the root cause of religious people's superior charity, trust, and civic involvement, the channel through which it is conveyed is *membership in the church community*, and the best predictor of these civic virtues is regular attendance at church.

The aspect of religiosity that builds civic virtues, then, is *church attendance*, Putnam and Campbell's data suggest. "Once we know how observant a person is in terms of church attendance, nothing that we can discover about the content of her religious faith adds anything to our understanding or prediction of her good neighborliness."[43]

One clever academic study of religious pilgrims published in the *Quarterly Journal of Economics* bolsters the idea that participating in religious activities with a religious community *causes* the good effects.[44]

The Hajj Effect

People who go on religious pilgrimages—such as American Jews traveling to Israel, Catholics hiking the Camino de Santiago, or Muslims making the Hajj to Mecca—will tell you how life-changing these events were. Social scientists, though, have learned not to trust this sort of claim: People can be trusted to describe (a) their current situation and (b) what they did; but people often mis-assign cause and effect even in their own lives.

To determine the effect of pilgrimages, you couldn't simply compare the characteristics of pilgrims and non-pilgrims, because there's a pretty strong selection bias—that is, more devout people are more likely to make pilgrimages. Ideally, you would compare people who go on pilgrimages and those who try to go on pilgrimages, but fail to go, through no fault of their own. So these researchers, David Clingingsmith, Asim Ijaz Khwaja, and Michael Kremer, turned to Pakistan for their data.

Mecca is in Saudi Arabia, and Saudi Arabia can allow only so many people to come for the annual mass pilgrimage known as the Hajj. To control numbers, the Saudis parcel out Hajj visas to every country with a significant number of Muslims. Each country gets to determine how to distribute its own quota of Hajj visas. As of 2011, Pakistan gives out its Hajj visas on a first-come-first-served basis. Previously, Pakistan had doled out the visas by lottery. This lottery provided the researchers with their opportunity.

The researchers polled Pakistani Muslims who had received the visas and went on the Hajj, but they also polled those who entered the lottery but didn't get a visa and thus stayed home. Then they compared the two groups. What they found: Hajj participation "increases belief in equality and harmony among ethnic groups and Islamic sects and leads to more favorable attitudes toward women." In other words, attending a religious event with coreligionists from around the world fostered greater solidarity among Muslims. But just as important, it didn't foster animosity toward non-Muslims. "Instead," the researchers wrote, "Hajjis show increased belief in peace, and in equality and harmony among adherents of different religions."

Communal religious observance, it seems, has pro-social effects.

Religion is different in very important ways from other sorts of community organizations, but one of its obvious and significant roles is the same: a way to meet other people, an opportunity to take on responsibilities, an environment where members can help shape the world around them, a source of support and encouragement, and a font of personal and moral guidance.

Church is a hub of friendships for churchgoers. "[A]lmost half of jointly attending couples form the majority of their friendships with fellow parishioners," Wilcox found in his research. When you recall how loneliness is arguably the most important health risk for Americans, this is a pretty powerful endorsement of church. Wilcox's data suggested that these friendships are the largest reason that church attendance promotes marital happiness.[45]

As we discussed above, nonchurchgoers are more depressed, more likely to be in poverty, more likely to die of despair. Nonchurchgoers are less likely to be connected to their community, and frankly less likely to see the value of community. Again, these risks are greater for the working-class unchurched than for the wealthier unchurched.

Robert Nisbet's definition of *alienation* seems to perfectly describe a big chunk of nonchurchgoers: The alienated individual "not only does not feel a part of the social order; he has lost interest in being a part of it."[46] Sure enough, Pew's research found that religiously unaffiliated people were far less likely to believe it was important to belong to "a community of people who share your values and beliefs."[47]

Of course, some perfectly secular places have strong community ties and intense civic involvement. They tend to be the wealthy and highly educated places.

Here's one way to look at it: In secular America, civil society is a high-end good that most people can't afford. Churchgoing people have access to civil society regardless of income.

And that Ramadan study—where longer fasts correlated with lower incomes but more happiness—showed that wealth and happiness really are separable, as long as you have religion.

Put another way, the two entrances into the crucial networks that provide meaning and support in life are (a) to be part of the elite, and (b) to go to church. Either one will do. "The civic difference between Americans who attend church nearly every week and those who rarely do so," Putnam and Campbell found, "is roughly equivalent to two full years of education."[48]

A crucial difference, though: Joining the elite isn't something available to everyone. It never has been. Joining a church, on the other hand, has much lower barriers to entry.

At least in theory, that's true.

Places without Church

"Wherever two or three are gathered in my name," Jesus said, "I am there among them."[49]

Christianity, the dominant religion in the United States, is inherently communal. It is also inherently familial. To be sure, private prayer and a personal relationship with Christ are central and indispensable to Christianity. But while this one-on-one relation with God is at the core, Christian churches have long understood that this core cannot be left bare—"it is not good for man to be alone."[50]

Humans, not being angels, need a support structure if we are to keep our hearts focused on the divine. As Genesis establishes, the most basic support structure—the first layer around that core—is marriage and the family. Around that layer is the parish, the congregation, the local community that gathers together in a building to worship—in the case of the Abrahamic religions, to keep the Sabbath as a community.

Abrahamic religions are all intensely communal. To take my church, the Catholic church: The individual's relationship with Christ is built on the foundation of sacraments. None of the sacraments can be self-administered. They all require a minister (in the case of marriage, the husband and wife are the two ministers). Baptism and marriage both typically involve further community involvement: Godparents or a best man and maid of honor officially play the role of witnesses to these sacraments. The sacrament of Reconciliation requires confession to another person—a priest. The most regular sacrament, the Eucharist, is quite obviously communal (it's called "Communion," after all) and this rite, in which a community drinks from the same cup, is part of a remembrance of the Last Supper, shared by a platoon of Christ's closest friends.

Some of these elements of Catholicism turn off some Protestants, but many Protestant sects are very communal in their own distinctive traits. Speaking in tongues, as some charismatic Christian denominations do, calls back to a biblical episode featuring large crowds in Jerusalem. Your average evangelical congregation has a dozen or so "ministries" and tries to supplement Sunday's service with small groups during the week.

Nothing could be more obvious than the communal nature of Judaism, whose self-understanding is as a chosen *people*. In Islam, prayer is understood to have more force when offered together with fellow believers than when offered alone. Consider the Hajj.

Religion, like every worthwhile thing in life, needs community. "[T]rying to believe without a community of believers," author Mary Eberstadt wrote, "is like trying to work out a language for oneself."[51]

The three things here—family, faith, and community—are so intertwined in human nature that all three must be understood as both causes and effects in mutual reinforcement. Eberstadt (wife of Nick Eberstadt, who wrote on the men dropping out of the labor force) argues in her book that we should regard the secularization of America as a bitter fruit of the erosion of family. Family provides the context in which religion makes sense, she writes. "Family and faith are the invisible double helix of society, two spirals that when linked to one another can effectively reproduce, but whose strength and momentum depend on one another."[52]

So it's hard to have faith without family. It's hard to keep families strong without faith. It's hard to keep families or faith strong without communities to support them. But communities are built *of* families, and the strongest communities are often kept together by shared faith.

When you see this interdependence, it sheds a new light on the suffering working class and the guy who doesn't go to church, doesn't get married or can't stay married, and maybe has dropped out of the workforce. Brad Wilcox summed up this plight with a paper aptly titled "No Money, No Honey, No Church."[53]

Charles Murray wrote of the "virtue" of religiosity, which his fictional working-class "Fishtown" lacks. It's easy to read this as an attack on the working class—they're *vicious* rather than *virtuous*. But enduring religiosity requires community, and no individual has total control over his own religiosity, because no individual by himself can build a community. By definition, that takes other people.

And while Jesus will be there, the Bible says, if only "two or three" are gathered, a church community is going to be much more robust with greater numbers than that.

A small congregation can be more intimate and more cozy, but a sclerotic, inconsistent, and shrinking congregation is also liable to lose its function as a valuable network of support, encouragement, modeling, and purpose.

Even though church has a higher purpose than social networking— i.e., eternal salvation—the lack of a more tangible, immediate benefit will reduce its draw. Distilling the insight in Nisbet's *The Quest for Community*, essayist Fred Donovan Hill wrote that when institutions "lose their functional roles in the larger society they will inevitably decay." Hill continued, "If an institution becomes less than vital to the economic and political operations of a society, then that institution is going to decline."[54]

It's another Catch-22: If your neighbors aren't going to church, the spiritual and worldly benefits of church diminish. But why would your neighbors go if there's insufficient community there?

In this light, recall the people of Fremont County, Iowa, the rural county that is a social capital desert, with churches regularly closing. The middle-income whites there, with their sparse attendance, could be understood as the seed mentioned in Jesus's parable, tossed by the planter, that lands on the footpath or on the rocky ground. The seed lacks good soil in which to take root and grow.[55]

Can we blame the seed for where it lands? Surely man has free will, and there are famous stories of humans persisting in and strengthening their faith all alone. Saint Patrick was a slave left alone in a field with sheep in pagan Ireland as a boy, and he prayed without ceasing until he could escape—eventually returning as a bishop and a missionary. So we shouldn't deny people individual agency by saying their environment *determined* their outcome.

Yet we know that environment *helps* determine our outcomes. That's why parents work hard to find the right school and community in which to raise their children. If people thought environment didn't help determine outcomes, they wouldn't expend so much time and money to obtain a great environment—family, school, neighborhood—for their children. They'd just say, "Hey, kid, make good decisions."

Those of us who find ourselves in good families and strong religious communities know that we benefit from both of these things, which is one reason we serve these institutions. If we benefit from our local congregation, ought we look less with scorn and more with pity and concern on those who live where the strong religious communities have dried up?

Closing Churches, Crumbling Communities

The same phenomenon we see in rural communities like Fremont County and Buchanan County is also visible in urban neighborhoods: When religious institutions shut down, the poor, working class, and middle class suffer as communities fray.

A study of closing Catholic schools suggests a cause and effect.

Catholic schools are closing at a ferocious rate across America. Half of them have closed since 1960.[56] In the Archdiocese of Chicago, for instance, about 87,000 students attended the archdiocese's schools in 2013, compared with 300,000 in 1965. Researchers Margaret Brinig and Nicole Stelle Garnett studied the effects of urban Catholic schools closing.[57] They acknowledged that schools often close because communities are crumbling, but they looked for evidence of communities crumbling *because* schools were closing. In short, they looked for Catholic schools that closed because of some random or unexpected problem in the parish—such as a priest-specific problem—that didn't reflect a broader community malady. The researchers found a very pronounced negative effect. In neighborhoods where Catholic schools unexpectedly shut down, residents reported more public drinking, drug dealing, and drug use, and more teenagers causing disturbances.[58] Graffiti, litter, and abandoned buildings became more prevalent.[59]

Most important, after a parish school closed unexpectedly, people in that neighborhood were less likely to agree that "people around here are willing to help their neighbors," or "this is a close-knit neighborhood," or "people in this neighborhood can be trusted."[60]

Disorder, distrust, and fear all rise up when a Catholic school leaves an urban neighborhood, this study suggests. In a wealthy neighborhood, full of highly educated people, there are other institutions to take the place of church, perhaps—a country club, a public school crawling with involved parents, yoga for mom, and travel basketball for Sean.

But for the part of America that lacks the resources to plug into these institutions, losing the institution of the church leaves them alienated.

ב

Seek the *shalom* of the city to which I have carried you into exile.
Pray to the Lord for it, for in its *shalom* will be your *shalom*.

Perhaps the oddest aspect of this divine order is that it is an order to
exiled Jews. They are clearly not at home in the city.

The Hebrew word translated as "city," *ir*, carries a negative connotation. Babel, an ungodly creation, is the first *ir* in the Bible.

So the Lord is telling the Israelites to look after the *shalom* of something that is very much not theirs. They are strangers in a strange land,
but their own *shalom* depends on the *shalom* of this strange land.

The current city is not the Promised Land, yet it commands the
attention and the labors of the exiles.

CHAPTER 8

Overcentralization

How Big Business and Big Government Erode Civil Society

So, how did we get here?

Deaths of despair, such as suicide, overdose, and alcohol poisoning. Men dropping out of work, out of the entire labor force, and out of society altogether. A retreat from marriage, and births out of wedlock becoming the norm. Life spans shortening. Inequality skyrocketing. Economic mobility fading.

These are the symptoms of an American Dream that is dead in much of the country.

The oxygen the Dream needs—social capital—is scarce in those places. Civil society has dissolved in huge swaths of America. Local community is a notion without a reality there. Historically, "civil society" in America has really meant "church." So the erosion of civil society is largely the collapse of churches.

Half the problems we think of as problems of poverty are problems of eroded civil society. Half the problems we think of as problems of modernity are really problems of eroded civil society.

This is a plague of alienation.

Because secularization and the erosion of local community are the conditions of our culture's economic and social woes—and the conditions that gave us Donald Trump—then the question of who killed the American Dream is really the question of *who killed civil society?*

It's tempting to finger a single cause, but we need to acknowledge that local community and civil society have many foes, who have chipped away with many tools.

Conservatives will blame the welfare state—and that's not wrong. Liberals may blame capitalism—and that's not totally incorrect. If we try to blame Left or Right, though, we will fall into error and miss half the culprits. Even sorting the culprits—the enemies of civil society—by ideology or party will mislead us.

The best starting point here is one particular term for the churches, bowling leagues, swim clubs, and other institutions this book has focused on. That term is *middle institutions*. They are *middle* not between Left and Right or between upper class and lower class. They are *middle* between the whole society and the individual. They are *middle* between the central government and the citizen.

The erosion of civil society that the previous chapters has spelled out, then, is the disappearance of the middle institutions. There are two forces that pull us away from the middle in this regard: centralization on the one hand and atomization on the other. You could also call them collectivism and individualism. If we all go our own way, our little platoons fall apart. If we are all lumped together, our little platoons are consumed by the whole army.

In chapter 3, we mentioned the progress since 1955 as a matter of these two seemingly contradictory forces—individualism and centralization. This progress was real, but progress usually comes at a cost. The next two chapters will study the harms of these forces. We will get to the hyper-individualism in the next chapter. Let us start with the overcentralization.

A Centralizing Century

Modernization often yields centralization, politically, economically, and culturally. Conservative thinker Yuval Levin wrote a book in 2016 titled *The Fractured Republic*, which delved into the forces of centralization and individualism, and he pinned centralization largely on modernization.

Citing political scientist Ronald Inglehart, Levin wrote that economically, "modernization generally involves the growth of large, industrial manufacturers at the expense of small, local producers." In government, "an increasingly centralized and uniform set of rules and institutions replaces ad hoc, often localized practices, and the scale of government action increases." And culturally, "modernization tends to replace localism and traditional attachments with mass culture. It displaces the small and near-at-hand with larger, often more distant entities."[1]

Over the last century, in fits and starts, America has seen a great centralization of government, culture, and economics. Small and local businesses dotting Main Street have been replaced by large national chains corralled into shopping centers. Governments have taken over what churches and voluntary groups used to do. State governments have taken over what towns and counties used to do. Most of all, the federal government has taken over what everyone else used to do.

The most consequential centralization, probably, has been on the political and governmental front.

"The conflict," Robert Nisbet wrote in *The Quest for Community*, "between central political government and the authorities of guild, village, community, class, and religious body has been, of all the conflicts in history, the most fateful."[2]

This didn't merely *happen*. There was a philosophy behind this.

Progressivism and "New Nationalism"

After Abraham Lincoln, no American politician is claimed as solicitously by both parties as is Teddy Roosevelt. Teddy can swing both ways because he doesn't fit neatly into the contemporary political spectrum. He was sometimes "Left" and sometimes "Right."

He advanced a growing federal regulatory state and a more aggressive foreign policy. He was a radical change-maker, but he was also a champion of conformity. He saw America's future as one of bigger government *and* bigger business.

Running through these seeming alternations between Left and Right, though, there's something consistent: Teddy Roosevelt was a champion of centralization.

Roosevelt seized on the spirit of the age, which professed that science enabled great solutions to society's problems—if only people of goodwill were given enough power. Armed with this confidence, TR moved to increase government's role in daily life and in industry, and to consolidate that power in the federal government.

Promising a "New Nationalism," Roosevelt argued that for many issues, the public interest "can be guarded effectively only by the national government."

"The New Nationalism," Roosevelt would say, "is impatient of the utter confusion that results from local legislatures attempting to treat national issues as local issues. It is still more impatient of the impotence which springs from overdivision of governmental powers. . . . This New Nationalism regards the executive power as the steward of the public welfare."[3]

In Roosevelt's Progressive Era, a confidence in science and power underlay a ferocious push for both centralization and rethinking of old ways of doing things. The progressives believed that things previously left to happenstance and the uncoordinated decision making of millions of individuals could now intelligently and rationally be *planned*, to the betterment of everyone.

You can see how this idea of planning and centralization would weaken local communities and weaken the middle institutions. *Heck, those middle institutions and small platoons could be made irrelevant with good enough central planning. Certainly, the inconsistency and redundancy of tens of thousands of towns and parishes and millions of clubs could be fixed with some regularization.*

In the Progressive Era, this idea had many champions, among politicians happy to take on more power, among businessmen who lamented competition as wasteful redundancy, and among intellectuals who fancied themselves the wise planners. The *New Republic* magazine was founded back then with a vision as ambitious as the magazine's name would suggest. Founding editor Herbert Croly wrote with optimism that the central government could become "responsible for the subordination of the individual to the demand of a dominant and constructive national purpose."[4] Along the way, this would involve the subordination of smaller and more local entities to this "national purpose."

This government centralization has been at the heart of American progressivism, even to this day. It was taken for granted in the New Deal. It was explicitly an aim of Lyndon Johnson's Great Society. It was behind Obama's ambitious agenda.

"We know what works," President Obama said in 2015, in arguing for more federal spending and more federal programs to prop up the industries of the future. "We know what we have to do. We've just got to put aside the stale and outmoded debates," Obama would say, so that we can "write the next great chapter in our continued advance."[5]

In this centralizing mind-set, history is a story of progress, wherein one's duty toward one's neighbor is step by step moved away from the local and personal and into a massive, efficient, central, and unitary power.

The Things We Do Together

"Government," former Democratic congressman Barney Frank is often quoted as saying, "is simply the name we give to the things we choose to do together." It's a telling line not only in that it glosses over the nonconsensual nature of many government actions (think of the TSA), but more important because it erases or ignores most of the things humans actually *choose to do together*. This isn't a petty semantic critique of Frank or the politicians who approvingly quote him. Frank's line really captures a widespread view that something counts as "public" only if it is owned and controlled by the government.

The view that *public* matters are and ought to be *government* matters has been behind America's centralization. It's almost a psychological difference between the Left and the Right, and it's one that often pits progressives against civil society and local community.

"Conservatives don't really get that some things are 'public,'" economics scholar Mike Konczal, a man of the Left, wrote in 2013, "and it's hurting their ability to handle the challenges of the early 21st century." As an example of conservatives denying the public nature of social ills, Konczal cited yours truly. I had argued, as he paraphrased it, that "the current safety net provided through the federal government, in [Carney's] mind, is better provided by private, civic 'voluntary organizations.'"[6]

Konczal didn't in this space contend that the federal government would be better than civic or local groups. He was making a moral argument, not a practical one. He charged that when I say a church or community group ought to be the first line of defense to help a community member in need, I am thus denying the "public" nature of that need. This assertion confused me when I read it, but I've since found it all over progressive literature.

Arlie Russell Hochschild, the liberal Bay Area baby boomer who spent months in Louisiana to try to understand the American Right, displayed this same mind-set.

In her book, she describes a "community of some 350 residents" who loved their place on the bayou, "in what they called a 'piece of heaven.'" Bayou Corne was filled with "modest homes" and residents "got on with their neighbors," who were "Cajun, Catholic, and conservative."

When she got to the part about community crawfish boils, I have to admit I started to envy the people of Bayou Corne. What a lively, robust life that community had built! But Hochschild seemed to see it differently, as she described the life of a Bayou Corne resident as "a world nearly wholly private." I thought I had misread. What could she mean? These weren't folks living behind gated drives and locked up in their McMansions. These were people whose life was built around neighbors.

But by "nearly wholly private," this liberal author explained she meant "one as far as [possible] from government taxes and regulation."[7]

Only taxes and regulation make something "public," in this view. Neighborliness, shared culture, and shared faith are "private," the reasoning goes. You're not *doing things together* if government isn't part of it, according to this mind-set.

Elsewhere in Louisiana and later in the book, Hochschild visited a burgeoning church community at Trinity Baptist Church, with summer camps, a snack bar, recovery programs for addicts, and sports teams. She saw a giant slide teeming with children. "The Trinity giant slide reminded me of the imaginatively designed Dolores Park in the Mission neighborhood of San Francisco and the public programs offered by the San Francisco Recreation and Parks Department."

To Hochschild, she wrote, "'public' services and programs were an almost entirely positive thing." She lists all the summer camps, "city-sponsored volunteers," services, activities. "Such programs are open to people of all races and creeds, filling the same cultural space, it occurs to me, filled by the church programs I was discovering in Lake Charles."

In her mind, Trinity Baptist was *displacing the public square* instead of *being the public square.*

"That's the gist of the liberal deep story," which conservatives have a hard time understanding, Hochschild writes, "and the right can't understand the deep pride liberals take in their creatively designed, hard-won public sphere as a powerful integrative force in American life."[8]

When she writes of "a large public square," she means government-controlled.

There's a legalistic way in which this is the right definition. The word *public* often literally means *government-run*—public schools, public funds, public office. But that narrow legal definition isn't the way most people use it in most contexts.

We say "public" when we mean *something that is the responsibility of or belongs to everyone in a given community.* The common usage includes things open to the general population, even those things run and owned by a private entity—particularly if that private entity is subject to significant control by its members. A swim club meets this definition. So does a Protestant congregation. Even a Catholic parish, where the hierarchy reigns, largely meets this definition when you consider the influence volunteers have over how things actually run. If we let the legalistic definition subsume the standard understanding, we are curtailing the public square.

Hochschild, Konczal, and others on the left perhaps can't understand that the folks of Trinity Baptist, Salt Lake City, and Oostburg see the church schools and the church slide as *part of the public sphere* and an integrative force. There's no admission charged on Sundays. The slides and coffee shops and concerts and sports teams at these churches tend to be open to all comers, not merely believers. Even those who are exclusive when it comes to worship (see the Mormon Temples) are inclusive when it comes to other events. The "gentiles" I met around Salt Lake City spoke fondly of bringing their kids to the monthly potlucks the local Latter-day Saints church would throw. The recovery and aid programs that Hochschild described and that most churches have are open to all needy people. Homeless atheists or Catholics aren't turned away from Trinity Baptist.

A mind-set that won't count these institutions as "public" is a mind-set that diminishes community and civil society. It's behind the ideology that has undermined civil society, and thus helped cause the alienation at the root of the problems discussed in this book.

Government necessarily plays a role in the safety net, in regulation, and in fostering civil society. In many ways, central government is indispensable to the safety net. Groups that help the poor will be among the first to say that. But when government gets too big and too intrusive, it undermines all its aims—or at least undercuts its own gains—by crushing civil society.

Tocqueville had warned America that this would happen, that America's egalitarian mind-set and democratic structure would tend toward this centralization. The central government in such a state, he wrote, "works willingly for their happiness; but it wants to be the unique agent for it."

"I Don't Believe in Charities"

Chittenden County is near the northwest corner of Vermont, and it sits on the banks of Lake Champlain. In 1981, the Chittenden County chapter of the United Way hosted a star-studded banquet for the organization's fortieth anniversary: Vermont's governor, Richard Snelling, was there, as was the local mayor, a self-proclaimed socialist named Bernie Sanders. Sanders had dedicated his career to expanding the government safety net, and United Way is the largest coalition of charitable organizations in the country, so you would think there'd be common cause here. But that wasn't how Sanders saw it.

"I don't believe in charities," Mayor Sanders told the assembled fund-raisers and philanthropists. Sanders, the future U.S. senator and presidential candidate, rejected the "fundamental concepts on which charities are based," the *New York Times* reported at the time, "and contended that government, rather than charity organizations, should take over responsibility for social programs."[9]

This wasn't some weird personal quirk of Sanders's. This mind-set is held by whole groups of people, for whom Barney Frank's saying—that government is the things we do together—is *aspirational*. It's rooted in human psychology and the nature of politics, as Tocqueville noted: "Among democratic peoples it is only by association that the resistance of citizens to the central power can come about; consequently the latter never sees associations that are not under its control except with disfavor."[10]

Big Government and civil society are natural rivals, and the growth of one often means the diminution of the other.

It may not be a coincidence that the twentieth-century decline in church attendance in the United States immediately followed Lyndon Johnson's Great Society. The Great Society's "Unconditional War on Poverty"—a barrage of legislation that expanded federal food stamps and disability insurance, created new welfare programs, and birthed Medicare and Medicaid—helped reduce poverty rates in the United States and had many other material benefits in many lives. Some Great Society programs were efforts to juice community organizations in poor neighborhoods, but the big War on Poverty programs were a declaration that it fell to central government to care for the poor, the sick, and the elderly. Often, this meant relieving churches of these duties. So people who saw church as a way to serve the poor might find church less crucial as the federal government displaced it. In the Catholic church, vocations to the priesthood dropped off dramatically after the 1960s.

You can't *blame* the centralizers of the 1960s too much. They saw, for instance, that Uncle Sam was the only one really willing and able to take a pickax to Jim Crow and institutionalized segregation. "States' Rights," a decentralization argument at heart, was deployed in those days to defend "Whites Only" diner counters and schools. Segregation wasn't some local eccentricity we could allow to stand. It was deeply immoral and destructive to America's social cohesion.

Centralizing the social safety net, similarly, provided clear material benefits. Centralization sent more money flowing into care for the poor and the elderly through Medicaid, Medicare, Social Security, unemployment insurance, food stamps, welfare, and disability benefits. Also, the federal government redistributes geographically better than local institutions do. That is, poor regions are better able to get the wealth from wealthy regions when a central taxing and spending power is involved. Finally, churches and private charitable organizations are subject to economic cycles—during downturns, people are less able to donate, leaving these institutions strapped for cash when the most people are the most needy. The federal government, in contrast, can be *countercyclical*: It can print its own money, or in a downturn it can borrow at low interest rates, thus bringing *more* money to the table during recessions or disasters instead of *less*.

These economies of scale are arguments for moving aid programs into the hands of the central government. Beyond the practical virtues, centralizers often make a moral argument, and it's one that directly attacks the idea of community organizations and individual charity. It's Teddy Roosevelt's idea that it only makes sense to fight such an important fight on the largest scale possible. If feeding the hungry and housing the homeless are left up to communities and organizations, then what are you, a lady in Waukesha, doing to alleviate the poverty of a family in Tuscaloosa? Only by making these aid programs as universal as possible (and we don't have a global government yet, so the national government will have to suffice), and running them on tax dollars, do we get every American of means contributing to the relief of every American in need.

Centralizers often see government explicitly as a *replacement* for community.

Franklin Roosevelt, for instance, saw Social Security as a more thorough substitute for bonds of community and family. On the third anniversary of Social Security, in 1938, Roosevelt, in a radio address, told of a man who worked long and hard to support a family and a household. "His security, then as now, was bound to that of his friends and his neighbors." But the Industrial Revolution and modern life made things more complex, Roosevelt said. "Where heretofore men had turned to neighbors for help and advice, they now turned to Government."[11]

When central government grows past a certain point, civil society retreats.

Crowding Out

Kristina Ribali works with the downtrodden people of southwest Florida. Her employer, FlourishNow, finds the single mothers, the men who have dropped out of the workforce, and the homeless, and tries to help them.

"One of the single biggest problems we saw," she told me, "was the dissolution of the family, the erosion of community, the 100 percent dependence on government." These were linked, she argued.

Government programs often create incentives that pull people away from other crucial institutions. Disability benefits, and the strings attached, keep some people from joining the workforce. Welfare, historically, has broken up families. And the impersonal nature of these benefits often creates a personal alienation.

These individual-level effects reflect a wider phenomenon: the welfare state's crowding out of civil society. There is some academic debate over crowding out, but the evidence is strong that government spending reduces private charity.

Jonathan Gruber is an economist who became famous in recent years for his role in crafting and selling the Affordable Care Act. Before his Obamacare fame, Gruber—a liberal—studied the effects of federal welfare programs on churches' charitable activity.

"Churches in the U.S. were a crucial provider of social services through the early part of the twentieth century," Gruber wrote with coauthor Daniel M. Hungerman in a 2006 paper for the *Journal of*

Public Economics, "but their role shrank dramatically with the expansion in government spending under the New Deal."

While the causality needs proving, the correlation is obvious: As the federal safety net grew, church charity fell. Church spending on outside programs (a rough estimate of churches' charitable work) was two and a half times the size of local and state government spending on welfare or charity in 1926, according to Gruber and Hungerman.[12] Then, "church charitable activity fell dramatically starting in the early 1930s, at the same time that the role of the government grew through the New Deal," the authors wrote.

It's probably obvious why you can't jump straight from that correlation to a conclusion about cause and effect. The 1930s featured the Great Depression, and so many of the ordinary people who would be funding church programs through charitable gifts were much poorer and thus less able to give. So Gruber and Hungerman developed an ingenious method to disentangle the Depression's effects on charity from government crowding out.

They studied the contemporary yearbooks and annual reports of thousands of churches and compiled their annual charity spending into a database. Then they looked at who the local congressman was. Why? Not all congressmen have the same amount of clout when it comes to delivering federal funds. More senior members bring home more bacon, and members of the Appropriations Committee are also far more adept at funneling taxpayer money to their districts.

It turns out that church charitable spending dropped a lot more in the districts of powerful pork barrelers than it fell in other parts of the country. That excess decrease of charitable spending in the districts of big spenders, the authors posited, was due to the big federal spending. "The New Deal crowded-out at least 30% of benevolent church spending," Gruber and Hungerman concluded after crunching the numbers.

Hungerman also studied the opposite phenomenon: How does church spending on the needy change when government welfare *retracts*? Looking at welfare reform in the 1990s, he crunched the numbers and determined that "decreases in government expenditures lead to significant increases in church activity."[13]

If a conservative laments this crowding out, there's a common response from the Left: *Are we supposed to provide suboptimal aid to the poor in order to preserve your church soup kitchen?* I've repeatedly encountered this retort from angry liberal economists. They think the loss of civil society institutions is nothing compared with the gains from a more robust federal safety net.

They wave away as airy sentimentality—at best—the notion that poor people need more than just cash, food, and housing, and they come pretty close to Sanders's idea that charity shouldn't really exist. At least they believe that there's nothing lost if a church soup kitchen is replaced by a government program providing food stamps or cash for the hungry.

But this misses out on the less obvious but still crucial benefits civil society institutions provide.

As an analogy: If a centralizer viewed the attendance at the popular local diner in its most direct material way, he might say, "These people need food and coffee. If we deliver to them groceries and a coffee machine, they can get these material needs more easily!" And it might work. Maybe government could buy and deliver to people the breakfast and coffee they want, relieving them of the need to go to the local diner. Hunger and grogginess in that town would go down. But the town would lose the diner.

Losing the diner means losing a meeting place. Over the years, this would weaken the connections between neighbors. You may say, "There's nothing keeping neighbors from getting together anyway, after they've finished their breakfast and coffee at home. Heck, now they can meet at a park or wherever they want, because they are liberated from their need to go to the diner!"

While this sounds rational, it also obviously ignores how human social interaction works. Our more obvious and more immediate needs bring us together, and the coming together fills the less obvious but still very real needs. We come together for food, drink, or security, and we end up gaining from camaraderie. Deprivation in these less obvious needs is often not noticeable in the short run but is devastating in the long run.

When institutions, including local church congregations, have a less visible role in the material needs of a community, many in the community feel less drawn to them. I am writing, not mostly about the *needy* turning away from institutions, but about the formerly *needed*—the average community member who sees church or some other organization as the means through which she serves her neighbor. "To exist and to be vital," Charles Murray wrote in his 1988 book *In Pursuit*, "little platoons must have something to do."[14]

When people don't see the immediate purpose of belonging to institutions, they turn away from those institutions. Then they lose the less obvious, less immediate benefits of community, such as the sense of purpose, the modeling, the camaraderie, the hidden safety net, the prods to take on tasks one might never think of on one's own. While being less obvious and less immediate, these benefits of community are crucial, and their loss is costly.

So we cannot chalk it up as nothing or as mere sentimentality when government crowds out charity and civil society.

The collapse of civil society has wreaked havoc on the needy and the working class, leaving families, communities, and politics in the disarray in which we find them. The trade-off isn't that the poor all get fed at the cost of Aunt Gertrude losing some volunteer opportunities. The trade-off is that there is more money to ensure the poor get fed, and yet less social infrastructure around which the poor and working class can raise intact families, find meaningful work, and access the good life.

"Government is not in the business of restoring families and restoring lives," says Ribali, who spends her days helping families and adults get out of poverty.

At best, the project of government centralization has left fewer Americans hungry and more Americans alienated. This doesn't count as caring for the poor. If Bernie Sanders disagrees, he should take a lesson from his favorite religious leader, whose social teaching Sanders claims to share: Pope Francis.

Include the Poor

Pope Francis is probably the favorite-ever pontiff of the American Left, and Bernie Sanders visited him during Sanders's 2016 presidential run, expressing agreement with "Catholic Social Teaching." But read Francis's social teaching closely and you see a huge chasm between Sanders and Francis. The pope, you see, is worried about alleviating alienation and abandonment, not merely material suffering.

When Francis writes of the poor, he focuses mostly on the problem of their "exclusion." Francis wants to make them less poor and less hungry, of course. But like Jesus, Francis also wants to bring them to the same rooms, same tables, and same communities as the rest of us.

In *Evangelii Gaudium*, an apostolic exhortation he published in 2013, Francis launched his discussion of poverty with a section titled "The Inclusion of the Poor in Society." We are each individually obliged to become "an instrument of God for the liberation and promotion of the poor, and for enabling them to be fully a part of society."[15]

Federal welfare programs are inherently impersonal. They don't work toward *inclusion*, and they often work toward *exclusion*. Giving people a check is often a good and necessary thing, but it doesn't tend to pull them fully into society. In some welfare programs, such as Social Security Disability Insurance, the check is contingent on *not* having a job. Throwing money at the poor, it turns out, is often adverse to welcoming them into society.

And to the degree that these welfare programs crowd out local institutions that have the power to *include* the poor, then the poor are more excluded.

Subsidiarity

Behind Francis's thoughts on care for the poor is a key concept in Catholic social teaching, and it's a concept that warns against overcentralization: "subsidiarity."

If you read or listen to Catholics discussing social matters, you will sooner or later come across the words *solidarity* and *subsidiarity*. Politics today being what they are, you can use a count of these words to guess the ideology of the speaker. If she says *solidarity* a lot, but not *subsidiarity*, she's probably a liberal. If she leans on *subsidiarity* and gives *solidarity* short shrift, she's probably a conservative.

Most of this book, though, has been about solidarity. The force that binds people together in a common cause and purpose is solidarity. Pope John Paul II wrote of solidarity that "it is a firm and persevering determination to commit oneself to the common good; that is to say, to the good of all and of each individual, because we are all really responsible for all."[16]

Pope Benedict XVI had a good and accessible description of solidarity:

> *To love someone is to desire that person's good and to take effective steps to secure it. Besides the good of the individual, there is the good that is linked to living in society: the common good. It is the good of "all of us," made up of individuals, families and intermediate groups who together constitute society.*[17]

Solidarity is taking the love of our neighbor to a collective level and seeing society's good as our own good. Solidarity is often used as a guard against the excesses of individualism or dog-eat-dog capitalism.

Subsidiarity is the other side of that same coin. It is the notion that for every social problem or need, there is an appropriate level of society or government to address it—an appropriate scale on which each duty should be executed.

In the Gospel, there's a telling episode. When Jesus is asked what man must do to attain eternal life, he agrees with the questioner that it is to love God and love thy neighbor. The follow-up question is a loaded one: "Who is my neighbor?" This is where Jesus tells the story of the Good Samaritan.

There is a robbery, and the victim is left bleeding on the roadside. The Samaritan is a foreigner, yet he *loves* this man by helping him, healing him, bringing him to the safety of an inn. He doesn't delegate the caretaking until a few days later, when he leaves the victim (and some cash) with the innkeeper.[18]

This parable doesn't mean one shouldn't call an ambulance in this case in modern America. The Samaritan would have been morally obligated to do so had calling a professional been an option. Instead, this says that the immediate needs of the needy ought to be addressed by those immediately present—and often physically proximate. This principle isn't simply grounded in a reading of one Gospel passage. Subsidiarity is, among other things, a recognition that people are really cared for only when they are cared for on the human level, and that the larger and more distant the entity administering care, the more loveless and thus less effective the care will be.

Subsidiarity often demands wide dispersion of the duty to care. This is contrary to the centralizing impulse of modernity and progressivism. It is anathema to the central planner, who wants things *regulated*.

Regulation

As children in Elgin, Illinois, fell asleep to visions of sugar plums on Christmas Eve in 2017, it was a frigid fifteen degrees outside, and the winds, already ten miles per hour, were picking up. By midday on Christmas, winds were twenty miles per hour, making it feel like seven degrees below zero in that Chicago suburb. The brutal cold would last all week, as a frozen conclusion to a frigid month.[19]

In this suburban tundra lived a Good Samaritan named Greg Schiller. Schiller turned his unfinished basement into a sanctuary from the deadly cold for the homeless of Elgin.[20]

"I would stay up all night with them and give them coffee and stuff and feed them," Schiller told a local reporter. Schiller played movies. He called it a "slumber party."

But the government saw right through Schiller's words and deeds. It knew what he was really up to: using his home as an emergency shelter for homeless people who would otherwise freeze to death. And this it couldn't stand.

"Mr. Schiller's house does not comply with codes and regulations," the city's spokeswoman explained, "that guard against potential dangers such as carbon monoxide poisoning, inadequate light and ventilation, and insufficient exits in the event of a fire."

"They shut me down," Schiller explained, "and said I have 24 hours to return my basement to storage and take down—I have several cots with sleeping bags for everybody—or they'll condemn the house."

The e-mail from the city threatened that "the City will take additional enforcement action to compel the removal of the unlawful basement sleeping area."

The city explained that "Elgin has lawful shelters that provide a safe space for people to go throughout the year," but Schiller said he opened his basement up because one shelter was closed.

The city's message to its citizens was clear: *Saving the homeless is not your job. Hands off.*

It was also a fine demonstration of how Big Government kills civil society through regulation. Regulation is necessary, but it is also in tension with civil society—not at all times, in all ways, in all places, but at least in its central conception.

The Elgin story, being about local government, highlights another tension in any discussion of centralization. Like *north* and *south*, the term *centralized* is a relative one. Addressing something on a national level is less centralized than addressing it on a global level. State power is less centralized than federal power. Local government is less centralized than that. And leaving more things up to institutions of civil society is even less centralized.

Sometimes, though, empowering some entity on a fairly low rung of the centralization ladder—such as a local government—actually diminishes the autonomy of whatever is on the next lower rung.

In any event, we can consider regulation to generally be a centralizing force. *Regulation* is about making things *regular*, uniform. The champions of more regulation in the early twentieth century included massive businesses, which would laud the "rationalization," economies of scale, and efficiency that government management of the economy could bring about. Competition was "redundancy" in the eyes of these rationalizers, and nothing was worse than inefficiency. This was the era in which eugenics and industrial socialism took hold of many intellectuals' hearts and minds. Centralization, Teddy Roosevelt and his friends in industry would argue, was only rational, since modern science gave us the tools to know what is best for everyone.

Subsidiarity, on the contrary, involves vesting power at the local level with a number of freely acting institutions. This approach is at odds with the central-planner views of rationalization and economies of scale.

If the local American Legion post is running youth baseball, while First Methodist Church is running the soup kitchen and the Knights of Columbus operate the neighborhood pool, who's actually *in charge*?

Letting communities run themselves necessarily means different places will do the same things in different ways. This is the sort of hodgepodge that regulation and rationalization are supposed to avert.

That's the conceptual tension between civil society and regulation. Often there's no tension in reality, because often regulation can be a matter of imposing needed standards on private actors so as to protect people from harm—such as requiring serious efforts to keep rats out of a restaurant kitchen. But in practice, regulation often does weaken local community and civil society.

One-size-fits-all safety rules crafted with restaurant chains in mind get applied to soup kitchens and shut them down. Mom-and-pop businesses die in the womb, strangled by red tape and bureaucrats. It's a story that happens every day across America.

A family in the Bay Area, for example, bought an old firehouse with plans of turning it into a brewpub and Portuguese bakery. This is exactly the sort of establishment that can anchor a neighborhood and bring neighbors together. They knew they would deal with regulation about food hygiene, fire safety, kitchen safety, and the safety of customers. It's long established that local governments will police such things with regulation. What the family was unprepared for: how much government authorities would force them to change the property *on the outside*. A local architect wrote on the plight:

> *Mandatory parking requirements, sidewalks, curb cuts, fire lanes, on site stormwater management, handicapped accessibility, drought tolerant native plantings . . . It's a very long list that totaled $340,000 worth of work. They only paid $245,000 for the entire property. And that's before they even started bringing the building itself up to code for their intended use. Guess what? They decided not to open the bakery or brewery.*[21]

Instead, they opened a commercial print shop. Yes, print shops are a valid part of commerce, but they don't form community hubs in the way a bakery or a brewpub does.

Parking requirements are a ubiquitous regulation and they perfectly capture the problem here. County and city governments often require businesses, especially restaurants and bars, to build parking lots for the customers. The fear is that a new coffee shop or bakery will bring in so many customers who will clog the street parking spots and annoy the neighbors. The result is that you can't just stick a diner or bakery in the middle of a neighborhood. That means it's harder to have a neighborhood coffee shop or a corner pub. These establishments must be built for cars rather than for humans, and for a large area—everyone who might drive there—rather than for a small neighborhood whose locals might walk there.

There are shelves and shelves of books and articles documenting how suburbs and sprawling cities are built not on the human scale but for cars, and how this undermines community. Some of this inhuman development is just the free market in play—people often *want* car-centric suburbia separated from business. But much of this is the result of misguided government planners and overbearing government regulation.

You can see this centralizing effect of Big Government in all corners of the economy. After the 2008 financial crisis, Congress passed the Dodd-Frank Wall Street Reform and Consumer Protection Act to regulate banks. The great irony was that the Big Banks (while fighting over the details) largely welcomed the regulation, calling the burdensome rules a "moat" that would protect them.[22]

Meanwhile, the law seems to have demolished community banks. Two scholars at Harvard found, in 2015, that community banks had shrunk significantly as a portion of the banking industry as Dodd-Frank was implemented. Community banks may not be that important to the ordinary banking consumer, who is fine with Bank of America. But for local businesses and farms, community banks are indispensable, in part because they know the community on a personal level.

"Community banks generally are relationship banks," the Harvard scholars wrote; "their competitive advantage is a knowledge and history of their customers and a willingness to be flexible." But regulations, by their nature, are impersonal, the authors noted. "This is sometimes a problem, particularly in a regulatory system that reflects Big Bank processes, which are transactional, quantitative and dependent on standardization and mark-to-market accounting practices."[23]

Businesses based on relationships, on knowing one's neighbors, don't fit in in this world of centralization, regulation, and rationalization. That makes it very hard for community-oriented businesses to arise.

New York City mayor Michael Bloomberg is another iconic Big-Government meddler. He banned smoking, he taxed soda, and he regulated fat content in food. It was inevitable that he would become the enemy of civil society efforts to feed the hungry.

Sure enough, when New Yorker Glenn Richter showed up in early 2012 at Ohab Zedek synagogue on West 95th Street to collect bagels for donation to local homeless shelters—as he had done regularly for two decades—Richter was told that such behavior was illegal. You see, Mayor Bloomberg had issued regulations requiring every institution serving food to disclose the salt content of the food it was serving. Donated bagels didn't have their nutritional information stamped on them. Donating any food for the homeless at all was not kosher (so to speak), the mayor explained. "If they did in the past," Bloomberg barked, "they shouldn't have done it. And we shouldn't have accepted it."[24]

Juan Carlos Montes de Oca, a cosmetology student in Arizona, had a similar experience in 2017. Montes de Oca decided to serve the poor by using the talent he was acquiring: cutting hair. A homeless person has many needs, and grooming may not be the most pressing concern, but it is a real concern. So Montes de Oca began cutting homeless people's hair for free.

This, of course, couldn't stand. Arizona's Board of Cosmetology launched an investigation into this unlicensed cosmetology occurring outside a licensed salon. Such activity posed "a real risk," the board's executive director said. "What, after all, could be more dangerous than living on the street with a potentially bad haircut?" a local reporter wryly asked.[25]

Big Business

The impulse to centralize government power doesn't come from nowhere, and it didn't take hold in America randomly. Yuval Levin puts the Progressive Era push for Big Government in the context of another great wave of centralization: the Industrial Revolution.

It was the rise of Big Businesses and economic consolidation that "created pressure for corresponding political reforms," Levin writes in his 2016 book *The Fractured Republic*.[26] The animating idea behind that era's Big-Government progressivism was that "America's government needed to keep pace with its growing, changing economy."

The stories we tell ourselves of the Progressive Era often portray Big Business and Big Government as rival forces pressing against each other. But that's misleading. Big Business and Big Government were (and are) both conceptually the same and self-reinforcing. That is, as Levin makes clear, industrialization and economic consolidation are an instance of *centralization* just as the progressive's reaction—a more robust regulatory state—is centralization.

And viewing the different big guys as rivals ignores how they reinforce each other: Industrial consolidation gives political support to government consolidation. Meanwhile, bigger government—through regulations, mandates, taxes, and spending—crowds out smaller business, thus building a "moat" around the big guys.[27]

Bigness begetting bigness is also the story behind the history of labor unions in the United States and Britain. The Industrial Revolution brought in new scientific methods to increase the efficiency of production. A truly rational businessman, freed of the irrational superstitions and sentimentality of the past, the argument went, would understand that labor was merely another input, like capital, feedstock, and equipment. A modern producer wouldn't have one machine do three things. Three machines, each specially crafted for a specific task, would do three things.

If people are merely another input, they should be seen similarly to factory machines, fabled management expert Frederick Taylor argued. Rather than an artisan cordwainer making a shoe—so inefficient!— each employee would specialize and be a role player in making the shoe. Why make three whole pairs yourself when you could punch the lace holes in one hundred pairs, and some other guy could install the rivets in one hundred pairs, and so on?[28]

Big Business arose largely from the efficiency gains from this Taylorism, which transformed manufacturing from *a person making a thing* to a factory, using people as machines, making things. Individualism faded away in favor of a sort of collectivism. The workers' response was just as collectivist: organizing into the modern American-British labor union. Workers who were treated not as individuals would in turn not treat their employer or their employer's customers the way individuals treat one another. Work no longer was an institution to which they belonged; instead it was simply an exchange: labor for payment. *Relations* gave way to *transactions*. They now would demand as much as they could from management and give as little as they could get away with—working to the letter of the agreement.[29]

It was a dehumanizing, vicious circle, where big collective entities reduced individuals to cogs.

Walmart's America

The growth of Big Business and the consolidation of industry, like other forces of centralization, tend to erode civil society and local communities. It's a cliché, but it's true, that Walmart and vast shopping centers of national chains crowd out mom-and-pop shops. Free-market advocates will point out that Walmart brings unprecedented selection and far lower prices to people who need them, arguing that everyone is better off for having more money left over after buying necessities.

"[N]ostalgia for Main Street is misplaced—and costly," wrote Cornell economist Louis Hyman in 2017. "Small stores are inefficient. Local manufacturers, lacking access to economies of scale, usually are inefficient as well. To live in that kind of world is expensive."[30]

It's the same with Amazon replacing local bookstores and Home Depot replacing local hardware stores. Measured in terms of short-term material well-being, the rise of Big Business is a winner for everyone.

The consumer is offered far more choice and far lower prices. The champion of free enterprise will say it's mere sentimentality to lament the loss of mom-and-pops to these far more efficient enterprises.

This argument may sound familiar. In form, it's the same argument put forward by defenders of the centralized welfare state when they are confronted with crowding out. They point out how the federal government's economies of scale and national reach deliver more efficient aid, just as Big Business's defenders point to lower prices.

Both defenses of centralization often ignore the real costs. Sure, there's plenty of mere sentimentality in the lamentations about the old drugstore and mom-and-pop corner store. But often the corner store and Main Street constitute a much more cohesive local community than does a strip mall with massive warehouse stores.

There's something rational about the shopping center—plenty of parking and you can do all your shopping in one trip. Car-centric shopping centers might fulfill the immediate need of shopping, but they can murder the more hidden benefits of a walkable Main Street, such as the serendipitous encounters among friends and neighbors that form the bonds of community.

The Great Good Place is the title of Ray Oldenburg's 1989 study on the disappearance in America of the "Third Place," the casual hangouts that form the heart of communities. The Third Place could be a local bar, a coffee shop, a roast-beef-sandwich restaurant with six tables, the chairs at the back of the local barbershop, a commandeered card table in a local grocer's shop, or a bowling alley.

Economic centralization is a chief culprit in the disappearance of these places. Big chains replace local places, and their economic efficiency doesn't allow for lingering, local variety, or much personality at all. Local planners centralize retail in a shopping center or a mall, to bring order to the hodgepodge, pell-mell scattering of shops amid homes that more organic development might have wrought.

"The locally-owned lunch counter soon enough finds itself competing with a newly-built, fast-food non-place," Oldenburg writes, using an apt name for establishments that exist strictly for commerce, but not as a *place* to be and meet and run into a neighbor. "In its decline, the old diner continues to enjoy the trade from its loyal customers, an assortment of regulars for whom it represents much more than just a place to eat. But the real place fails to attract the others."[31]

Again, the efficient delivery of the obvious and immediate need (food) doesn't provide the less obvious but just as necessary need—community.

Oldenburg's meticulous study of places (which we will discuss more in the next chapter) turns up explicit guidance that advises planners against building third places. In a grim-looking volume titled "Efficient Drug Store Management," Oldenburg came across the advice, "In this day of heavy unionization and rising minimum wages for unskilled help, the traditional soda fountain should be thrown out."[32]

Economic centralization and government centralization (higher-minimum-wage laws and more workplace regulation) dovetail efficiently to bring about a less human place. The lost bonds of community weren't just *nice* things to have. As this book has explained, they are essential for the good life.

Economic centralization, then, is another force for alienation. But it's not the only one. The opposite tendency is also dangerous.

CHAPTER 9

Hyper-Individualism

How the Modern Economy and the Sexual Revolution
Erode Civil Society

President Obama in 2012 went to Roanoke, Virginia, to argue for a tax increase. He ended up planting the seed from which a thousand Republican attack ads and stump speeches would bloom.

"If you were successful," Obama said, "somebody along the line gave you some help."

There was a great teacher somewhere in your life. Somebody helped to create this unbelievable American system that we have that allowed you to thrive. Somebody invested in roads and bridges. If you've got a business, that—you didn't build that. Somebody else made that happen.[1]

"You didn't build that" became a rallying flag for the GOP and Mitt Romney's eventual campaign. Throughout the summer, Republicans trotted out small businessmen to declare, "I did build that!" invoking the heroic image of the self-made businessman. It was classic "gaffe politics," trying to take an ill-considered turn of phrase from the other guy and turn it into something meaningful and big.

Obama's syntax and grammar were muddled, and he was probably saying the businessman hadn't built "this unbelievable American system." His policy demand was higher taxes, to fuel more subsidies and more federal programs. We can set aside his muddled meaning and his favored policies, though, and focus on the oddness of the Republican response.

The "I did build that" campaign portrayed the creation of a business as a solo enterprise, undertaken by a brave individual pulling him- or herself up by the bootstraps.

Just as one can't actually pull oneself up by one's bootstraps (think about it for a moment), of all things a person could do unassisted, building a successful business is one of the last. Almost every business will need investors or partners or employees. Almost every successful businessman or businesswoman learned from a mentor, a teacher, or an old boss. You may need a local banker who believes in you, or a landlord willing to take a risk on you.

But on a more basic level, commerce (with the telling prefix *com-*) is inherently interpersonal. Almost every business needs suppliers. Every business needs customers. A business without customers would not be much to brag about. But there's much more.

Sometimes people point to the iPhone as the brainchild of the late Apple CEO Steve Jobs—a great creation of a great mind. Even if we set aside the hundreds of engineers and designers who worked for him, the Chinese manufacturers, and the sub-manufacturers who actually make the components—even if we say, "Jobs *hired* these people to do this work, so he still gets the credit"—Steve Jobs still didn't make the iPhone a success.

Think about what makes your smartphone useful. First, there's the mobile phone service. This depends on cellular technology, which has been constantly upgraded for decades, and an amazing network of towers and companies. Steve Jobs didn't build that.

Otherwise, I use my phone mostly for e-mail (not an Apple invention) and Twitter (same). What makes the phone most valuable is the sort of things that economists call "complementary goods." Complementary goods are a central concept in business and economic theory, which is itself a hint that the Great Man idea of industry is too myopic.

Yet in 2012, this "I did build that" message stirred many heart-strings, probably for the same reason Ayn Rand's novels excite many readers. Something in this message resonates with a big chunk of Americans. Heck, *Little House on the Prairie* is largely about a family that sets itself apart from other families, and Pa and Ma make it all work on their own.

Individualism runs deep in the American psyche. It is an essential element of American Greatness. It's part of what makes America exceptional. It's easy to miss how exceptional American individualism is if you've always been surrounded by it.

I came face-to-face with it in 2004, in a conference room in Berlin. Through a trip organized by a German think tank, I found myself part of a small group being briefed by a top German government official. She told a story that went like this:

> *Europe historically was populated by two types of people. The first type all followed the rules, worked together, and kept order. The second type all liked to go their own way, take risks, and test boundaries. Then one day, the second group all got on a boat and sailed to America.*

This is a great account that helps explain why America is America. It also explains why America is prone to going to extremes when it comes to individualism.

Virtue is a mean, Aristotle explained. The preceding chapter explained how *overcentralization* has harmed America. At the same time (and we'll discuss later how this isn't a contradiction) *hyper-individualism* has been a problem.

If the middle institutions are the necessary element for the good life, then the hypertrophy of either extreme is a threat. American alienation is, in large part, due to a hyper-individualism that has taken hold.

The Me Generation

Leaning on the notion that "blondes have more fun," Lady Clairol Ultra-Blue Cream Hair Lightener launched an ad campaign in the mid-

1960s featuring actress Rosemary Rice Merrell riding off with a handsome man in a handsome convertible, and inexplicably driving into a lake for a fun afternoon. If driving one's convertible into a lake seems a bit reckless, that was the point. "If I've only one life," Merrell said, rolling out the product's new motto, "let me live it as a blonde."

Legendary essayist Tom Wolfe latched on to that formula, "If I've only one life, let me live it as a _____," as the perfect motto of what he called "the Me Decade." It wasn't mostly about hair color, Wolfe argued. The idea appealed to a growing and radical notion of self-determination, which required stripping away what society expected of you or imposed on you. This required self-examination, in private and public. In short, it required tons and tons of focus on *me*.

The unstated premise, the philosophical principle, beneath "If I've only one life, let me live it as a _____" was one that upended an unstated but universal idea that undergirds moral codes and social expectations around the world. Wolfe called it "man's age-old belief in serial immortality." Wolfe wrote:

> The husband and wife who sacrifice their own ambitions and their material assets in order to provide "a better future" for their children . . . the soldier who risks his life, or perhaps consciously sacrifices it, in battle . . . and, for that matter, most women upon becoming pregnant for the first time . . . are people who conceive of themselves, however unconsciously, as part of a great biological stream. Just as something of their ancestors lives on in them, so will something of them live on in their children . . . or in their people, their race, their community—for childless people, too, conduct their lives and try to arrange their postmortem affairs with concern for how the great stream is going to flow on.[2]

That one owes a debt to posterity was a central notion for America's Founders. The ideology that would undermine it, however, was also baked into our form of government, Alexis de Tocqueville would argue. "Thus not only does democracy make each man forget his ancestors," Tocqueville wrote, "but it hides his descendants from him and separates him from his contemporaries; it constantly leads him back toward himself alone and threatens finally to confine him wholly in the solitude of his own heart."[3]

This individualism is more deeply rooted in all of Western political philosophy, some argue. Thomas Hobbes and John Locke have convinced Europeans and Americans that the point of politics is to preserve the autonomy of the individual from any claims by others. This view plants the idea, as author Patrick Deneen put it in an interview, that "[n]ot only must all relationships ultimately be the result of the free choice of the sovereign individual, but, in order to preserve the autonomy of the liberated self, those relationships must be permanently revisable and easily exited."[4]

This is key: Individualism doesn't always mean literal isolation—relationships can be part of this. But the relationships in an overly individualistic world are always contingent, and easily broken. Permanent relationships, this thinking goes, are not compatible with true freedom.

However deep the roots of this phenomenon, its fruits have been most visible in the United States for the past fifty years. From the late 1960s until today, individualism has been the trend in American culture. Many keen social observers have noted this tendency. "In the past half century," Robert Putnam writes in *Our Kids*, "we have witnessed, for better or worse, a giant swing toward the individualist . . . pole in our culture, society, and politics."[5]

Putnam has documented and others have concurred that participation in civil society is falling. Loneliness (a consequence of hyper-individualism) is measurably growing in the United States. Recall the Brigham Young University psychologist who found that "Americans are becoming less socially connected and experiencing more loneliness."[6]

Individualism's triumph over cohesion since the late 1960s is a central theme of Levin's *Fractured Republic*. Levin paints it at first as a reaction to the conformity that ruled during the Great Depression and World War II, when solidarity and national cohesion were seen as indispensable to carry the country through dark times. After the war came prosperity, and with it the liberating sense of defining oneself and living for oneself.

America has recovered from some absurd experiments in individualism during the 1970s—New Age religion, divorce as something to celebrate—but it hasn't really retreated. Two decades into the twenty-first century, we are still clearly in an age of individualism.

When Robert Putnam measured the decline of social capital in the United States, he spotted a pattern of individualism eroding civil society involvement. He found declines in all sorts of community activities but steeper declines in some types than others. "Strikingly," Putnam wrote, "the forms of participation that have withered most noticeably reflect organized activities at the community level." He went on:

> *The verbs describing these modes of involvement . . . reflect action in cooperation with others: "serve" "work" "attend." Each of these activities can be undertaken only if others in the community are also active. Conversely, the activities . . . that have declined most slowly are, for the most part, actions that one can undertake as an individual. . . .*
>
> *"[C]ooperative" forms of behavior, like serving on committees, have declined more rapidly than "expressive" formers of behavior, like writing letters.[7]*

These cooperative, organized, political, or community activities were at the center of the decline.

Free-market capitalism, the sexual revolution, the isolated sub-urban home, the ability to escape into technology, the retreat from marriage, the retreat from organized religion—these are all expressions of individuals' total freedom to go their own way and do their own thing. And as with anything taken to an extreme, individualism can be a vice. Specifically, the vice of hyper-individualism results in people's splitting away from institutions of civil society, which in turn causes those institutions' sclerosis. The end of the tale is alienation.

Capitalism

The amazing wealth of America as a nation is tied—in fact and in legend—to our deep sense of individualism. Free-market capitalism with a relatively modest safety net (compared with western Europe's) is about as individualist as an economic system gets. You're free to invent without permission, to set your own prices, to shop around, to play sellers off each other, to set your own standards. Americans are also, more than those in the Mediterranean countries, responsible for funding our own retirement, more responsible than Brits for our own medical bills, and more responsible than Scandinavians for our kids and for a rainy day.

The Little House novels became national classics because they brought this rugged individualism to a logical conclusion: a man and his wife raising their kids by the sweat of their own brows.

Besides its being the greatest generator of wealth, there are many other moral arguments for free-market capitalism. For one thing, in a free market, nobody is coerced by the state to engage in commerce he doesn't want to undertake, and nobody prevents two consenting adults from trading between themselves. This properly respects the dignity of the individual.

One satisfying trait of free enterprise, in contrast to more managed economies such as that of Russia or Saudi Arabia, is its meritocracy, which can act as a leveling agent. This cuts against the critiques of capitalism that paint it as the path to Big Business raking in huge profits. Such large profit margins, in fact, are possible only when a company is protected by barriers to entry, and that often requires regulations, subsidies, and government protection.

The *point* of free enterprise is *small* profit margins, not large ones. In a free market, if you mark up the price of your wares too far above the cost of producing and distributing them, someone will undercut you. The small profit margins for the sellers mean great savings for consumers. That saving by consumers is the real reason America is so wealthy—after we buy what we need, we have money left over for other things. Spending that money, in turn, stimulates more productivity by those who want to capture our surplus.

This keeps businesses, even the titans of industry, on their toes. Anyone can undercut them. Nobody is safe.

While the social safety net grew in meaningful (and often harmful) ways after the 1960s, commerce was generally and steadily loosed from the fetters of state control in this period. The managed economies of the war era were scrapped. Nixon's experiments with wage and price controls would seem unthinkable now. Airlines went from a command economy to a free market. Taxes were cut. Because of de-regulation, simplification, and tax cutting, as Levin put it, "a nation of big, powerful institutions was giving way to a nation of smaller, more humble players competing intensely in a highly dynamic, if therefore less stable, economy."[8]

Capitalism tends to cast down the mighty and lift up the lowly. In 2007, the four largest companies in the United States, by market capitalization (that is, the aggregate value of all the shares of their stock), were, in order, Exxon, General Electric, Microsoft, and AT&T. In 2017, the four largest were Apple, Google, Microsoft, and Amazon. Microsoft first entered the top four in 2001. General Electric in 2018 was dropped from the Dow Jones stock index.

"Dynamism" and "creative destruction" are two descriptions of the free market's tendency to upend the current order. There is no royalty in American capitalism.

But go down into the Mon Valley, over to Fayette City, and inside Vargo's Newsstand to see what stands in the rubble after the creative destruction. Home builders and other manufacturers got their nails and other steel goods cheaper when foreign factories began competing with Pittsburgh Steel's Monessen plant. But cheaper nails aren't much consolation to the sons of the men who used to make nails, and who now idle away at an empty Vargo's as their old town rots around them.

It's not just trade, and it's not just a story of the companies that go out of business. Unpredictable and uneven earnings—a sign that capitalism constantly demands the delivery of value and never allows for laurels-resting—are connected to unpredictable and uneven *wages*, particularly for the working class.

Companies with more stable earnings pay more stable wages. When those same companies experience instability in earnings, wages become less stable. That's the finding of Michael Strain, an economist at the American Enterprise Institute, a supporter of free enterprise, and a friend of mine. While corporate profit fluctuation is fine in itself, household earnings fluctuation isn't.[9]

"Earnings instability lowers household welfare," Strain writes in typical economist-speak, "because risk-averse households prefer stable to unstable earnings, even if average earnings are the same." That is, predictability is very valuable to a family with a mortgage, and has to decide whether to send Meg to Catholic school or get piano lessons for Brendan.

Sam, a Cambodian immigrant in my Maryland neighborhood, lived this experience. He was a realtor back in the day, making decent money. "If you average it out," he told me one day, "one sale of real estate can equal three months of earning."

These high earnings didn't make his wife feel secure, though. She wanted him to change jobs to something where he would earn a salary—a predictable paycheck every two weeks.

Sometimes people say this is just wired into women's psyches, or at least wives' psyches—a sort of feminine risk aversion. It's better understood, though, as an adaptation to family.

Family life is tied up with stability. The practical virtues of the family as an institution are the virtues of predictability and long-term planning: routines, unconditional love, the permanence of marriage, sacrificing in the present for the sake of a very distant future. It's fitting that one's work adapt, too. So Sam left real estate for loan processing.

It's a traditional progression, but it's harder today. A stable job at a firm—a fitting match for family life—is less common today because the stable job at the firm was often economically inefficient from the perspective of the owner. It's another instance of America's move away from attachment to institutions and toward a sort of individualistic free agency.

The workplace—an institution of civil society—is less prominent in Americans' *work* today. As a result, the economy is less fertile for the formation of family.

The Gig Economy

"The research shows that ideally," the executive told me as I worked late one night at the office, "the company would have very few full-time employees. Most of the time, the gap would be made up of contractors. In lean times, you would be down to the core of only employees."

Coming from the boss, this struck me as an odd thing to share with a junior employee at the company. I was, however, intrigued by the business sense of it. To my young ears in 2001, this seemed cutting-edge and brilliant. The idea has taken hold in the intervening decades, and it's part of a bigger idea that has grown in importance, especially in this day of smartphones: the Gig Economy.

When my wife doesn't feel like lugging our six kids along to the grocery store, she can now order the milk and peanut butter and coffee on her phone and have them delivered, from almost any store. Back in the dark days of 2010, the food came in a big truck operated by the grocery store. These days, a Toyota Camry or a Chevy Volt or some other ordinary car pulls into our driveway and out steps some contractor—often a neighbor—whom the app had selected to do the shopping for us. She (most of them are women) hands us our groceries and goes to deliver her other loads, getting in a few runs and making a few bucks on her day off, or maybe before picking up her kids at school.

There's no formal relationship between this shopper and the store. There's no employee-employer relationship between her and the de-livery app. And we may never see her again. She's a contractor. She puts in as many hours as she feels like and gets paid cash for as many deliveries as she makes. She could walk away tomorrow, and the app could cut her off tomorrow.

If it did cut her off, there are competing apps she could work for. She could drive for Uber or Lyft, or she could work for a different de-livery service. Heck, she probably does that already, piecing together people and deliveries of produce to make a few bucks, at whatever pace she wants.

This is the Gig Economy: amazingly fluid, without the downtime, the unused capacity, or the unmet demand of the old-fashioned way, which may have involved owning trucks and having full-time employees.

The Gig Economy is a perfect capitalist microcosm of our age of individualism: no entangling alliances or permanent commitments. Easy come, easy go. Two or three parties come together on the occasions when they can derive mutual benefit. Then they go different ways. No strings attached. It's like free love, but for groceries and a $5 surcharge.

This less attached, more individualistic arrangement isn't just at new-economy app-driven businesses. "Over the past two decades, the U.S. labor market has undergone a quiet transformation," business writer Danny Vinik noted in *Politico* in 2018, "as companies increasingly forgo full-time employees and fill positions with independent contractors, on-call workers or temps—what economists have called 'alternative work arrangements' or the 'contingent workforce.'"

The growth of contingent work could account for the entire growth of the job market from 2005 to 2015. This seems to be the wave of the future.[10]

Tyler Cowen wrote of this shift in *Average Is Over*, which we discussed in chapter 3. Technology has brought new efficiencies to the economy, giving consumers savings and convenience, and giving workers flexibility. But there are clear downsides to the loose attachment here.

Today's young people, Cowen writes, "take freelance and part-time service work," and it is "less likely that their first or even second jobs will count as potential 'careers.'"[11]

The downside of being a "contingent" worker shouldn't be measured simply by reduced paychecks or by unpredictability. It's another erosion of civil society, because a workplace is for many the most important institution of civil society. Especially these days, work is often a person's leading source of friendship, top occasion for mentoring or being mentored, and biggest informal safety net. When work is contingent, spotty, and on-demand, it lacks some key traits of a true institution of civil society: reliability, regularity, and long-term duration.

A hyper-individualized capitalism is currently taking us toward a world where workers are available when needed, but no lasting attachment is formed. Work can't form an institution of civil society, because work is no longer a *place* or a *company* or *colleagues*—it's a series of *gigs*. With no lasting attachment, and no long-term investment, young people are less likely to find mentorship and training. They are less likely to find the work stability that is fitting for family life.

This is part of a bigger development among young American adults, who are increasingly *contingent* in all their connections—with employers, with romantic partners (less marriage), and with religion. Everywhere we look, we find a lifestyle very different from, and less connected to institutions than, that of two generations ago.

Wired Suburban Havens

Capitalism isn't the only driver of hyper-individualism in the United States, of course. Simply the shape of the modern world plays a role. To return to *Hillbilly Elegy*, it's important to remember that most of the story took place not in the hills and hollers of Appalachia, but instead in the flat, neat grid of suburban Ohio.

Vance's family, he tells us, came from Jackson, Kentucky, where poverty and violence were always the norm and where drug overdoses were increasingly a plague. Despite all its pathologies, as Vance told it, Jackson was tight-knit, or at least had been before being overrun with opioids. "Jacksonians say hello to everyone," Vance writes, "and willingly skip their favorite pastimes to dig a stranger's car out of the snow."[12]

Vance's grandparents left the holler in the 1950s, along with millions of others from Appalachia. Many of these émigrés from Kentucky and West Virginia settled in Middletown, Ohio. "In 1950s Middletown, my grandparents found themselves in a situation both new and familiar," Vance writes. "New because they were, for the first time, cut off from the extended Appalachian support networks to which they were accustomed; familiar because they were still surrounded by hillbillies."[13]

A clan that had never seen the need for many bourgeois virtues now found itself in a situation where families were more isolated. "In the mountain homes of Jackson," Vance explains, "privacy was more theory than practice. Family, friends, and neighbors would barge into your home without much warning. Mothers would tell their daughters how to raise their children. Fathers would tell sons how to do their jobs. Brothers would tell brothers-in-law how to treat their wives. Family life was something people learned on the fly with a lot of help from their neighbors."[14]

Things were different in suburbia.

"In Middletown, a man's home was his castle." Vance's grand-parents "brought an ancient family structure from the hills and tried to make it work in a world of privacy and nuclear families." This world of privacy and nuclear families is an individualist world, and absent robust institutions of civil society, it can be an enemy of social cohesion. For Vance's class of hillbillies, the cultural changes of the later twentieth century resulted in social isolation, and thus "social decay."[15]

For the upper class, where motivated parents shuttle their children around to activities and the castle tends to have both a king and a queen, suburbia's isolation is manageable (even if not desirable). The modern marketplace means the wealthy can afford to pay for things that used to be available only through tight-knit social networks. When Senator Lee, from Utah, put out his study on civil society's collapse, his chief economist explained this dynamic:

> We used to need our neighbors and our fellow church congregants more, for instance, for various forms of assistance, such as child care or financial help. Today we are better able to purchase child care on the market and to access credit and insurance. Freed from these materialist needs, we have narrowed our social circles to family and friends, with whom social interaction is easier—especially thanks to the Internet—and more natural. But the wider social connections filled other, non-materialist needs too, and those have been casualties of rising affluence.[16]

When we got a puppy in 2012, I would ask our neighbor to swing by and let her out in our yard if we were going to be gone all day. We have since moved away, and now my wife uses an app that summons a dog walker—whom we may never meet—and provides a code for a lockbox. It's quick, anonymous, and simply transactional. There's no relationship needed. Money and technology have made relationships less important for dealing with these small practical issues.

Think about the things you count on your neighbor or roommate for, or used to, at least. A ride to the airport? Take an Uber. A cup of sugar? FreshDirect! Any small arrangement of convenience, either regular or in a pinch, for which you might count on a neighbor, you can now pay someone to come on demand. This is both a cause and a mitigating instrument of an erosion of neighborliness that can arise when suburbs become isolating and atomizing.

You can mind your own business, keep to yourself, stream any movie, and never have to face a neighbor, and so you're less likely to do so. When you do leave the house, it's from your attached garage, and you drive to a central strip mall that serves an area much larger than your neighborhood. It's a rarity, then, if you even run into a friend while out and about. You don't need an evening stroll for exercise because you pay for a gym or a home gym. The serendipitous encounters with neighbors become rarer and rarer as our lives are increasingly bespoke, made *contingent* on our whims and tastes.

I have a few very close friends who are introverts, for whom the preceding paragraph sounds like heaven. And it is nice that people have the option to be hermits. But there are societal costs to our reduced connection.

The shape of America's sprawling suburbs "is pushing the individual toward that line separating proud independence from pitiable isolation," wrote Ray Oldenburg, a tireless scholar of how places fit into social life, "for it affords insufficient opportunity and encouragement to voluntary human contact."[17]

Specifically, his study has found a small and diminishing supply of "third places"—places besides work or home, such as a coffee shop, a bar, a lively barbershop—where a person can walk, and run into friends and neighbors, gaining camaraderie with neither plans nor a long drive.

Give a man nine hundred television channels plus the ability to stream any show ever made, a fine espresso machine in his own kitchen, and some hermetically sealed windows to keep in air-conditioning and heat, and he has little reason to go out. Chance encounters with neighbors disappear, and with them real friendship with one's neighbors.

"Increasingly," Oldenburg writes, people "are encouraged to find their relaxation, entertainment, companionship, even safety, almost entirely within the privacy of homes that have become more a retreat from society than a connection to it."[18] (Americans, notably, are buying bigger and bigger homes: The average new home in 2015 was about 2,700 square feet, compared with about 1,700 in 1982.)[19]

Here's one more telling number: In the late 1940s, 90 percent of beer and liquor was consumed at bars or restaurants or other public places. By 1990, the portion had fallen to 30 percent. Neighborhood pubs disappeared at a similar rate over that same time.[20]

Writing on the death of the local bar as a symptom of American loneliness, journalist Elle Hardy noted, "Around 10,000 local haunts have closed over the last decade, predominantly in Midwest and Appalachian towns like Huntington. In 2014, they were closing at the rate of six each day."[21]

This can be seen as another case of a capitalist-fueled individualism—*you can buy all the entertainment you need rather than get it from social intercourse*—eroding local community and society.

Once again, the effects are unequal. The disappearance of these common things means the wealthy can still afford some of them, while the poorer cannot. "In the absence of an informal public life," Oldenburg writes, "living becomes more expensive. Where the means and facilities for relaxation and leisure are not publicly shared, they become the objects of private ownership and consumption."

But when we talk about the wealthy—with their big homes and fancy TVs and espresso machines—buying their way out of civil society, we run the risk of misstating things. The fact is, the affluent are less socially isolated than the working class. College-educated and higher-income families increasingly live among other college-educated and high-income families, and *these* suburbs just have more civic engagement. Their PTAs are overflowing with involved mothers and fathers. The local libraries have more events and better attendance. And again, despite the reputation of the decadent godless elite, the pews are more crowded at the churches in wealthier parishes and towns.

In modern suburbia, building civil society requires more deliberate effort and work. This work is harder for single mothers, who are the norm in working-class America. This work is harder if you don't have a car, or two cars. Being a youth basketball coach may be impossible if your boss gets to set your hours every week, an arrangement more common among the working class.

Replacing the small town or the tight-knit urban neighborhood with the sprawling and isolating suburb has generally contributed to atomization and thus the erosion of civil society across the board, but certainly not evenly.

Modern suburbia has made civil society more expensive.

We can't end our discussion of American individualism after discussing only capitalism and suburbia, though. There's another, more intimate story to tell here.

The Sexual Revolution

In no realm of life has individualism been more celebrated, and the liberation from community expectations been trumpeted more loudly as *progress*, than in sex. The 1960s and 1970s grip the public imagination these days as times of tumult and change for many reasons, but most legendarily for the sexual revolution.

"Free love" was a spasm, to be sure, but the march of individualism and the erosion of institutions in the realm of sex and family have been lasting. No-fault divorce in every state has made marriage more of a *contingent* relationship. The Christian teaching forbidding sex before marriage was never observed fastidiously, but now it's something of a punch line in popular culture. Talk of chastity or abstinence has become the object of derision among many progressive commentators who, in a lukewarm echo of Freud, posit that prudery and "repression" are the real problems facing American sexual culture today.

"Sexual liberation" is another manifestation of the extreme individualism that has defined America since the 1960s, and, like the other cases of individualism, sexual liberation has worked to disintegrate family and community and erode civil society.

This isn't mere moralizing. Sexually transmitted diseases, including deadly HIV/AIDS, exploded after the sexual revolution started. Out-of-wedlock births spiked. Children raised outside marriage became the norm in the working class. And if you trust the economic studies of one of America's most powerful women, sexual liberation also exacerbated poverty.

Janet Yellen served as a chairwoman of the Federal Reserve's Board of Governors. Before that, she was a preeminent scholar in economics, whose research included inquiries into how poverty and inequality connect to the retreat from marriage.

"In 1970 a permanent cure to poverty in America seemed on the horizon," Yellen and her coauthor (and husband), George Akerlof, wrote in a 1996 paper for the left-leaning Brookings Institution. "Federal poverty warriors appeared to be gaining ground, and decisions by state courts regarding abortion and by state legislatures regarding the availability of contraception seemed to be giving poor families the tools to control the number and the timing of their children."

But things didn't go that way, obviously. Recall the post-1970 collapse of the family and community that we discussed in chapter 5: marriage disappearing so that about half of all children are born out of wedlock.

Why has this happened? Yellen and Akerlof studied the data and arrived at an unexpected answer: "The Answer: No More Shotgun Marriages."

The authors pinned the explosion in out-of-wedlock pregnancies on the cultural separation of three things that had traditionally gone together in America: family formation, sex, and marriage.

As leftist Christopher Lasch had put it, "Efficient contraceptives, legalized abortion, and a 'realistic' and 'healthy' acceptance of the body have weakened the links that once tied sex to love, marriage, and procreation."[22]

What happened in the 1960s and 1970s that drove these things apart? You could easily say the sexual revolution, and that's correct.

But Yellen and Akerlof wanted to know what *external* factor drove this cultural shift. They pinned it on a "technology shock." Specifically, they cited "increased abortions and use of contraceptives."

Here's the most important passage:

> *Before the sexual revolution, women had less freedom, but men were expected to assume responsibility for their welfare. Today women are more free to choose, but men have afforded themselves the comparable option. If she is not willing to have an abortion or use contraception, the man can reason, why should I sacrifice myself to get married? By making the birth of the child the physical choice of the mother, the sexual revolution has made marriage and child support a social choice of the father.*[23]

This argument may be a bit jarring to the modern eye, but Yellen and Akerlof aren't the only scholars making it. Anthony Giddens is arguably the most renowned sociologist in the world. He has published about three dozen books and has served as director of the London School of Economics. He sits in the British House of Lords and is officially a baron. Just as Yellen is more associated with the Democratic Party in the United States (President Obama made her Fed chair, and she served on Bill Clinton's Council of Economic Advisers), Giddens is tightly bound up with the left-of-center Labour Party in UK politics.

The ubiquity of contraception, Giddens wrote his 1992 book *The Transformation of Intimacy*, "signaled a deep transition in personal life. . . . [S]exuality became malleable, open to being shaped in diverse ways, and a potential 'property' of the individual." Contraception, Giddens wrote, spurred a "progressive differentiation of sex from the exigencies of reproduction."[24]

This has changed the nature of a romantic relationship in a way consonant with an age of individualism. Now, Giddens writes, dating has become the type of relationship "entered into for its own sake, for what can be derived by each person from a sustained association with the other; and which is continued only insofar as it is thought by both parties to deliver enough satisfactions for each individual to stay within it."

This is very different from an idea of permanent marriage, which is entered into together with a whole community, and which used to be the accepted social context for sex. It is also very different from any robust institution of civil society, which one stays in not only for one's personal gain but partly out of a sense of a commitment to a community—the common good. This is instead a contingent relationship, transactional even, between two individuals who never sacrifice their independence.

How does this species of individualism—the liberation of sex from marriage and family formation—erode civil society in America? In a few ways. Most directly, it drags men away from marriage, which has become less necessary for men who are seeking sex.

But in the separation of these things, we once again return to class differences. As sex, marriage, and procreation are separated, they aren't all separated equally across different classes. If you look at the Chevy Chases of the world, you find an out-of-wedlock birthrate that looks more like Salt Lake City than it does like the rest of the country. The elites, like the religious, are more likely than the working class to wait until marriage to have children, and to have more lasting marriages.

The biggest chisel splitting sex, procreation, and marriage is birth control, which isn't always used effectively. The frequent failure of birth control users, however, somehow doesn't undermine the cultural view that sex and procreation are separate things. The reader here may think, "Birth control is perfectly reliable, in my experience." But that's something you would say only inside an elite bubble.

Sociologist Mark Regnerus took up Giddens's research in a 2017 book titled *Cheap Sex*. Regnerus noted that "contraception's failures are not random, but track with socioeconomic status."[25] That is, college-educated women with high-income college-educated parents are less likely to botch their contraceptive use. Yet these elites are the ones who set the social norms.

So working-class and poor women take their cues from culture that tells them sex and family are separate. But in their own lives, sex is more likely to yield babies, thanks to imperfect use of contraception. The result is broken families.

There's another way, less direct but just as important, in which the sexual revolution—another species of individualism—has eroded civil society. Namely, the sexual revolution has helped power America's secular revolution.

Secularization is a matter not simply of *individuals* turning away from religion, author Mary Eberstadt argues in *How the West Really Lost God*, but of a *society* turning away from religion. Eberstadt likes to call secularization "the replacement of a Christian ethos with an ethos that explicitly rejects Christian thinking."[26]

Contemporary popular culture holds that casual, frequent, and consequence-free sex is the norm and fine. This is certainly an ethos that explicitly rejects Christian thinking. It's also an individualistic ethos that has great appeal to young men. If you have to choose between plentiful worry-free sex and church, then church is fighting an uphill fight. In other words, the sexual revolution has meant there's more in theory to gain (pleasure-wise) from a non-Christian ethos than there used to be. Thus, the sexual revolution is a direct attack on the central institution of civil society in America.

And so in this discussion of the enemies of civil society in the United States, we've arrived at perhaps the most powerful enemy: secularization of American culture.

Secularization

Religion has plenty of enemies in America. Some commentators like to pound the pulpit and declare that religion is repressive and backward and needs to be crushed. Others are gripped by paranoid fear of some imminent Christian theocracy. More widespread—and more closely connected to the matter of atomization in America—is the idea that religion is fine, but one ought to keep it behind closed doors.

A discussion of the secular crusade in America fits into a discussion of hyper-individualism because secularizers' arguments often boil down to *keep it to yourself*. The secularizing of America also belongs in this discussion because it neatly shows us how hyper-individualism can imply its opposite, overcentralization.

Driving religion out of public life has been a central aim of parts of the American Left. Some hold firmly to a notion of purity, that religion should be contained to private lives and worship, and that the public square should not be tainted with religion.

Religion as a matter of personal belief, the secularizers would say, *is fine. But keep it to yourself.* This is an effort to turn religion into an *individual, private* experience. That is, they want to make sure churches aren't part of civil society.

"Americans for the Separation of Church and State" for two and a half decades was a major force on the left and in the courts, advancing an all-encompassing vision of "secularism." The founder, Barry Lynn, launched the group in order to diminish the strength of "powerful, wealthy churches."[27]

Lynn would say his principle was that "mixing of religion and government is toxic and unconstitutional," as a *Washington Post* profile put it. But when you looked at his actual agenda—and generally at the agenda of secularism's proselytizers—you see that his aim was far broader: to prevent the mixing of religion and public life altogether.

Lynn was distraught over the prospect of the Supreme Court ruling in favor of a baker in Colorado who was sued for not participating in a gay wedding. That violated secularism, Lynn and the secularism army argued. This is confusing if you believe that this secularizer was trying to fight the "mixing of religion and government." Is that baker somehow an agent of government?

Instead, this secular crusade is an effort to stick the state deep into the lives of religious people who venture into the public square. The Colorado case wasn't about a man who refused to serve gay clients. It was about whether government could force someone to *participate* in a ceremony and make expressions against his religious beliefs. If *allowing* the baker to live his life according to his own beliefs somehow violates this idea of "secularism" and "separation," then there is no tolerance for personal expressions of—or even adherence to—religion or its teachings in public.

The government thus tries to transform religion into a private experience for the individual, and sometimes the government and its allies are pretty explicit about this demand.

Strings Attached

"I'm tired of religious groups operating secular enterprises (hospitals, schools)," liberal writer Kevin Drum wrote at the beginning of 2012, "hiring people of multiple faiths, serving the general public, taking taxpayer dollars—and then claiming that deeply held religious beliefs should exempt them from public policy."[28]

Drum was weighing in at the beginning of the public debate over an Obama administration rule that required employers, including religious employers such as Catholic schools, to cover 100 percent of the cost of every type of contraceptive. This included non-reversible sterilization and also morning-after contraception, which is found by many studies to act as an abortifacient (that is, the drug acts after fertilization).[29]

There was a significant, but not necessarily crucial, factual error in Drum's argument: The contraceptive mandate had nothing to do with "taxpayer dollars." It was a mandate that applied to nearly all employers, including, amazingly enough, an order of nuns.

Drum's attitude toward taxpayer dollars, even if inapt in the context of the contraception mandate, is important more broadly in the erosion of civil society.

It's fairly common to argue that federal money ought to come with strings attached, lest taxpayers be left subsidizing undesirable—but perfectly legal—activities. Companies aren't supposed to use government money to hire lobbyists. Conservative politicians often try to curb what types of goods poor people can buy with food stamps. And liberals try to make sure tax money doesn't subsidize religion or discrimination. "Discrimination" in the eyes of a bureaucrat might in the eyes of a religious institution simply be the Christian teaching on marriage.

And here we see a danger of government's growth: As government increases its "generosity," funding more and more things, this "no tax dollars for religion" rule crams religion into a smaller and smaller corner of society.

Returning to the contraception mandate, though, the argument here is even more ambitious: You lose your right to operate under your religious moral code once you get out into the "secular" world and start hiring people regardless of faith and "serving the general public."

Once an institution with religious origins, such as a Catholic hospital or Catholic school, begins allowing patients or students of other faiths, according to this thinking, the institution has to shed its beliefs. Religions, in general, do not allow for this divorce from conscience. You can't do something you know is wrong just because the rest of society thinks it's right. Providing birth control violates Catholic teaching and morning-after contraceptives or elective sterilizations offend the morals of many conservative Christians.

The question here isn't whether religious employers can or should prohibit their employees from using birth control. The question is whether the government should force religious employers to violate their own conscience. The argument is, in effect, *You're not allowed to have a religious conscience if you enter into the public square.*

The Obama administration made essentially this argument in court. Defending the mandate against a suit by the family-owned national crafts chain Hobby Lobby, the administration argued that businesses do not enjoy the First Amendment's freedom of religion. It was impossible, the administration argued, "that for-profit corporations exercise religion within the meaning of the Free Exercise Clause."[30] Businesses, even those owned entirely by one family, exist for a certain purpose, and that is not religious. *Businessmen and businesswomen are free to have their own beliefs, but they had better not bring those beliefs into the marketplace.*

As Justice Anthony Kennedy characterized the administration's position, "for-profit corporations have no standing to litigate what their shareholders believed."

Put another way, individuals can generally be free of government coercion to violate their conscience, but if those individuals *come together* and form a legally recognized institution, they might lose that freedom of conscience. The contraceptive mandate is one instance of a widespread effort to impose this rule. The ACLU has sued Catholic hospitals to try to force them to perform abortions. Catholic charities have been driven out of the adoption business because of opposition to gay marriage and out-of-wedlock cohabitation. State governments have targeted bakers, florists, and photographers whose religious views won't allow them to participate in a gay wedding.

This crusade is based on the argument that you're allowed to believe what you want to believe, but you need to leave your beliefs out of the marketplace and out of the public square. "I do my religion on Sunday," as Democratic congressional leader Nancy Pelosi succinctly put it when discussing the mandate.[31]

To understand this brand of secularism, you need to combine the phrase "separation of church and state" with Barney Frank's definition of government. If "government" is the name for everything we do together, as Frank says, then the entire public sphere of daily life must be seen as belonging to the "state." Thus religious entities must be seen as inherently "private," and if they try to open their doors— say, by opening a hospital that takes all comers—then they have stepped their unworthy religious foot on the sacred ground of state.

This effort to curb public exercise of religion became a central battle in the 2012 election thanks to the debate over the contraceptive mandate. The Obama campaign saw this as a perfect campaign issue, and to illustrate the issue, conceived the ultimate heroine of progressive hyper-individualism, and named her Julia.

Life of Julia

"The Life of Julia" was a slide show intended to convey how women's lives had been improved by President Barack Obama's policies. Julia is a cartoon character who goes through various rites of passage, with Obama's federal government as her only companion through most of life.

It's a perfect story of atomized alienation. There is no other human in the slides of Julia's first three decades of life. There's just a lonely young woman without a face who is cared for marvelously by Washington, D.C.

Who needs friends, family, or neighbors when you have the president and his beneficent federal mandates, subsidies, and regulations?

And at the heart of this story, two slides zoom in on the sexual revolution.

Julia works as a Web designer, and "Thanks to Obamacare, her health insurance is required to cover birth control and preventive care, letting Julia focus on her work." That's the contraceptive mandate.

Then, in her thirties, "Julia decides to have a child," and the federal government makes sure she gets "maternal checkups, prenatal care, and free screenings." Considering the total absence of any other humans in Julia's life to this point, the reader is left to assume that this is some sort of virgin birth with the child conceived by Uncle Sam, as no father or stepfather ever arrives.

A lone, faceless, friendless, parentless, unmarried woman is ushered from cradle to grave by a benevolent state. It's not merely a tale of atomization, it's also a tale of the sort of centralization and collectivism we discussed in the previous chapter. And while these two things are opposites in some regards, they are in fact inseparable.

Two Sides of the Same Coin

"Collectivism and atomism are not opposite ends of the political spectrum," Yuval Levin wrote in *Fractured Republic*, "but rather two sides of one coin. They are closely related tendencies, and they often coexist and reinforce one another—each making the other possible."[32]

"The Life of Julia" is clearly a story of atomization, but it is one made possible by the story of centralization: The growth of the central state in this story makes irrelevant—and actually difficult—the existence of any other organizations. Julia doesn't need to belong to anything because central government, "the one thing we all belong to" (the Democratic Party's mantra in that election),[33] took care of her needs.

This is the tendency of a large central state: When you strengthen the vertical bonds between the state and the individual, you tend to weaken the horizontal bonds between individuals. What's left is a whole that by some measures is more cohesive, but individuals who are individually all less connected to one another.

Tocqueville foresaw this, thanks to the egalitarianism built into our democracy: "As in centuries of equality no one is obliged to lend his force to those like him and no one has the right to expect great support from those like him, each is at once independent and weak.

"His independence fills him with confidence and pride among his equals, and his debility makes him feel, from time to time, the need of the outside help that he cannot expect from any of them, since they are all impotent and cold."

Tocqueville concludes, "In this extremity he naturally turns his regard to the immense being that rises alone in the midst of universal debasement."[34]

The centralizing state is the first step in this. The atomized individual is the end result: *There's a government agency to feed the hungry. Why should I do that?* A progressive social philosophy, aimed at liberating individuals by means of a central state that provides their basic needs, can actually lead to a hyper-individualism.

According to some lines of thought, if you tell a man he has an individual duty to his actual neighbor, you are enslaving that man. It's better, this viewpoint holds, to have the state carry out our collective duty to all men, and so no individual has to call on any other individual for what he needs. You're freed of both debt to your neighbor (the state is taking care of it) and need (the state is taking care of it).

When Bernie Sanders says he doesn't believe in charity, and his partymates say "government is the name for the things we do together," the latter can sound almost like an *aspiration*—that the common things, and our duties to others, *ought to be* subsumed into government. The impersonality is *part of the appeal*, because everyone alike is receiving aid from the nameless bureaucrats and is thus spared the indignity of asking or relying on neighbors or colleagues or coparishioners for help.

And when we see the state crowding out charity and pushing religious organizations back into the corner, it's easy to see how a more ambitious state leaves little oxygen for the middle institutions, thus suffocating everything between the state and the individual.

In these ways, collectivism begets atomization.

Christopher Lasch, the leftist philosopher, put it in the terms of narcissism. Paternalism, and the transfer of responsibility from the individual to a bureaucracy of experts, fosters a narcissism among individuals, Lasch argued.[35] Children are inherently narcissistic, and a society that deprives adults of responsibility will keep them more childlike, and thus more self-obsessed.

It's also true that hyper-individualism begets collectivism. Hyper-individualism doesn't work as a way of life. Man is a political animal and is meant for society. He needs durable bonds to others, such as those formed in institutions like a parish, a sports club, or a school community. Families need these bonds to other families as well, regardless of what Pa in *Little House on the Prairie* seemed to think at times.

The little platoons of community provide role models, advice, and a safety net, and everyone needs these things. An individual who doesn't join these organizations soon finds himself deeply in need. The more people in need who aren't cared for by their community, the more demand there is for a large central state to provide the safety net, the guidance, and the hand-holding.

Social scientists have repeatedly come across a finding along these lines. "[G]overnment regulation is strongly negatively correlated with measures of trust," four economists wrote in MIT's *Quarterly Journal of Economics*. The study relied on an international survey in which people were asked, "Generally speaking, would you say that most people can be trusted or that you need to be very careful in dealing with people?" The authors also looked at answers to the question "Do you have a lot of confidence, quite a lot of confidence, not very much confidence, no confidence at all in the following: Major companies? Civil servants?"

They found, among other examples:

High-trusting countries such as Nordic and Anglo-Saxon countries impose very few controls on opening a business, whereas low-trusting countries, typically Mediterranean, Latin-American, and African countries, impose heavy regulations.[36]

The causality here goes both ways. In less trusting societies, people demand more regulation, and in more regulated societies, people trust each other less. This is the analogy of the Industrial Revolution's vicious circle between Big Business and Big Labor: The less trust in humanity there is, the more rules crop up. And the more rules, the less people treat one another like humans, and so on.

Centralization of the state weakens the ties between individuals, leaving individuals more isolated, and that isolation yields more centralization.

The MIT paper, using economist-speak, concludes there are "two equilibria" here. That is, a society is headed toward a state of either total regulation and low trust, or low regulation and high trust. While both destinations might fit the definition of *equilibrium*, the one where regulation replaces interpersonal trust is not a fitting environment for human happiness.

On a deeper level, without a community that exists on a human level—somewhere where everyone knows your name, to borrow a phrase—a human can't be fully human. To bring back the language of Aristotle for a moment, we actualize our potential only inside a human-scaled community.

And if you want to know what happens to individuals left without a community in which to live most fully as human, where men and women are abandoned, left without small communities in which to flourish, we should visit Trump Country.

ר

Seek the *shalom* of the city to which I have carried you into exile.
Pray to the Lord for it, for in its *shalom* will be your *shalom*.

This order to seek the flourishing of the city comes after specific instructions about caring for oneself and for one's family. This is an order to look after others.

The very work of seeking the flourishing of the city is connected to one's own flourishing. This tells us something about how we live out God's plan for us. God wants us—for our own good—to labor for others, specifically for the people and things around us, physically.

These are areas where we can see, materially, the impact of our labors, and in these labors lies our own flourishing.

CHAPTER 10

The Alienated

Trump Country

"Things have changed so much that I often feel like a stranger in my own country."

This was a sentiment I encountered at every Trump rally I attended. Bob Garrett Sr. in the Charlotte area made this lament regarding the lack of patriotism and of hometown pride. Joseph Kubash, a paper mill worker I met in West Allis, Wisconsin, lamented erosion of America's work ethic. Others in Iowa, New Hampshire, Virginia, and Ohio expressed the same feeling.

This view turned out to be one of the best predictors of Trump support. Most Americans don't feel like strangers in their own country, according to a 2017 survey by the Public Religion Research Institute in conjunction with the *Atlantic*.[1] Among the white working class, however, about half do. When we parse the white working class (defined as those without college degrees) further, we see a very interesting correlation.

Trump supporters in the white working class were 3.5 times more likely to feel like a stranger in their own land than were working-class whites who didn't support Trump. That's an extraordinary correlation, stronger than almost any other indicator pollsters could find. Even support for deporting illegal immigrants was less correlated with Trump support in PRRI's survey.

While some old guys in Make American Great Again hats complaining about cultural changes may have meant something like "too much rap music on TV" or "women don't know their place," there were also plenty more valid reasons for Americans to lament cultural shifts, and the previous chapters covered them.

A retreat from marriage is a cultural shift that most social scientists would say is negative, even if it goes hand in hand with a good change (increasing social and economic liberation of women). Increasing geographic segregation by income and education is a harmful cultural change, even though it goes hand in hand with a good change (decreasing racial segregation).

And while some dedicated secularists may object, people falling away from church and organized religion had bad effects among the working class, even though religion has been a source of division and exploitation throughout history.

So Trump's election *was* driven by cultural concerns. More precisely, though, Trump support was about cultural alienation. People turned to him to fill a void left by the erosion of civil society. "Trumpism," commentator Alex Wagner suggested after noticing how Trump rallies resembled religious revivals, could be "endowing certain Americans with a sense of solidarity and support that were once found in institutions like the church (or marriage)."[2]

A quick reminder, though, as we discuss election results and "Trump Country": By the general election in 2016, a vast majority of Republicans had come around to Donald Trump. Many would choose anyone but Hillary. Others had grown fond of the man. By the end of Trump's first couple of years in office, after two Supreme Court picks and a tax cut, many other right-leaning Americans embraced him. This book isn't about those later adopters, though.

This book has mostly studied the results of the early primaries to sort out who was Trump's *early core support*. When we have looked at general election results, we have been most interested in the voters or places that shifted from Democrat to Republican—the voters who would have stayed home or voted Democrat had Trump not been the nominee.

So on this question—who was Trump's *early core support?*—different studies found wildly differing results. You may recall those who said "economic anxiety" was the cause, and those who said they could prove that there was no economic anxiety, just racism at the heart of Trump's earliest support.

What distinguished these two classes of studies? The studies that found no or little connection between economic woe and Trump support were polls of *individuals.* Those finding that economic woe predicted Trump support were studies of *places.*

As a *Washington Post* headline aptly put it: PLACES THAT BACKED TRUMP SKEWED POOR; VOTERS WHO BACKED TRUMP SKEWED WEALTHIER.[3]

This is one reason we couldn't tell the story of Trump without discussing community. The story of how we got Trump is the story of the collapse of community, which is also the story behind our opioid plague, our labor-force dropouts, our retreat from marriage, and our growing inequality.

The core Trump voters weren't the people dying, obviously. They weren't even necessarily the unhealthy ones. They weren't necessarily the people drawing disability payments or dropping out of the workforce. Trump's core voters were these people's *neighbors.*

Trump's win—specifically his wins in the early primaries and his outperformance of Mitt Romney—is best explained by his support in places where communities are in disarray. Many traits characterized Trump's early core supporters. This chapter will explore them, and we will see how closely they are all tied to alienation.

"I Just Rely on Myself"

"Outside of your family," the Center for the Study of Elections and Democracy asked Americans in 2016, "who would you turn to first if you needed help with" child care, finances, a ride to an appointment, advice on raising a family, and other matters for which people often turn to their neighbors, their church community, or other institutions that play an intimate role in their lives.[4]

Maybe you rely on a next-door neighbor for a ride, but for life advice you turn to a church friend. Maybe you turn to work colleagues for financial advice. For some matters, people replied, "I just rely on myself."

Trump voters—as compared with Ted Cruz voters, or Bernie or Hillary supporters—answered, "I just rely on myself" the most.

The Center also asked a few questions about one's social and family life and used the responses to group voters into two categories: socially connected or not socially connected. Trump voters were significantly less socially connected.

There's plenty more data like this, charting loneliness and social disconnection in Trump's early core support.

Community strength depends directly on trust. When people like Robert Putnam talk about "social capital," a big part of it is how much you can trust others and how much trust other people put in you. Trump's core supporters did not express much trust in their fellow men. You may recall pollster Emily Ekins, who divided up Republican voters by various traits and then identified Trump's earliest, most ideologically sympathetic group, which she labeled the "Preservationists." That group was, by far, most likely to say, "People are looking out for themselves" when asked, "Would you say that most of the time people try to be helpful, or that they are mostly just looking out for themselves?"

Cultural commentator Emma Green described Trump's base, and the Trump-era base of the Republican Party, as "voters who are becoming more disillusioned with and detached from political and communal life."[5]

Also recall that Trump's core supporters weren't necessarily poorer than other voters. But they lived in *places* that were worse off, culturally and economically, than other places.

Trump's core supporters were, with their votes, largely casting a vote that America was not currently Great, and that the American Dream was dead. By this, what they mostly meant was that the path to the good life had been shut down. And while they probably wouldn't have said it this way, they saw things this bleakly because of what was most immediately surrounding them: communities that had lost the connective tissue that ties individuals together and is indispensable for raising a family and getting ahead.

This alienation was acute in the realm of politics.

The Political Animal

Earlier, we noted Aristotle's proclamation, "Man is a political animal."[6] Americans, particularly conservatives and libertarians, sometimes bristle at this idea, as they imagine it prescribes nanny-statism or elevates politics above the individual or family life. But if we use an older meaning of *political*, the meaning Aristotle may have had in mind, it's a very conservative idea.

The Greek phrase translated as "political animal" is ζῷον πολιτικόν. The adjective *politikon* comes from the noun *politike*, which may be best understood as meaning *the public things*—the shared things. Aristotle's notion is pretty similar to the line in Genesis, "It is not good for man to be alone."[7] We live fully as humans only when we live in community. But man-in-community isn't merely man with companions. We naturally want not only to control our own lives but to shape the world around us. Shaping the world around us is the *politics* that is natural to man, and where that activity isn't available or availed of, that is political alienation.

I saw my first sign reading THE SILENT MAJORITY FOR TRUMP at an early Trump rally in Rock Hill, South Carolina. The claim to be part of "the silent majority" is a clear cry that one feels disenfranchised—one feels that he has been stripped of his political voice.

The liberal critic will respond, *Yes, old white men no longer run the show, and that makes them bitter.* This isn't totally false, but if we sneer too much about the white guys who lost their privilege, we miss that there is a real poverty here when it comes to cultural connection and the political life.

"People like me don't have a say in what government does" is a bleak sentiment in a democracy. Trump's core supporters (the "Preservationists" identified by pollster Emily Ekins) were the most likely to strongly agree with this statement. As much as 25 percent of this core Trump group "strongly agreed," compared with less than 15 percent of those who got behind Trump later, in the general election.[8]

"I never really got involved, because it was so hopeless before," Joseph Kubash, the paper mill worker, told me outside a Trump rally near Milwaukee. Kubash was supporting Trump in the primaries, over Ted Cruz and John Kasich. About forty years old, Kubash told me he had never voted before. In 2016 he was standing in line for hours to attend a rally during a primary election.

I encountered this sentiment again and again across the country, Trump supporters who said they felt they previously had no voice in politics.

Trump tapped into that sentiment. He suggested that in the past, the other side hadn't simply *won* but that the system had been rigged. The other side had *cheated*. So when Trump peddled birtherism—the racially infused conspiracy theory that Obama wasn't born in the United States—when he attacked both parties as cliques of insiders serving foreign elites, when he declared the media an enemy of the people, and when he launched his other attacks on the crucial institutions of American democracy, it resonated with the feeling of political alienation. Something illegitimate had happened, according to this view, robbing the people of their rightful power. (Of course, the "resistance" and George W. Bush's critics similarly banged this "illegitimacy" drum during Republican administrations.)

While Trump's most ungrounded and conspiratorial campaign themes tapped into disenfranchisement, so did his most important and insightful argument during the Republican primary: The GOP no longer represented its base but instead had come to be the tool of some powerful special interests. Trump argued that most Washington politicians advanced the interests of the lobbyists, and he was largely correct. The Republican Party, ostensibly representing half the country, was really a lever of power wielded by a small group of insiders.

The elites of both parties long favored more immigration, free trade, and more military adventurism. The more populist, less internationalist positions were common throughout the country, but not in Washington. In this sense, Trump was right that the political system wasn't really representing the people.

Ironically, after the talk of a "silent majority," Trump ended up winning the White House with a minority of the vote—only 46.4 percent of the popular vote, losing to Hillary Clinton by more than two million votes. And Trump's talk of fraud and conspiracies against the majority were almost all fables, and destructive ones at that. But that this talk *worked* should tell us how Americans feel about their political system.

My Night at Occupy Wall Street

It wasn't in Fayette County, the Charlotte exurbs, southwest Virginia, or industrial Milwaukee that I most directly encountered political alienation. It was in Manhattan's Zuccotti Park in October 2011. Nothing prepared me better for understanding Trump's appeal than my night camping out at Occupy Wall Street.

The memorable protest movement had begun a month earlier. Hundreds of mostly young people had literally occupied this park in New York's financial district. Tents dotted the park, a drum circle played almost constantly, and hundreds of protest signs were scattered about. On an unusually warm Columbus Day weekend, I slept in the park with the occupiers.[9]

I eagerly attended the "General Assembly" on Sunday evening, ready for some barn-burning socialist diatribes. Most of what I heard at the "Assembly," though, sounded like mundane logistics. ("The Occupy Sanitation Committee meets at 9 a.m., every day except Tuesday and Thursday.")

Running an occupation, rather than a mere protest, involved tons of logistics. There were committees for safety, sanitation, community relations, media relations, and so on. Some volunteers manned a dishwashing station (enabling reusable cups and dishes, thus minimizing trash). Others ran a library, with books radical and less radical. This wasn't what I had expected.

Before heading up to New York, I had visited an "Occupy D.C." gathering at Freedom Park, a couple of blocks from the White House, where I had a half-dozen conversations with these Beltway occupiers.

What are you protesting? I asked.

One D.C. woman brought up the Obama administration's lax enforcement of the Dodd-Frank law's Volcker Rule, governing proprietary trading by banks. Another occupier demanded a new Authorization of Use of Military Force for America's drone strikes in Yemen and continued fights against al Qaeda. It was a sort of wonk-hippie protest.

The occupiers in New York were different. I had gone there looking for common ground. Maybe we could talk about war, including Obama's war in Libya. Maybe we could talk about corporate welfare and bailouts. That wasn't to be.

While some folks I spoke with at Occupy Wall Street got very theoretical (*Abolish the notion of the employee!*), my typical conversation there went like this:

Q: What are you protesting?
A: Wall Street and Big Business control our government.
Q: And what is the government doing that you dislike?
A: Keeping out the voices of the people, and getting in bed with the lobbyists and fat cats.
Q: What specific policies do you object to?
A: *Citizens United*, and the lack of campaign-finance reform.
Q: Okay, we've established that the Big Business lobbyists are behind closed doors with government, and the regular guy is locked out. What do they do in that smoke-filled room that you dislike?
A: Hand control of our government over to Wall Street and Big Business.

There was no *there* there, it seemed. I was hoping for answers like "bailouts" or "deregulation" or "tax cuts." Instead I got process complaints. I concluded that these occupiers simply lacked the policy chops to really go deep. They should probably read more *Congressional Quarterly* and less Rawls, I thought.

Sleeping on the flagstone was rough, and I was up before dawn. Once there was daylight enough to read, I toured the park and took a census of all the signs. I was surprised that Wall Street wasn't the dominant issue the protesters addressed. Instead, the most prominent topic on the occupiers' signs was campaign finance, money in politics, and undue influence by corporate lobbyists.

I began to see in the morning gloaming that this was a protest not about policy but about *politics*. They were upset not over Volcker Rule implementation but over a deep disenfranchisement. They wanted to have a say, and they didn't have a say. It would be easy to shake your head at liberal busybodies wanting to micromanage the economy, but there was something nonideological and frankly primal in their frustration.

The occupiers, above all, felt they had been deprived of the opportunities to work their political muscles, to shape the world around them, to actualize their potential as political animals. To hark back to Charles Murray's *In Pursuit*:

> *Much of what we observe as rootlessness, emptiness, and plain unhappiness in contemporary life, may ultimately be traced to the many ways, occasionally blatant, more often indirect and subtle, in which social policy has excised the option of taking responsibility, the need to make an effort, or both—the ways in which social policy has, in a phrase, taken the trouble out of things.*[10]

The laborious work of the General Assemblies and the sanitation committee wasn't just necessary logistics in the service of protests and speeches by Marxist philosophers. This community-building toil was half the appeal of the occupation. The very fact that it took *effort* was the point. That's what these millennials were missing in a world where so much was arranged *for* them.

Occupier Julia Shindel, when we spoke, mostly focused on the participatory decision making, the building of a civil society right there in a park. "Extremely intoxicating," she called it. The direct democracy and the ability to shape the world around them were satisfying. For the twentysomething millennials washing dishes and collecting trash for a community, being *needed* by one's friends and new neighbors was invigorating.

Building a mini-society in the park was a microcosm of their political protests. "The hollowing out of our political institutions" was the evil against which occupier Rob Eletto was agitating. "This is a movement for direct democracy, rather than corporatocracy," Sinead Lamel, an occupier, told me during the General Assembly. Lamel, like others there, let slip her ambitious dreams of the Occupy movement—as an institution of civil society—persisting, and forming a permanent new culture with its own politics. Of course this heaven on Earth never came to be, and that winter Occupy scattered to the wind.

I ran into some former occupiers in 2016 in New Hampshire, where they were propelling Bernie Sanders to his stunning win in the first-in-the-nation primaries. Again, Sanders and his supporters spoke more about process—campaign finance—than about substance.

But what we may be tempted to diminish as "process" and "logistics" could also be called "participating in a community." A Bernie supporter named Sierra who was in Philadelphia for the Democratic Convention in 2016 wore a backpack with a patch reading LOVE THE PROCESS. What did that mean, I asked? "Democracy in action," she said.

"If this campaign is about anything," Sanders said, "it is about revitalizing American democracy—making sure that every American knows how powerful he or she is to determine the future of this great country."

At the 2016 convention in Philadelphia, many Bernie supporters were there trying to still win the nomination for their man. Most, though, had other goals. "I'm more interested in meeting grassroots organizers and making any connections that are useful to organizing on the ground moving forward," Sanders delegate Tascha Van Auken told me. "His message from the beginning," Van Auken, a New Yorker in her late twenties, said of Sanders, "is that no matter who is elected, the important part is that the grass roots becomes more active and builds networks, and builds a movement that lasts beyond the campaign."

"He empowers us," said middle-aged Bernie supporter Lynn Guido on the streets of Philadelphia during the convention. "He encourages us to be part of the solution."

Occupy Wall Street and the Bernie Sanders campaign were seen mostly as socialist crusades, aiming for a higher minimum wage, breaking up Big Banks, and nationalizing industries. For many of the adherents, though, these movements were about addressing political alienation.

As progressives and socialists, the Occupiers believed the solution to this real problem involved centralizing power, which chapter 8 showed to be a real enemy of civil society and thus counterproductive for alleviating alienation.

But of course progressives and socialists weren't the only Americans suffering from a sense of political alienation. For the rest of the alienated, 2015 brought their champion.

"A Strong Leader"

"The country is going to hell in a handbasket," Trump supporter Janice Areno down in Louisiana said in 2016, "and we need a strong leader to get back on track."[11]

That was a concise statement of a ubiquitous sentiment, and it helped explain why the alienated, suffering from the collapse of community and thus being cut off from human politics, would turn to a politician who talked and acted like a strongman.

In debates Trump wasn't a debater so much as a "counterpuncher." If Jeb Bush criticized some policy or utterance of Trump's, Trump would respond with an unrelated, often personal insult. The message was clear: *Don't mess with me.* That appealed to voters looking for "a strong leader." At his rallies, Trump would complain that disruptive protesters weren't treated more violently. He praised brutal governments such as Vladimir Putin's and Rodrigo Duterte's for being "strong."

People in broken communities saw the culture around them crumbling, and many concluded that a strongman was needed to put things back together.

"The appeal of Trump arose from the pervasive sense of helplessness by a broad swath of Americans," conservative author Patrick Deneen aptly put it, "especially those who have suffered most from the dissolution of families, churches, communities, and a range of constitutive bonds."[12]

Trump made outlandish promises, implying he would wield power beyond what the U.S. president possesses. Those promises often came in the context of disenfranchisement talk: "Your government betrayed you," Trump said in late October in Cambria County, Pennsylvania—coal country—"and I'm going to make it right."

Just as Occupy Wall Street turned to the central state for relief from alienation and disenfranchisement, Trumpism offered a strongman to restore things to their proper order. The contradiction should be obvious, though.

The disenfranchisement Americans have felt is not really a matter of the federal government being taken away from the people—Washington was always too distant, always too large for any individual or family to have meaningful sway. Modern disenfranchisement was really the disappearance and erosion of the layers of society where an individual and a family *can* make a difference.

But once that middle layer of society is gone for long enough, many people—especially those most affected by its absence—can no longer imagine it or see its value. Instead, knowing in their hearts that they are political animals made to shape the world around them, they look to the most visible level of politics (because it's the one that is still there and not fading) and imagine that it's at *that* level that they're supposed to live their potential as political animals.

The contradiction is that strengthening the central government often just exacerbates the root problem by further eroding civil society. A more powerful central government harms local governments and voluntary organizations by crowding them out, by regulating them out of business, by demanding ideological conformity, but also in another important way that Occupy and Trump embody: by stealing people's attention and affection from the community.

Since the chaotic 2000 elections and the 9/11 attacks, Americans have spent more and more of their attention on national politics.

Elections for Congress, for the Senate, and even for governorships have become increasingly nationalized. Wave elections, in which one party sweeps elections across the country, used to happen now and then, but in most years, the hundreds of different local shifts in politics tended to cancel one another out on the national level. Now, wave elections are the norm.

We had waves in 2006, 2008, 2010, and 2014—that's four out of six. The non-wave years, 2012 and 2016, were the exceptions.

As national politics steal the spotlight, people's affections and allegiances swing away from their communities or parishes or towns or counties, and toward their political party or ideology. The Trump era has shown clearly how this drives polarization, thus weakening the ties that bind and bolstering the things that divide us. It's not so much that ideology and partisanship divide people against their neighbors (increasingly, Americans cluster geographically by ideology anyway). It's mostly that national politics take people's attention away from their communities, thus weakening communities and civil society.

"The new nationalism that imbues a large swath of current Republican sentiments has little use for subsidiarity and federalism," my AEI colleague Ryan Streeter wrote in early 2018. "From the Tea Party election of 2010 to the election of Donald Trump as President in 2016, Republicans have been sending people to Washington with hopes of solving big national problems."[13]

Around the same time, conservative commentator Erick Erickson took to the Internet with a video imploring his fellow conservatives, especially conservative Christians, to attend more to local matters and less to national issues.[14] When I encouraged this sentiment on Twitter, criticizing some Religious Right groups for being consumed with national politics, one typical response I got was: *We wouldn't be consumed with the federal government if the federal government weren't consumed with us.*

"It wasn't a city council in Mississippi that went after the Little Sisters of the Poor," a friend wrote on Twitter. "It was our federal government."

This is the vicious circle of centralizing government power: The more power the central state takes away from civil society and local community, the more individuals have to spend their attention on the central state. The more everyone's attention shifts toward the central state, the more local communities and civil society are neglected. Community erosion leads to a demand for a central state, and so on.

And this shift of power and attention to the central state doesn't merely make the central government more powerful. It results in heightened partisan polarization, and more gridlock, yielding more frustration and more demand for someone strong enough to get things done.

Politics seem more fractious than normal in the 2010s. Alienation and the shift of political attention from the local to the nation explain that fracture. On a national level, political debates will inherently be less human—you just don't *know* the people a country away. The debates will also inherently be more frustrating—too many people fighting over too few levers of power.

Local institutions of civil society allow for more pluralism, more voice, and more human-level politics. Centralized politics raise the stakes and make the ordinary man feel powerless.

Old Soldiers, Cops, and Working Men

"They've been screwing me ever since I came back from Vietnam." Those were the first words Larry Lyles ever spoke to me. I met him after a Trump rally, and I asked him whether he thought the American Dream was really dead as Trump had said. His thoughts turned immediately toward the federal government, and the Department of Veterans Affairs and its predecessor, the Veterans Administration.

This was a sentiment I ran into at every Trump rally I attended during the primaries. Drew Brandenburg was an Afghanistan vet at a rally in Hickory, North Carolina. I spotted him because of his service dog, who was there to help with Drew's post-traumatic stress disorder. "Gunshot wounds . . . I went through a lot of explosions," he told me. Brandenburg was an Obama voter in 2008, but now he was firmly in the Trump camp. He thought veterans were ignored by Washington and that Trump would be different. "I support him because he will help the veterans more than anyone."

In West Allis, a working-class suburb of Milwaukee (household income and educational attainment here are both well below the national average), CJ LaRocke and David Suminski stood at the front of a long line waiting to get into the Trump rally ahead of that state's GOP primary.

"One hundred percent disabled vet," LaRocke, also an Obama voter in 2008, called himself at least three times during our conversation. He served eighteen months in the "Red Devils" Brigade in Vietnam, he said. He lost his leg in 2010 and has a prosthesis—"it was Agent Orange. . . . Did the VA care about it? No."

LaRocke recounted a string of exasperating dealings with the VA, including a heart attack he says the VA denied was a heart attack, sending him home.

Suminski then took LaRocke's case to his congressman, Paul Ryan, at a town hall in Kenosha. Pointing to LaRocke, Suminski said, "He just had a quadruple bypass. He's a hundred percent disabled vet. He has Agent Orange in his system from Vietnam, and the VA will not pay five million for his heart operation." Suminski griped that Ryan gave a weak response.

LaRocke also told of his Marine vet son who can't get a job, and "can't get food stamps," and "can't get Obamacare," as Suminski put it. "They get denied" for unemployment, LaRocke said.

Gary LuMaye, at the same rally, described himself as "80 percent disabled." A generation younger than Suminski and LaRocke, he's a Gulf War veteran who blew out his back during a flood on the frigate USS *Gary*. LuMaye spoke about abuse of welfare benefits, but fiercely defended his disability and veteran's benefits.

Veterans are perhaps the most stereotypical group of Trump supporters. Trump loves to talk about making America respect veterans again. And Trump did exceedingly well among them. While Republicans John McCain and George W. Bush carried the veteran vote with 54 percent and 57 percent in 2008 and 2004,[15] respectively (exit polls didn't ask about veteran status in 2012), Trump pulled in 60 percent of veterans.

More tellingly, Trump tended to overperform in the early GOP primaries among vets. In Virginia and South Carolina, for example, exit polls showed him winning by more among veterans than among nonveterans.

Trump's consistent invocation of veterans and his success among them was a piece of a larger effort. Police were the second piece. Cops, like veterans, stand for the tough, gritty, blue-collar workers who are accustomed to manly work, but who have been mistreated by politically correct politics and media.

The third, and maybe most interesting piece of this blue-collar triumvirate is the union man, particularly the factory worker. Trump appealed directly to him, and did better among union households than any Republican in a generation.

So what was Trump's appeal to these groups? After all, Trump avoided combat (bone spurs) and certainly had a life nothing like a factory worker's or cop's.

For one thing, Trump delivered an appealing pitch to these groups in simple terms: *You are real men, tough men, who were disrespected by a PC society that needs to get tougher.*

There's another, richer explanation, though. Think of veterans like Brandenburg, LaRocke, Suminski, and LuMaye. They lived and worked in an environment, the military, that was more tight-knit than anything most nonveterans will ever experience. This is especially so for those who saw combat—they fought shoulder to shoulder as a band of brothers. Solidarity and unity of purpose were the unavoidable reality of their daily lives in the military. They lived and fought and toiled in literal "little platoons."

And then they lost it. It's one of the most common stories in America: A war vet comes home to parades but then progressively finds himself a stranger in his own land. We can blame, as Trump did, a culture that doesn't respect veterans. But it's just as useful to look at the inevitable loss of fraternal cohesion and of solidarity. Those things hold up servicemen when they're in the service. Then they disappear.

"While post-traumatic stress disorder (PTSD) gets lobbed around like a grenade in a china store as an explanation for why soldiers are killing themselves at an endemic rate," former soldier Benjamin Sledge wrote in a 2018 essay, "I believe the answer is much simpler. We're lonely and lack the emotional intimacy we once had with our brothers in arms."[16]

It was partly to address this post-discharge alienation that organizations like the American Legion and Veterans of Foreign Wars arose. These Veterans Service Organizations (VSOs) became core institutions of civil society all across America. For the vets, the legion hall or the VFW lounge became the hangout, the "third place" where, without having to plan anything, a man could find camaraderie with men of similar experience. The VSOs also have a higher purpose. They were hubs of community service. The American Legion sponsored youth baseball in towns across America, plus debates and activities like Boys State.

Men who fought wars together came home and built communities together. But in the current era, these old institutions are fading.

"We're just trying to survive," Wookie Leong told me at the American Legion Post 8, a humble building on Capitol Hill in Washington, D.C. "But you gotta have the people. And we don't have the people like we used to." Leong, enjoying a beer at the bar of the Post 8 lounge, was a past commander of the post. A Vietnam vet with a long gray ponytail, he was just roped back into being vice chair, as the post is short on active members.[17]

I heard a similar story outside an increasingly empty Post 268 in Wheaton, Maryland. Navy vet Mark Boles, wounded in Normandy, recalled the days when "you couldn't get a seat" at that suburban legion hall.

In 2018, the American Legion boasted 1.4 million members, which is impressive on the surface, but there were 3.1 million Legionnaires in 1992. In a generation, the membership has halved. Plus, as Leong would tell you, a small minority of those members are active. "They sign up," Leong says of younger Iraq and Afghanistan vets, "but we never see them."

VFW said in 2015 it has about 6,500 posts. That's down from 9,200 in 2003, and 11,100 in 1993. In other words, almost half of the VFW posts that were around twenty years ago have closed. Meanwhile the

American Legion has been losing about seventy-five posts a year since 2000, according to a 2013 *New York Times* article.[18]

So these days, veterans are less likely to have those friendly institutions of civil society and familiar "third places." Instead, compared with veterans of decades past, they have an extensive infrastructure of increasingly comprehensive veterans benefits guaranteed by—and often provided by—the federal government. This ever-expanding system of federal benefits has been the Legion's tireless lobbying agenda for decades. So it's possible VFW and the American Legion lobbied themselves into partial irrelevance by shifting some of the safety net and insurance function they used to perform over to the federal government.

And when you listen to Lyles, LaRocke, and LuMaye, you can hear how inhuman and unresponsive a partner the federal government is.

Today's veterans, who once lived a solidarity most of us will never know, and whose parents or grandparents may have come home from the world wars to a vibrant community where veterans formed a hub of civic life, are now too likely to live in a world of alienation, where their help and support are supposed to come from a massive, inhuman, inefficient bureaucracy.

Can you blame them for believing the American Dream is dead?

Union Solidarity

"Today the American working class is going to strike back, finally," Donald Trump said after midnight, in the wee hours of Election Day.[19] It was his final rally of the campaign, and the state he chose was auspicious: Michigan. Since George H. W. Bush in 1988, no Republican had carried the state. Democrats had won Michigan in six straight elections. Obama twice won it by double digits.

The former factory worker in Michigan was the stereotypical Trump voter in the standard media account. Trump had been promising since before he won the nomination that these working-class whites from Michigan were his people, and he'd bring them into the GOP.

The truth is more complicated than the stereotype: Hillary Clinton won among union households in Michigan, according to exit polls. Still, Trump dramatically outperformed previous Republicans with that demographic. Trump got about 500,000 votes from union households in Michigan compared with Romney's approximately 430,000. That 70,000-vote increase is far more than Trump's 10,000-vote margin in the state. In other words, Trump won Michigan by outperforming among union households.[20]

It seems likely (poll data aren't as clear) that Trump's gain in union households also accounted for his margins in Wisconsin and Pennsylvania, and thus gave him the White House.

Trump's protectionist talk and critique of free trade help explain this shift. Foreign trade—particularly with China—hit some parts of the country and some skill sets very hard. The studies showed that competition with China didn't merely set a lower equilibrium wage for low-skilled workers forced to move into the service sector—it destroyed towns. We saw it in Fayette County, and if you've driven through Detroit, you've seen it, too. Beautiful homes crumbling to the ground. Street after street with commercial lots all boarded up.

Things didn't just get a bit poorer—the places died. But not everybody left. Those who stayed suffered the social woes of less marriage, less childbirth, less church, more drugs, more alcohol, more disability. In short, community and family crumbled in these places.

One institution that the working class lost was the labor union. The labor union is not merely a lever for negotiating higher pay and benefits. It's also an institution of civil society. "Solidarity," a catchphrase of the labor movement, is a human virtue. Lashing your fate to the fate of fellow men is a core part of *belonging* to something, and thus a key source from which people derive both support and meaning. While the white-collar worker may be chummy with his bosses and his underlings, the factory floor is apt to be a more alienating workplace. So the blue-collar union injects solidarity and camaraderie into a potentially inhumane environment.

Shared purpose, shared experience, and shared values are the things that make institutions rewarding and attractive. Aside from pay, a key difference between a union manufacturing job and a non-union manufacturing job is stability. Unions (at their strongest) provide job protection, long-term contracts, and pensions. This stability can create the sense of permanent belonging that is the foundation of community and family.

So in this way, Trump's relative success among union households is one more instance of his appeal to those who have lost key institutions of civil society, and thus find themselves alienated.

Immigration and Community

"I'm a Trump supporter because I agree that mass immigration, both legal and illegal, has been a detriment to the average American citizen." Those were Bob Garrett Jr.'s first words when I met him outside a Trump rally.

Indeed, immigration was the most important single policy matter catapulting Trump to the Republican nomination. The most notable part of his campaign announcement in Trump Tower was his description of immigrants from Mexico: "They're bringing drugs. They're bringing crime. They're rapists. And some, I assume, are good people."[21] His central campaign promise was a wall along the U.S.-Mexico border. His most notorious policy proposal was a moratorium on Muslim immigrants.

This anti-immigration stance distinguished Trump from the elites of both parties. It's also why so many critics are willing to chalk Trump's victory up to racism. Trump didn't talk about immigration as a policy wonk, to put it mildly. His talk was clearly racially tinged. And among his supporters, racism and racial discomfort are undeniably parts of the anti-immigration sentiment Trump tapped into.

But if racism is tied up with a policy view, that ought not bar us from examining other motivations and concerns behind that view.

For example, racism was a central motivation behind Planned Parenthood's founding and its agenda of birth control and abortion. We shouldn't ignore that when discussing birth control and abortion, but it obviously can't be the beginning and the end of our debates over those matters.

Bob Garrett Jr., for instance, cited the effect immigrants have on supply and demand of labor. "There's a flood of people, and a minimum amount of jobs," he told me, thus mass flows of immigrants drive down wages and employment rates. This wasn't the only concern among those who liked Trump and wanted less immigration, but polls showed it to be a top concern.

We can't deny that racism, in more acute or more diffuse ways, plays a role in American views on immigration. Humans, after all, are fallen creatures and prone to prejudice and to distrust of the foreign and the different. But we should also see wariness about immigration, especially in Trump Country, as bound up with alienation and the erosion of community bonds.

Seemingly unchecked immigration, for one thing, adds to the sense of political alienation we discussed earlier in this chapter. "A nation without borders is not a nation at all," Trump declared early in the primary campaign. "We must have a wall. The rule of law matters."[22]

Immigration control is the idea that we, as a people, *control who we are*. Under the widespread perception that we don't or didn't have any border enforcement (which is a gross exaggeration), Americans have no power of self-determination. If the people in a democracy cannot control their membership, do the people really control their politics?

But as always, we need to return to the local level to really understand alienation. Immigration policy is, by its nature, a national policy issue handled by laws and law enforcement at the federal level. But immigration, like most things, has its effects on a very local stage—on the community level.

The Tower of Babel

Some analysts concluded that Trump support and anti-immigration sentiment were highest where immigration was lowest;[23] this analysis fed the conclusion that Trumpy immigrant haters were ignorant rural whites getting their attitudes from too much Fox News.

This analysis, though, was too simple, and thus flawed. There was a complicating factor here. It turns out that immigrants flock to wealthy places, where the jobs are, and those wealthy places were places where Trump did poorly.

Look at Virginia, for instance. The two counties with the highest immigrant population are Fairfax and Loudoun Counties right near D.C., with 32 percent of Fairfax being foreign-born and 27 percent of Loudoun being foreign-born, according to the 2010 census.[24] Sure enough, Fairfax and Loudoun were Trump's two worst counties in the GOP primaries: He lost them by 15 and 12 points respectively while carrying the whole state.[25]

So what if we controlled for income and education? That is, what if we separated out counties by income and education level, and *within those groups*, we compared Trump vote and immigrant population?

Political scientists Brian Arbour and Jeremy Teigen did something like that (but more complicated). Looking at all the early GOP primary states, they found that controlling for income and education, the higher the immigrant population, the higher the Trump support.[26]

Put simply, among wealthy counties, those with a higher portion of immigrants voted more for Trump. Among middle-class counties, too, those with a higher portion of immigrants voted more for Trump in the early GOP primaries. And so on.

If Arbour and Teigen are correct, it tells us something about alien-ation. The simplest conclusion is that native-born voters in high-immigrant places were part of Trump's early core support, backing him in the primaries over the other Republicans such as Rubio, Cruz, and Kasich.

If the early Trump vote was an expression of alienation and a re-action to weakening community ties, this makes sense. It's not that immigrants are bad at community—you could say the opposite, because immigrants who live near immigrants of the same background tend to be more close-knit than the average Americans. Instead, we can say that new immigrants in a community, especially a smaller com-munity, can make community solidarity and cooperation harder to achieve.

Most obviously, there's the Tower of Babel effect. While hearing many languages as you walk down the streets of Geneva or Manhattan can be exhilarating, a common language is a pretty fundamental precondition of community. Literally being able to speak to others, especially in one's first language, is pretty important for forming bonds and doing things together.

Also, people born in different parts of the world will have different customs, traditions, and celebrations. This erects challenges to cohesion.

For instance, I have a neighbor from India. He and I talk on the sidewalk regularly, about India, about American politics, and about immigration, in fact. He is a Hare Krishna. While most immigrants to the United States are Christian, the immigrant population is disproportionately non-Christian: Compared with natives, immigrants to America are 15 percent less likely to be Christian, and ten times more likely than natives to be Muslim or Hindu.[27]

Why does my neighbor's religion matter? After a few months of driveway chats, and him occasionally giving me a ride to the metro, I invited Mr. Patel for a beer on my back deck. This is the most normal way I get to know a guy.

But Mr. Patel, for religious reasons, doesn't drink alcohol. That's admirable, but it creates a barrier to our bonding. Coffee? No. Tea? Nope. Herbal tea? Sorry.

So for months, I was frustrated. Finally, I had to approach him with an awkwardly direct question:

"Mr. Patel, I would like to have you over for a drink, but what liquids do you actually consume? I've got some lime La Croix."

No dice. He said the waste of putting water in *cans* and *bottles* violated his religious obligation to care for creation.

Finally, he suggested "water with some lemon or lime in it." So I sent my kids off to the grocery store to pick up a lemon and a lime, I filled a couple of big pitchers with water, and after my kids went to bed, Mr. Patel and I finally got to know each other over many glasses of gently citrified water.

This shows that it isn't impossible to bridge cultural gaps, but that it takes a lot of effort, and has a lot of potential pitfalls. It's reasonable to infer, then, that cultural differences tend to weaken community bonds.

If I serve pork hot dogs at a cookout, will my Muslim neighbors even want to be there? If I grill cheeseburgers, does that appeal to any of my non-American neighbors?

We have a similar challenge at our local parish, which is extremely diverse, with parishioners from Central America, South America, East Africa, West Africa, South Asia, and the Pacific islands. When the more established families in the parish—mostly U.S.-born African Americans, Irish Americans, and Italian Americans—plan a community activity, it's tricky to plan one that appeals to all the cultures we have. One fall event is built around watching a Redskins game, which has little appeal to half of our immigrant parishioners.

By virtue of our mostly being Catholic and all sending our children to Catholic schools, we have enough solidarity to establish strong community ties. Still, the diversity that fills our parish with pride also presents obstacles.

Finally, there are norms. Another neighbor has loud parties a few times a year, with very amplified Latin dance music going into the evening on Saturdays and sometimes on Sundays. I appreciate these events, as they often revolve around Catholic observances such as a First Communion or the Feast of Our Lady of Guadalupe. Still, late-night outdoor Latin dance parties on a Sunday night are not exactly the norm in bourgeois white Montgomery County.

If one wasn't used to these cultural differences, it's easy to see how a changing neighborhood would make the old folks feel like "strangers in their own country."

Is this racism? You could call it that or not, depending on your definition of the word. Should people get over it when their neighbor has loud dance parties or keeps chickens? Probably. But the *should* is less interesting for our purposes than what people actually do and how neighborhoods actually change.

Diversity makes trust and social capital harder to come by, social capital expert Robert Putnam found. In the short term, at least, "immigration and ethnic diversity tend to reduce social solidarity and social capital." In high-immigrant and high-diversity areas, "[t]rust (even of one's own race) is lower, altruism and community cooperation rarer, friends fewer."[28]

That parenthetical information is key. Diversity doesn't cause balkanization and clustering—that would imply that *like* would cling closer to *like* and shun the *other*. What Putnam found, after thirty thousand interviews, was that in more diverse places, everyone is more likely to distrust everyone else. "Diversity seems to trigger not in-group/out-group division, but anomie or social isolation. In colloquial language, people living in ethnically diverse settings appear to 'hunker down'—that is, to pull in like a turtle."

Putnam found that even controlling for poverty and crime, diversity had this impact. That is, among equally poor or crime-ridden neighborhoods, diversity appears to come with negative effects on trust.

"You Have to Come with Respect"

Putnam had his critics. One pair of scholars said Putnam may have been conflating or blurring *diversity* and *transition*. That is, rather than diversity itself, it could be the instability of a community in transition that erodes trust and weakens community bonds.[29]

If you live in a major city, you've probably seen this very transition in a nearby neighborhood or your own. Filmmaker Spike Lee had a discourse on gentrification in Brooklyn and Harlem—college-educated white people moving into black neighborhoods and changing the norms. "You have to come with respect," Lee implored. "There's a code. There's people.

"You can't just come in when people have a culture that's been laid down for generations and you come in and now s**t gotta change because you're here?"

Spike Lee is expressing the sense of angst and dislocation of seeing one's own culture displaced, very locally, by a new one. He is talking about finding yourself, as Trump voters are prone to say, a stranger in your own land.

I spent a couple of days in 2016 in the Philadelphia neighborhood of Fishtown, after which Charles Murray named his abstract white working-class American neighborhood. Sure enough, the real Fishtown is historically a white, working-class Catholic neighborhood, made up of small row houses all sitting right on the sidewalks of narrow streets. Kids still ride their bikes and meet up at the park for stickball, but not as much as they did back in the day. Ask the old men at the retirement home there—old men who were born in that same building when it was St. Mary's Hospital—and they'll tell you they don't like the changes.

"Fishtown used to be Philly's best-kept secret," says Bubbles the barmaid working the morning shift at Les & Doreen's Happy Tap. "Now we have all the new people moving in."

"Yuppies," Bubbles calls them. Chris, a grandmother who has lived in Fishtown since 1970, calls them "hipsters." "If you are one, forgive me," she tells me, as we talk on her front stoop on Berks Street. "It's always been poor-to-middle-class, you know, working-class community," Chris says of Fishtown. Now it's changing. She doesn't mind the new people, but she warns that her husband, if he came out to the stoop, would rant about the changes. "He's not thrilled to death with the hipsters."

The new folks do things differently, Bubbles says. They don't say hi as they pass by. They chased Pokémon Go figures in the summer of 2016. And they all have dogs.

"In my day, we didn't have dogs," says Mary Margaret, Bubbles's more senior colleague behind the bar. "We had kids."

She's not wrong. In the main zip code of Fishtown, less than 14 percent of the population were children under fifteen as of 2016. As recently as 2000, the figure was more than 20 percent under fifteen. Going back to Mary Margaret's day, it was likely much higher.

Raising their kids, mostly in the Catholic church, was a unifying purpose for Fishtowners of old. It wasn't the hyper-driven raising of kids you might see today a few miles away in Montgomery County, Pennsylvania. But it was about raising kids right and according to certain values. That shared purpose helped make Fishtown a community.

The yuppie gentrifiers, especially as long as they have dogs instead of kids, don't share in that purpose and aren't taking up the same mantle as the old-timers. So it's not merely behaviors that are shifting. The entire *purpose* of the community is being rewritten.

In the long run, new cultures and new norms develop, and hopefully trust can return. But in the period of transition, at least, there's real struggle.

This hunkering down isn't a good thing, especially when it involves interracial distrust. Stating this relationship or explaining its mechanisms isn't advocating or defending the reaction. Also, no one should take this as an argument against immigration or diversity, or in favor of segregation. But if we're trying to understand our fellow Americans, all of the above material helps.

If your neighborhood is changing, if your neighbors don't speak the same language, if you don't share customs and norms, if you don't consume the same liquids, then the act of building community becomes more challenging. On average, communities in these high-immigrant places are weaker, and individuals are more isolated.

This can explain Trump's special appeal, in the early GOP primaries, in places that have more immigrants than other similarly educated or similarly wealthy places. It's about alienation.

The Americans

There's another intriguing aspect of Trump Country and ethnicity that bears on the questions of alienation and civil society.

You may recall the Village of Oostburg, Wisconsin, along with Orange City, Iowa, and western Michigan. What drew me to visit them during the Republican primaries was the large portion of the population that claimed Dutch ancestry. And in these places, the other half mostly claimed German ancestry.

From the same census question about ancestry comes a very interesting way to find Trump Country on a map. The Census Bureau's American Community Survey, after asking about race and Hispanic ethnicity, asks another question, which is left open-ended (that is, not multiple choice): "What is this person's ancestry or ethnic origin?" Below the question, in parentheses, the questionnaire explains, "(For example: Italian, Jamaican, African Am., Cambodian, Cape Verdean, Norwegian, Dominican, French Canadian, Haitian, Korean, Lebanese, Polish, Nigerian, Mexican, Taiwanese, Ukrainian, and so on.)"

About 7 percent of the country answers, simply, "America" or "American." They're not saying "Native American." This is not simply a claim to "American" citizenship. It is a claim to "American" ancestry.

For the 22 million Americans who consider their ancestry or origin to be "American," there are about 22,000 different explanations from sociologists and commentators.

Maybe it's an expression of patriotism. Maybe it reflects a nativist, anti-immigration sentiment. Some of it certainly reflects a weakened connection to one's ancestral traditions.

Plain old "Americans" are most prevalent in Appalachia, particularly Kentucky and West Virginia. Recall Buchanan County, Virginia, THE PLACE THAT WANTS DONALD TRUMP MOST, as the *Wall Street Journal* put it. A substantial 39.8 percent of Buchanan County lists its ancestry as "American"—that's about the same portion of Oostburg that reports Dutch ancestry.[30] In the opposite end of Virginia, in wealthy, highly educated Fairfax County, only 4.6 percent claim "American" ancestry.[31]

Sure enough, the sociologists who found that more immigrants meant more Trump votes—Brian Arbour and Jeremy Teigen—also found that these "unhyphenated Americans," as they call them, were overrepresented in places that voted for Trump early in the primaries. That correlation held up even when the authors controlled for income and education.[32]

So here's one more explanation for why some Americans won't go deeper in their roots than calling themselves American: They have shallow roots. One word for this sort of uprootedness is *deracination*.

Ethnic roots can foster the *belongingness* that is one of the great assets of community. Ethnic identities also, indirectly, foster a sense of purpose, because ethnicity serves to bolster religion.

Being "Irish" in America has many elements, including music and beer. But one of those elements is also the Catholic church. Do most Irish Americans go to Mass every Sunday plus every Holy Day of Obligation? Probably not. But for those Irish Americans who have stuck with the Catholic church, ethnicity plays a reinforcing role. This is even clearer among other Catholic ethnicities.

For the Dutch of Michigan, Iowa, and Wisconsin, membership in Reformed churches is central to their Dutchness. The German Americans who populate the Upper Midwest also have their Lutheranism and their German heritage bound inextricably inside their hearts. And for immigrants, this is all so much stronger.

If you can say about your background only that you're "American," this could reflect an absence of cultural and religious heritage. It means the invisible forces that give most people's lives meaning—God, history, tradition—are absent or diffuse. Especially among those of modest means and education, it indicates a life that is grounded only in the visible surroundings—the nasty, brutish, and short ordeal of human life absent connection to the higher things.

Ethnic customs, tales, music, and food are passed down generation to generation among millions of Americans. That is, they are transmitted through family. Ethnicity acts as another glue that bonds family members together.

Loss of ethnicity can be both a cause and an effect of family dissolution. The family without ancestral traditions, music, food, and faith could have weaker family bonds. Also, broken families or less tightly bound families are less able to pass along the traditions and identity from past generations.

On a bigger scale, passing along traditions and tales requires intact, stable communities. Absent that, people see themselves as being who they are where they are merely in a material sense—and that can be bleak and alienating.

Our "little platoons" traverse space and time. The people with whom we intimately identify include not only those we see, work with, and pray with regularly, but those who did so a generation before us. And if you're religious, you may perceive that they are still praying with and for us.

The deracinated lack this death-defying little platoon, too.

The irony is that we know the ancestry of most (or at least the biggest chunk) of these unhyphenated Americans. They're Scots-Irish. The Scots-Irish were émigrés from Ireland in the 1600s and 1700s, but they had come to Ireland (mostly Northern Ireland) as émigrés from England and Scotland. They were Presbyterians seeking to get out from under the Church of England.

Famously steely and pugnacious, in the seventeenth and eighteenth centuries the Scots-Irish settled the frontier, which was Appalachia. Somewhere along the way they lost their ethnic identity. Only 2.2 percent of people in Buchanan County identify as Scots-Irish, and only 1.1 percent identify as Scottish.[33] In truth, Scots-Irish is probably the ethnicity of a huge portion of that 40 percent of the county who claim their ancestry is simply "American."

And again, in the early 2016 primaries, as Trump ran against other Republicans like Ted Cruz, John Kasich, and Marco Rubio, you could predict Trump's support in a county by looking at the concentration of these deracinated Americans, who lacked ethnicity and, largely, religion.

Secularization Gave Us Trump

Once again, our exploration of America's current cultural and political tumult brings us to the front door of the church. And in Trump Country, it's an empty church.

To reiterate: We're not talking here about the nearly half of the electorate who voted for Trump over Hillary Clinton. That group includes all the most religious Americans, because conservatives tend to vote Republican. We're not even talking about the approximately 40 percent of the country that generally has approved of Trump's job as president.

"Trump Country" and "early, core Trump voters" don't mean Republican or conservative places. By these terms, I mean the places and people that early on heavily favored Trump over his Republican rivals—many of whom were more measurably conservative or more openly Christian—such as Ted Cruz and Marco Rubio. Trump Country is largely the places that never had use for conservative Republicans or establishment Republicans, but stood and cheered when Trump came on the scene.

Trump was preaching that the American Dream was dead and that he alone could bring it back. This resonated among the alienated, those without strong ties to their neighbors and civil society, and, most important, those without a church community.

To recall the numbers:

In early GOP primaries, Trump did twice as well among Republicans who *never* went to church as he did among Republicans who go to church the most often. In one early national poll Trump *trailed* Cruz by 12 points among evangelicals who went to church weekly, but *led* Cruz by 27 points among other evangelicals.[34]

Trump's best county in the pre-April primaries was Buchanan County, Virginia, 3,028th in religious adherence out of 3,143 counties in America, putting it in the bottom 4 percent.[35]

So to answer the question that Washington commentators have thrown about since early 2016, "What gave us Trump?": The secularization of America gave us Trump.

This is ironic, because so many secular liberal commentators had seen secularization as a path to cultural peace in America.

As numbers rolled in year after year showing more religiously unaffiliated Americans, more atheists, and lower church attendance, there were audible cheers. The secular elites' unease with Christianity had birthed a slew of books during the Bush years warning of Christian theocracy.[36] They were now finding relief as pews emptied. There was hope in some circles that the United States was finally adopting northern Europe's secularism.

Liberal writer Peter Beinart in 2017 noted how some of his colleagues on the left

> predicted that this new secularism would ease cultural conflict, as the country settled into a near-consensus on issues such as gay marriage. After Barack Obama took office, a Center for American Progress report declared that "demographic change," led by secular, tolerant young people, was "undermining the culture wars."[37]

Beinart, on the other hand, came to see secularization as a negative force in America. His lament wasn't from the perspective of a religious conservative. "As Americans have left organized religion," Beinart wrote, "they haven't stopped viewing politics as a struggle between 'us' and 'them.' Many have come to define *us* and *them* in even more primal and irreconcilable ways."

Beinart's focus was on political aspects of this shift: the increasing tribalism of party politics, racial identity politics, the intensifying culture wars. Beinart reported on a study finding that "among

Catholics, mainline Protestants, and born-again Protestants, the less you attended church, the more anti-immigration you were."

It's probably not a coincidence that Europe, much further along the path of secularization, has a more explosive and distrustful immigration dynamic, with more strife, more segregation, and less assimilation. For instance, in North America, 39 percent of people say immigration levels should be decreased, while in Europe that number is 52 percent. Only 8 percent of Europeans say they want more immigration.[38]

And back home, Beinart was right to see white nationalism bound up with secularization. We could also trace it to the deracination that leads so many Americans to deny any ancestry but "American." The human need to belong to something means people will try to fill a void when it exists. Take away church and heritage, and maybe you fill it with hometown pride, or a college community, or a swim club, or a PTA. But recall that those institutions are weaker or nonexistent in places with less education and lower incomes.

So a young man growing up in an alienating suburb that lacks community bonds, with no religious ties, and no heritage to give him a deeper sense of self, where will he turn? Recall how atomization goes hand in hand with centralization, and you see how he's more likely to look at himself and see his identity as his race and his nationality—because there's little in between himself and these mass groups.

This young man's heart is fertile ground for the weed of white nationalism, that ersatz identity that, lacking the roots in family, faith, and tradition of more organic ethnic identities, instead defines itself strictly against the *other*.

And once again, we see the fallout of alienation and community dissolution.

THE ELEMENTS OF TRUMP'S appeal and the contours of Trump Country tell a tale of alienation and loneliness. When we focus not on the places that picked Trump over Hillary in November 2016 (nearly half the electorate), but instead on Trump's most dedicated and earliest supporters (those who supported him over Cruz, Rubio, Kasich, et cetera, in the early primaries), we see a pattern that explains why his message appealed, why people thought the American Dream was dead.

Neighborly bonds are weaker in Trump Country. The sense of political disenfranchisement is stronger. The appeal of a powerful central leader is stronger.

Trump Country is where veterans and blue-collar workers live amid the rubble of fading institutions, and are left to interact daily with the cold, inhuman institutions of Big Government and Big Business.

Trump Country is full of communities in transition, where, in the words of Spike Lee, "people have a culture that's been laid down for generations" and new cultures "come in and now s**t gotta change."[39]

Trump Country largely lacks the color and depth that custom and tradition provide in so many parts of America's ethnic patchwork.

Most important, in Trump Country, even if expressions of religiosity are high, the churches are empty.

Given the lower income and education in Trump Country, this last one is devastating. Because church is and always has been the most accessible institution of civil society for the poorer and less connected, a culture where church has eroded is a culture where the poor and working class simply cannot afford community, which in turn means intact families are hard to attain.

The earlier chapters have shown the cultural and economic consequences. If we recall, as Robert Putnam of *Bowling Alone* laid out, that church is the largest and most important institution of civil society, and it is the wellspring of most of the rest of civil society, then the retreat of churches in America is the erosion of civil society in America. The erosion of civil society in America means the collapse of community in America. The collapse of community in America is the collapse of family, and the death of the American Dream. In this alienating wasteland, we get increased inequality, decreased mobility, and faded hope. Then we get even more broken families, even less churchgoing, and more deaths of despair.

CHAPTER 11

The Elites

The Village of Man

W hat a scene did we witness!" wrote Margaret Bayard Smith, publisher of Washington, D.C.'s first newspaper, and a preeminent literary and society figure in the nation's capital. The setting was the open house at the White House after Andrew Jackson's inauguration.

> The Majesty of the People had disappeared, and a rabble, a mob, of boys, negros, women, children, scrambling fighting, romping. What a pity what a pity! No arrangements had been made no police officers placed on duty and the whole house had been inundated by the rabble mob. We came too late.[1]

Smith described broken china and crystal, blood running down men's faces. It was, she suggested, the natural consequence of a populist president inspiring the populace. "Ladies and gentlemen, only had been expected at this Levee, not the people en masse. But it was the People's day," she wrote, "and the People's President and the People would rule."

This was how Washington society saw Jackson, whom President Trump would praise for having "confronted and defied an arrogant elite." Washington "society" is quite different in the 2010s from what it was in 1829. But "society" still exists in the nation's capital, and today's society folk were just as put off by Trump as Mrs. Smith's comrades were shocked by Jackson. If you wanted to find today's society figures, you could do worse than drive north by northwest from the White House up Connecticut Avenue about five and a half miles to the edge of D.C.

I'm talking, of course, about the Village of Chevy Chase, population 1,953, which encompasses the wealthiest neighborhood in the wealthiest region in the wealthiest nation in the history of the world.

But Chevy Chase isn't gaudy. "Stately" is a better word. The houses are large and charming, often with tricycles, soccer balls, and kids' croquet sets in the front yards. The brick sidewalks under the beautiful old oaks give a neighborhood feel to Chevy Chase. You don't have gated driveways in this village (except at Chevy Chase's country club, of course).

If your home is worth less than $1.5 million or your income is less than $420,000 a year, you'll drag down the village's averages. About two-thirds of the village—64 percent in 2015—had an advanced degree.[2]

These are the elites. They are ambassadors, authors, television stars, and revolving-door lobbyists.

Given the makeup of Chevy Chase Village, no one was surprised when Donald Trump bombed here in Maryland's Republican primary. On a state level, Trump dominated Maryland's primary election, pulling in 54 percent statewide, trouncing John Kasich and Ted Cruz. But in the Village of Chevy Chase, Trump won only 16 percent of Republican primary voters.

Chevy Chase's results echoed similar results in similar places throughout the country. In Virginia, where Trump won statewide, he lost badly in the suburbs close to D.C., finishing in third place in the tony town of McLean, garnering less than 20 percent. McLean is far larger than Chevy Chase, but otherwise it's similar. Among adults over twenty-five years, 83 percent have a bachelor's degree, compared with 25 percent nationally.[3] The median house in McLean has nine rooms and a value of $983,000.[4] The median household income is $190,000.

In the toniest precinct of McLean, the Chesterbrook precinct, Trump got less than 14 percent.[5]

This book has maintained the hypothesis that in the early primaries, a place that voted for Trump, such as rural Buchanan County, Virginia, should be understood as voting that the American Dream is dead. A wealthy place isn't expected to cast the pessimistic vote. If you have a million-dollar house and $200,000 household income, optimism seems in order.

You may recall that in only thirty-four counties in the entire country did Trump score below 20 percent in Republican primaries or caucuses. Most of those were Dutch or Mormon counties. The remaining were university-dominated towns or very wealthy counties or independent cities in northern Virginia: Alexandria (median household income $89,000, putting it in the top 1.5 percent of counties), Arlington ($109,000 median income), and Falls Church ($115,000).[6]

More telling than income, though, is educational attainment. Arlington is the most educated county in America. Alexandria (an independent city, but the equivalent of a county) is number two. Among adults age twenty-five and over, 32 percent and 25 percent, respectively, in Arlington and Alexandria have graduate or professional degrees, making them the top two large counties in America.[7] The City of Falls Church is a small independent city, so it doesn't make the rankings, but 43 percent of adults over twenty-five in Falls Church have advanced degrees.

One alternative explanation, with regard to Chevy Chase and northern Virginia, is that Beltway bandits were merely protecting their racket from a man who promised to "drain the swamp." That explanation isn't all wrong, but it misses the most important thing that made these highly educated high-income places around the country reject Trump early on: In these wealthy enclaves, the good life—deep satisfaction with one's current state and optimism about one's future—is more accessible. *The American Dream is alive in elite America.*

This book has argued, and the evidence has shown, that upper-middle-class, college-educated America is happier than working-class America. This cuts against the Hollywood story line that bourgeois white suburbia is secretly broken, repressed, and dysfunctional—that nobody is less happy in America than the college-educated suburban married families of four with white picket fences.

Religious conservatives have their own variation on this story: *Wealthy liberal elites are decadents whose ridiculous and impractical education drives them to left-wing politics, and their wealth enables perverse lifestyles that harm children and erode society. Send your daughter to Wesleyan and she'll end up like Lena Dunham, promiscuous and perverted, and ultimately unhappy.*

You can see similar story lines in movies like *The Ice Storm*, where overprivileged kids of soft and wealthy parents end up the worst off, and outwardly faithful and happy suburban couples attend swinger parties.

The elites of McLean, Greenwich Village, and Chevy Chase don't live particularly isolated, amoral lives, though. They tend to live family-focused lives tied up with community. And their communities are made up of other people just like them.

Elite Bubbles

"Wealth," Charles Murray writes, "enabled the development of an isolated new upper class. It did so first by enabling the new upper class to become spatially isolated. The price of houses in a neighborhood screens the people who can live there."[8] Murray's 2012 book, *Coming Apart*, charted the growing segregation—geographically and socially—of America's elites.

"Before the age of mobility," Murray contends, "people commonly married someone from the same town or from the same neighborhood of an urban area."[9] This had a leveling effect. Every town was likely to have its share of highly skilled and highly motivated adults, and those adults had a decent chance of marrying someone of perfectly mediocre or below-average skill or motivation.

But from 1960 to the current day, the elites' geographic mobility has increased immensely, and thanks in large part to what Murray calls "the college sorting machine," pairing off happens differently these days. The top kid in any high school is more likely to go to an Ivy

League school today. Women who go to Princeton are more likely to marry men who go to Princeton or Georgetown.

In terms of the skills, intellect, and habits that go hand in hand with college, *like* increasingly marries *like*.

The next step is that these elite couples self-segregate into elite neighborhoods. Today this clustering may seem normal, but things didn't look this way two generations ago. "During the late twentieth century," Princeton scholar Douglas Massey wrote after a detailed study of residential segregation in America, "the well educated and the affluent increasingly segmented themselves off from the rest of American society."[10] Murray in *Coming Apart* mapped these enclaves by identifying the zip codes populated mostly by adults with college degrees. Chevy Chase and environs were already heavily educated in 1960 (42 percent with degrees and $94,000 median income), but those numbers increased by 2000 (to 77 percent and $176,000). In Manhattan's Upper East Side, college degrees became three times more common from 1960 to 2000. Meanwhile, median incomes tripled as well.[11]

These enclaves sit in the D.C. suburbs, parts of Westchester County in New York, some slices of Manhattan, Silicon Valley, the North Shore suburbs of Chicago, Philadelphia's collar counties, Newton and Brookline outside Boston, and elsewhere. Much more than they were two generations ago, these neighborhoods are attracting the elites—the highly educated, the successful, and the affluent—from around the whole country. So skills, education, and wealth are less evenly sprinkled throughout the country, and much more crammed into these elite pockets.

In November 1963 the average price of a Chevy Chase home listed for sale in the *Washington Post* was $272,000, a little more than twice the average price for a new home built that year.[12] In 2016, the median Chevy Chase home cost $1.5 million, nearly *five times* the price of the average new home built in the rest of America.[13]

"[F]ewer affluent kids live in poor neighborhoods," Robert Putnam wrote in 2015, "and fewer poor kids live in rich neighborhoods."[14]

When wealthy and highly educated people pair off and then cordon themselves off in their own local communities, other communities suffer from the loss of the money and the skills.

These clustered elites, it turns out, take up with relish the work of strengthening their community.

The most famous resident of greater Chevy Chase is Supreme Court Justice Brett Kavanaugh. When the *Washington Post* dug into his adult life, it found that he volunteers at his church, coaches his daughters' CYO basketball teams, attends father-daughter dances (even bringing a neighbor girl who lost her father), and stops by the Chevy Chase Lounge occasionally for a beer.

Recall Chevy Chase's speaker series, its village holiday parties, its ten different volunteer-manned local committees. They build the institutions of civil society at a fierce pace, and it's no wonder.

The elite neighborhoods have plucked the would-be PTA presidents, the would-be small-town mayors, and the would-be leading local businessmen from hundreds of small towns and suburban and rural counties around America and jammed them into a few towns near Long Island Sound or a few blocks on either side of Connecticut Avenue.

I met Michael, chairman of Chevy Chase's Village Board, at a village meeting in 2017. He's a lawyer, a graduate of Harvard Law, and a former chairman of the antitrust section of the American Bar Association. Now he gives his time to the community, including the Catholic school his three daughters attended and the village where he's lived for forty years. Plenty of his neighbors, it turns out, are doing the same. "We have a very educated and very involved community," Michael says, making it clear that that's for better and for worse.

The village has all the markings of the good life. As we noted in chapter 1, about 95 percent of the children in Chevy Chase live with two parents who are married. The month of that presidential primary—April 2016—the village had zero violent crimes. The crime wave rattling the village then was four thefts in a month—copper downspouts in two cases. The only burglary year-to-date was a bike stolen from an open garage.

The police chief, you may recall from chapter 1, knows the local residents by name. The residents gather for talks by their neighbors, many of whom are at the pinnacle of their respective fields. Village Hall hosts Tai Chi classes, Saint Patrick's Day parties, and movie nights for the kids that allow the parents to go out for a date. Ten village committees are populated by a handful of volunteers.

One speaker at the village meeting gushed over the "Little Village Lending Libraries built by our jack-of-all-trades carpenter Gary." Gary is also the village treasurer and the former CEO of a technology company.

In addition to raising $600,000 to beautify the traffic circle, the villagers had formed "Friends of the Circle," which was holding a "pruning party" on the first Saturday in May, "to take on the over-sized azaleas."

This sort of community cohesion is the norm in wealthy, highly educated places. As far as we can tell from the outside, these people are doing something right.

The "Success Sequence"

While the best things in life are free, and money can't buy you love, there is a fairly depressing finding in sociology that wealth and happiness correlate. Specifically, the wealthier you are, the more likely you are to report a real satisfaction with your life, especially if your income is up to $75,000 (after that, the marginal return on another $1,000 of income flattens out).[15] Why would that be? Maybe all that sappy stuff is wrong, and having nice stuff really does make you happy.

If you look at the data, though, a different explanation emerges: Children from wealthier families are more likely to engage in the practices that make a happy and healthy life more likely. In short, they finish high school (and often go to college), they get married, they stay employed, and then they have children.

Some sociologists call it the *success sequence*. Isabel Sawhill at the liberal Brookings Institution made that term popular, and researchers find that young adults are less likely to follow the sequence today than they were in the 1960s.

Most millennials who had children by 2016 had children out of wedlock. The rate was 55 percent according to a 2017 paper by Wendy

Wang and Brad Wilcox.[16] Some millennial mothers later married the father of their children, while others didn't. Wang and Wilcox found that the sequence mattered.

"Young adults who put marriage first are more likely to find themselves in the middle or upper third of the income distribution," the researchers wrote, "compared to their peers who have not formed a family and especially compared to their peers who have children before marrying."

Following the rule *First comes love, then comes marriage, then comes the baby in the baby carriage* seemingly helped young people avoid poverty and made economic health more attainable.

School and work are part of the "success sequence" as well. If you finished high school, had a job, and got married before having a baby, you were nearly guaranteed to avoid poverty—only 3 percent of such people under thirty-five were in poverty, the study found.

Some liberal critics object that the "success sequence" is a lie and that poverty is really about just one of those steps: people with full-time jobs avoid poverty.[17] But all the steps matter—16 percent of those who (a) graduate from high school and (b) have a full-time job are nevertheless in poverty. If you focus instead on those who followed the entire sequence—(a) graduate and (b) have a full-time job, (c) get married, and then (d) have babies—the poverty rate drops down to 3 percent.[18]

Some commentators dislike "success sequence" talk because it sounds morally judgmental. It can come across like a scolding church lady telling a struggling young lady, "You wouldn't be in this mess if you just *lived right!*"

That inference of blame or moral culpability is unnecessary. If you like, you can understand this sequence as simply an instruction manual. Deviating from it is a mistake, and it's more likely to give you bad results. Messing up the order doesn't make you a bad person, and following the instructions doesn't make you a good person. But we shouldn't pretend the order doesn't matter or is just a matter of "different lifestyles."

One reason not to judge those who mix up the order of things is that environment appears to affect one's ability to hew to the order. That is, while your decisions are your decisions, it turns out your upbringing can make it easier or harder for you to make the decisions that lead to better outcomes. (Again, this is why elites and religious parents dedicate so much time to providing their children with a good upbringing.)

Most important, coming from an upper-income family seems to make it less likely you will have a child out of wedlock. And this brings us back to the lifestyles of McLean and Chevy Chase. Abstinence until marriage isn't a hard-and-fast rule in these places, but if you are a parent in the upper third of income, your children are half as likely to have a child out of wedlock as the children of parents in the lower third.

Marriage is more common among the elites, and the gap is growing.[19] College-educated men are half as likely to get divorced as those who never went to college.[20]

In general, elites hew more to conservative lifestyles. Obviously, there are exceptions, but the median number of sexual partners for a college-educated American male born in the 1980s is four. The median for his non-college-educated peers is six.[21]

The data are mixed on substance abuse. Most studies tend to find that alcohol and marijuana use is higher among children of wealthy families,[22] while opioid abuse is higher in the lower socioeconomic strata.[23]

We could go on and on looking at other indicators—criminality, unemployment, premature death, dropping out of high school—and we'd see a general pattern: Children brought up in highly educated, higher-income places and by such families have better results. This is the heart of America's economic mobility problem, when you think about it: Where you start out increasingly predicts where you end up.

So, why do elites' kids find it easier to make better decisions? Look at the local institutions of civil society.

Elite Institutions

Privilege is a term of increasing popularity in cultural and political discussions these days. Ask *Why do the children of elites do better in life?* and you're sure to get the answer: "because of privilege."

Fine. But that doesn't tell us much. What are the elements of that privilege? What are the mechanics through which this privilege works?

We can start with a specific instance of objectively better results among the highly educated and the wealthy: test scores in public schools.

One study in Chicago found a depressing fact:

Schools with the fewest low-income students score the highest on average.

As the percentage of low-income students goes up, the test scores go down. The pattern holds true at every income level, every year.[24]

This confirms what studies have found nationwide. Schools with more poor kids have worse test scores. Schools with fewer poor kids have better test scores.

Take eighth-grade math scores, for instance. In schools (like Langley High School in McLean) where less than 5 percent of students qualify for free or reduced-price lunch (a standard proxy for the portion of poor children in a school), the average score on the eighth-grade math National Assessment of Educational Progress is 307. Then as the percentage of poor children grows, the test scores drop. If the portion of needy children is between a third and a half, the average score is 282. For schools where nearly all students are on free and reduced-price lunch, the average score is 258.[25]

That range from 307 to 258 is very wide. A score of 299 or above demonstrates that the student is "proficient" in math. A score of 262 is the lower threshold for a "basic" understanding.[26]

So in the poorest schools the *average* student is *below* "basic."

Attending Langley High School, then, is a concrete *privilege.*

But how does it work? *Why* do public schools in wealthy neighborhoods produce such better results? Any teacher or administrator with experience across the socioeconomic spectrum will tell you that parental involvement is huge. Involved parents provide teachers with more feedback, more assistance. The schools with involved parents can have more extracurriculars, a more active sports booster club.

No one would assume that wealthy parents are just better and more selfless with their time. So why are they so much more involved? For one thing, they are more available. Marriage matters here: The wealthier and more educated your parents are, the more likely they are to be married to each other. The flexibility a two-parent household provides is considerable.

Also, white-collar work is often much more flexible than blue-collar work, in that you can set your own hours when you need to (as opposed to being told your shifts by your boss every two weeks) and work from home. If you commute by car, rather than waiting for a bus, you're more likely to be able to give an hour behind the counter at the school store.

Finally, our elite neighborhoods, through the college sorting machines, are plucking up the most dynamic, most energetic, most socially skilled people, marrying them to similar people, and plopping them all in the same town.

As a result, a school with involved parents becomes something much bigger than a mere "educational institution"—which can sound like a factory that produces children exposed to information. Lively and vibrant schools become real institutions of civil society.

That is, "good schools" provide connections, offer parents opportunities for meaningful service, provide support, and cultivate solidarity and lasting bonds among adults and children, and across the generations. These factors provide benefits far beyond the academic, but they also boost the academic effects.

And the effect of involved parents goes beyond the classroom.

Wealthy neighborhoods boost kids' outcomes through better schools, Robert Putnam wrote in *Our Kids*, but "also because other youth-serving institutions, like quality child care, libraries, parks, athletic leagues, and youth organizations are more common there than in poor neighborhoods like Kensington [a poor neighborhood of Philadelphia]. Well-developed social networks in a community provide an important resource for school leaders."[27]

Affluent children are twice as likely as poor kids to "have some sort of mentoring beyond their extended family," Putnam found.

If it takes a village to raise a child, we have to be more precise about what constitutes a "village." A government-funded and government-run school is not sufficient, it seems. A real "village" has active involvement from the villagers. In more affluent school districts, the public schools, like the private and religious schools, are *communities*.

This is the microcosm of the bigger story of happier, healthier lives for the wealthy and highly educated.

We know this because we know the exceptions to the depressing story of immobility. As Raj Chetty, the economist and expert on economic mobility, found, the greatest predictors of high mobility were on the local level—the amount of social capital in the local area and the share of intact families. If you grow up poor in a neighborhood with strong institutions of civil society, you have a good chance of doing well in life. But it's mostly the rich who live in neighborhoods with strong civil society.

When the American Time Use Survey asked Americans to rate their life satisfaction on a scale of 1 to 10, wealthier people were happier. It turns out that even independent of wealth, time spent in social activity significantly boosted happiness—and wealthier people were more socially active. A big part of what makes wealthier people happier, then, is that they are more socially connected than less wealthy people.

Trust—the glue that holds communities together—is simply greater in more affluent neighborhoods. While trust of others has generally fallen since the late 1960s, that fall has been uneven. "If you live in an affluent neighborhood," Robert Putnam wrote in *Our Kids*, "you are more likely to know and trust your neighbors."[28]

Wealthier neighborhoods are more likely to have parks, and parks are known to have a positive effect on happiness. The possibility of a quiet walk or a bench on which to read is part of it, but parks' role as neighborhood meeting grounds—as "Third Places"—is also central.

Throughout earlier chapters, we saw again and again how the less educated and less wealthy have less access to the institutions of civil society.

In general, poorer people "tend to be socially isolated," Putnam found, "even from their neighbors." The working class is less likely to do networking.

College-educated Americans ages thirty-six to fifty are 50 percent more likely than their non-college-educated peers to attend religious services. That means they're more likely to be embedded in the community of a local congregation.[29]

When it comes to secular institutions of civil society, the gap is even bigger: A majority of college-educated adults participate in book clubs, sports teams, or neighborhood associations while fewer than one in three non-college-educated adults do.[30]

Drilling down to even more basic institutions, we find that the pattern is the same: Almost all college-educated adults have a job. The unemployment rate among college grads was 2.2 percent in January 2018.[31]

And again, in the most elemental institution of civil society— marriage—the elites are overrepresented. But there's more. Alienation, as Robert Nisbet defined it, is not only absence from civil society but an inability to see the *point* of the institutions. Sure enough, non-college-educated unmarried adults are also twice as likely as their college-educated counterparts to say they don't want to get married.[32]

The best reason to graduate from college and make good money, it seems, is that it helps you get into the networks and neighborhoods that have robust institutions of civil society—which are the path to happiness and success for you and your children.

A Model That Doesn't Scale

So are there any problems with white-picket-fence America?

The fictional problems of the Chevy Chases and McLeans are that they're populated by decadent elites or stiffs who are repressed and depressed. If these tales are somehow true, then the elites are exceptionally good at hiding these facts. *Bravo.* All the data, though, indicate generally happy, intact families.

The problems that are visible every day in these places are over-involved adults who monopolize schoolteachers' time, lobby too hard for *their* vision of the new neighborhood park, or implement too many rules at the Home Owners Association. These are annoyances.

In themselves they should count as good problems to have, when you consider how alienated so many communities in America are. An overcrowded public square is far better than the alternative. A surfeit of social capital is better than a deficit.

So what are the *real* problems of the wealthy, highly educated elites? If they've figured out how to minimize (not *eliminate*) the bad outcomes of single motherhood, drug overdose, dropping out of high school or the labor force, and so on, don't they have the answer to living the good life? Can we just say, "The American Dream is alive and well, you just need to make the same good decisions that the people in Chevy Chase and McLean make"?

This doesn't work, it turns out.

To see why not, begin with those excellent public schools, which are often the center of community and family life. A good public high school often defines a town or a larger neighborhood.

Langley in McLean, with its great test scores, is a public school, but in practice it's fairly exclusive. Only 2 percent of all students there receive federally subsidized lunches, meaning there are almost no poor kids among the nearly two thousand students.[33] (Notably, Bethesda–Chevy Chase High School is far more diverse, demographically. Nearby Walt Whitman High School in Potomac, Maryland, is demographically more like Langley High School.)

More than 95 percent of the owner-occupied homes in McLean cost $500,000 or more, and Langley is one of the more expensive parts of McLean. Of the 17,000 homes in all of McLean, only 400 are houses for rent for less than $2,000 a month—and probably none of those are in Langley.[34] That is, the working-class kids can't "get into" public Langley High School, because their parents can't afford a house inside the district lines.

This is the norm in the elite communities. In the eyes of the urban and suburban elite, a big part of what makes "the best schools" the best schools is that the other parents are "like us." That is, there aren't too many working-class, less-educated parents. There's a racial dynamic here, of course.

"Urban whites," liberal journalist Jamelle Bouie wrote on Twitter, "are liberal up until it's time to integrate their schools."[35] More broadly, the elite places stay elite in part by excluding the nonelites.

It's not an option, sadly, to just make all high schools into Langley. Because having many involved, available, educated parents is so key, you can't make an okay school great by pouring taxpayer money into schools; developing better statewide and county-level school policies can do only so much.

The story of our public schools is merely a microcosm of the elites' self-segregation.

What allowed the relative economic and social equality of the 1950s and 1960s was an economic integration far more radical than what anyone would ever propose today. It couldn't be achieved by busing students, redrawing lines, or changing housing policies. (Though more affordable housing and different lines could help.) Today's segregation is powered by the college sorting machine, assortive mating, and the existence of local public schools and their effect on home prices.

So here's the problem of seeing the elites as a model: The elites are, by definition, a small group. Chevy Chase and McLean present a great model of the good life and an excellent path to success and happiness. The model is to do well in school, go to college, finish college, get a job, get married, have kids, move to a neighborhood of similarly educated people, build a career, be involved in your kids' lives, be involved in your community, send your kids to college—and repeat.

The problem, as business analysts would put it, is that this model doesn't *scale*. No policy, reform, or cultural movement could turn a majority of our population into the college-educated elite. Theoretically you could make college easier to get into and subsidize tuition to make it universally affordable, but if everyone went to college, college would lose much of its correlation with good life outcomes.

The inability to scale is deeper than a mere numbers thing, though. It's not simply that elites, by definition, are numerically few. Part of the problem is that America's elites in the twenty-first century seem to be extraordinarily bad at spreading the wealth—figuratively and literally. Growing economic inequality and immobility in America testify to this elite failure.

Infertile Virtue

Inequality in the United States is growing. Economic mobility is low. These facts alone suggest that our elites aren't sharing the wealth.

Now, here the elites may launch a politically driven defense. Chevy Chase, you may recall, is overwhelmingly Democratic and left-of-center. Fairfax County is among Virginia's most liberal counties. Increasingly, white suburban enclaves of highly educated families are center-left politically. College towns are further in that direction.

This suggests that the elites *want* to help the less well off. College-educated whites are more likely than non-college-educated whites to support a more expansive welfare state.[36]

But by cloistering themselves in elite bubbles, the elites are ignoring the message of Pope Francis. They are not "including the poor" in their parts of society. An uncharitable interpretation is that liberal elites support federal welfare because they want to pay their way out of their duty to personally care for the poor.

But you can't spend away the more important inequality: the *social* poverty growing outside the garden walls of the elites and marked by crumbling families and dissolving civil society.

This social inequality, as earlier chapters laid out, was far less in the 1960s (racial and gender inequality were far worse, of course). Between the upper class and the working class, there was a far smaller gap in marriage, in divorce, and in out-of-wedlock births. At the root of it all: In 1960, there was a narrower gap in social connectedness, including church attendance. Today, family life and strong community are increasingly a luxury good. And here we can blame the elites.

"The new upper class knows the secret to maximizing the chances of a happy life, but it refuses to let anyone else in on the secret," is how Charles Murray puts it.[37]

If the elites today possess virtue, there is something *infertile* about that virtue. There's no germination or spreading of their good habits.

Part of this book has been dedicated to showing my fellow conservative Christians that those liberal elites *practice* what we *preach*. They value work as a good in itself, they have fewer sexual partners, they get married, they have kids, they get involved in their kids' lives.

But the elites today often lack the courage to *preach what they practice*. This is a truth long noted by informed observers liberal and conservative, devout and atheist. You can see an instance in public school sex-education curricula. These curricula are drafted by baby boomers and inspired by the sexual revolution. It's an effort to liberate students from supposed sexual repression. But this is not the way the typical upper-middle-class college-educated parents apparently raise their own children. The elites, it would seem from the statistics, generally pass down (imperfectly, of course) the notions of monogamy, marriage, and family. What the elites might consider a bad set of choices by their own child, they chalk up as an "alternative lifestyle" among someone else's kids.

Those values, norms, and teachings that they pass down to their children but wouldn't want to *preach*—they're hoarding that wisdom. By doing so, they have failed to convey the map to success that has hardly needed to be articulated within their circles: Value work as a good in itself, postpone sex, get married, be involved in your kids' lives.

Those rules are less observed among the working class than they were two generations ago, while they are nearly as sacrosanct among the elites as they have ever been.

So perhaps we are looking at selfishness—the elites keeping the secrets to the good life to themselves, and holding too close to their vests their most valuable assets. Or it may be a lack of conviction.

Being nonjudgmental is another tenet of elite morality, and that may weaken the power of elite morality altogether. Perhaps if you are committed to the virtues of work, chastity, and monogamy merely as *best practices*, rather than as moral laws that reflect God's law, you will lack the conviction to preach what you practice. These best practices are not buttressed by a deep moral conviction but instead are complemented by what Murray calls "ecumenical niceness."

There's a more pernicious problem here, which some critics of our elites note. It's an ideological commitment to egalitarianism among elites that prevents them from seeing themselves as elites.

There's something unnerving about being called an *elite*. "The ruling class," conservative author Patrick Deneen wrote in 2018, "denies that they really are a self-perpetuating elite that has not only inherited certain advantages but also seeks to pass them on."[38]

Deneen writes of Ivy League schools and premier private liberal arts colleges where the students express a militant egalitarianism. The echoes of these elite college students' arguments are audible among the professional commentariat in New York and D.C., when they vociferously advocate redistribution yet blast the white working class as irredeemably deplorable.

"One is tempted," Deneen writes, "to conclude that their insistent defense of equality is a way of freeing themselves from any real duties to the lower classes that are increasingly out of geographical sight and mind. Because they repudiate inequality, they need not consciously consider themselves to be a ruling class."

American liberals are better than conservatives at acknowledging that "privilege" is a real thing. That for some people, circumstances and upbringing have made life easier—like a video game set to a lower level of difficulty. Harder for the Left to embrace, it seems, is the next step in this thinking: The privileged have *assets* that others do not have: Ivy League educations, excellent public K–12 educations, two educated parents, habituation toward delayed gratification, proclivity toward abstract reasoning.

To admit possession of these extraordinary assets could sound inegalitarian, especially if one calls such assets "virtues." To deny the unequal distribution of the assets, though, is not only erroneous but also selfish. When you admit that your upbringing and your environment have left you with extraordinary assets, including virtues, you run the risk of taking on your shoulders extraordinary obligations.

Granting that you have more money than others, and that you don't deserve such wealth—but stopping there—allows you to settle the score by paying your taxes and advocating more redistribution.

This reductive attitude toward inequality has the added comfort of justifying nasty judgments about the other side. "Highly touted commitments to equity, inclusion, and diversity do not only cloak institutional elitism," Deneen argues. "They also imply that anyone who is not included *deserves* his lower status."

In this light, it's easier to understand all of the efforts in recent years to say that the white working class deserves its suffering, and the Trump voters deserve no sympathy but are guilty of racism, cultural resentment, and revanchism. An elite class that won't admit to being elite feels no need to *include* the worse off whom they find distasteful. The gloating articles about the Republican voters who nevertheless take welfare have an inescapable conclusion: *We give these deplorables the money they need, but their vice and hate prevent them from being grateful for it.*

"They've chosen not to keep up," as the interviewer at Vox put it.

But what if what the working class—white, black, Hispanic, etc.— *needs* most isn't a check from the government but inclusion in community? And what if the most accessible form of community— the church—is under constant assault by both culture and the government? And finally, what if the elites frowning upon the deplorable poor won't *include* them in their community, citing their deplorability?

If the elites granted that they are elites—that they have been blessed with virtues, which in turn convey obligations—they might be more likely to share their most valuable assets with the less fortunate. But, at least according to critics like Deneen, the elites deny that their privilege conveys assets beyond the material, and thus they excuse themselves from owing anything besides a few bucks.

Noblesse without the Oblige

We're still not at the heart of the problem with our elites, though. Not sharing their road map of the good life is bad enough. But the elites also aren't sharing the most valuable thing they (we) have: our networks and our institutions of civil society. These institutions are the arenas where we all live out our human need to love and serve our neighbors, where we find a safety net and mentoring, and act as our support structure for the crucial task of raising families.

The increasing geographic segregation of the classes, as charted by Massey and explored by Murray, means that the elites are no longer living in communities with everyone else. That means we are keeping our most valuable asset from the people who need it the most, the poor and the working class.

A local community, and a human-scale institution like a parish, a swim club, a neighborhood, or a public elementary school, will always be the most responsive safety net a person can have. The elites are increasingly providing that safety net only for one another and not for the less educated and less privileged.

No combination of benevolent public policy, heavily funded public schools, and a robust government safety net can provide what only the institutions of civil society, operating on the human scale, can provide.

"Our commitment" to the poor, Pope Francis writes, "does not consist exclusively in activities or programmes of promotion and assistance . . . but above all an attentiveness which considers the other 'in a certain sense as one with ourselves.'

"Only on the basis of this real and sincere closeness," the pope explains, "can we properly accompany the poor on their path of liberation."[39]

If we are realistic, the only way to maintain "real and sincere closeness" with a person is to entangle ourselves with that person through the bonds of an institution—to live in community and to work toward common ends with that person.

"Man cannot give himself to a purely human plan for reality, to an abstract ideal or to a false utopia," Pope John Paul II wrote in an important 1991 encyclical that dealt with the problems inherent in the ideologies of both Marxism and capitalism. "As a person, he can give himself to another person or to other persons, and ultimately to God, who is the author of his being and who alone can fully accept his gift."[40]

Only in self-sacrifice can man live fully as man, Catholic teaching states. Some people sacrifice for an idea, but really, John Paul argues, we give up our lives only for other people—or for God. And that true sacrifice requires love, which in turn requires true human contact. Community bonds make that love real. And so these two popes show us that true *inclusion* of the poor—by living in community with them—is the only way to carry out our duty to serve the poor.

And there's evidence that this unwillingness to *include* is the seed of the elites' *infertile* virtue. Look at the younger generation. When we examine things like premarital sex, unwed pregnancy, and criminality, millennials, especially those from the Chevy Chases and Fairfax Counties of the world, show good outcomes. But it often looks as though these young people are merely *well behaved*. It's harder to say they're *virtuous*.

In *The Lion, the Witch and the Wardrobe*, the Pevensie children, after passing through the magical wardrobe, finally get the lay of the land when Mr. and Mrs. Beaver have them over to dinner. The Beavers share the good news: Aslan is on the move. After the Beavers explain that Aslan, the king, is in fact a lion, the worried kids twice ask about the danger: "Is he—quite safe?"

"Safe?" Mr. Beaver responds, "Don't you hear what Mrs. Beaver tells you? Who said anything about safe? 'Course he isn't safe. But he's good."

Elite America is raising well-behaved men and women, whom one can trust to be "safe." *Good* is another matter.

For one thing (and this argument is open to the charge that I am begging the question), look at religious affiliation. While wealthier and more educated Americans are more likely than those poorer or less educated to go to church regularly, religiosity isn't passing down to the next generation very well. More than one in three millennials claims no religious affiliation, a figure higher by far than that of older generations.

Among Americans earning six figures or more, "unaffiliated" is now a larger group than Catholic, evangelical, or mainline Protestant—that cohort has grown by nearly 50 percent since 2007.[41] This demographic shift was mostly driven by adults under age thirty in 2014, according to Pew data.[42]

So the elites' virtues are *infertile* in many dimensions. We can't spread our good outcomes outside our class boundaries. We are unwilling to spread our good habits and practices beyond our families and communities. We don't include the poor in our institutions of civil society. And some of our good behaviors, such as going to church, we are unable to pass down even to our own children.

It takes a village to raise a child, and the village of the elites does that very well. But to find something for the children born outside the elites' walls, we're going to have to visit the other village.

CHAPTER 12

The Church People

The Village of God

Windmills greet you when you drive into Orange City. These aren't the towering subsidized General Electric or Vestas windmills on which the politicians in Des Moines pride themselves. These are the squat, old-school four-blade windmills—with a window in the body—that scream Holland. The windmills don't actually *mill* anything, but they also aren't idle like the factories in western Pennsylvania. The windmills are teeming with children at this park in the center of Orange City, an oasis of civil society in the middle of Iowa's corn and soy.

The WELCOME TO ORANGE CITY sign is in the shape of a giant clog. Windmill Square itself has, near the beds of tulips, a six-foot-long hollowed-out clog that kids can climb in. In my visit to Orange City just before the 2016 Iowa caucuses, I dined at Nederlander's Grill, from where I drove down the road to Dordt College in Sioux Center, where Jeb Bush would be speaking.

Dordt is a Christian school, affiliated with the Christian Reformed Church of North America. It's named after the famed Synod of Dordt, held in the Netherlands in 1618 and 1619, which laid out as doctrine the Reformed church's five central teachings. The first couple I met at the Dordt College event, Harold and Wilhelmina Schelling, were elderly, staid, and not very talkative, but they did make a point of noting that Mrs. Schelling was named after Queen Wilhelmina, the monarch of the Netherlands for fifty-eight years, including both world wars.

At last count, 34,509 people lived in Sioux County, and 15,891 of them reported their ancestry as Dutch.[1] That's 46 percent. (Another 8,197 reported German ancestry.) Sioux County is by far the most Dutch county in Iowa—again, the county seat is called *Orange* City, named after William of Orange, and the national color of the Netherlands.

The color certainly did not create a kinship with Donald Trump.

A small cabal of freshmen women at the Dordt event, with names like Holly Hiemstra (the *stra* ending is ubiquitous among the Dutch) or last names like Vos or Van Der-something, were all Republicans, friendly, and they turned up their noses when I asked about Trump at this pre-caucus event.

One questioner at the Bush event, asking Jeb to contrast his views with those of the Republican front-runner, refused to even speak the front-runner's name. Instead he referred to "a man with initials 'D.T.'" The crowd broke into applause when Jeb pointedly declared that nobody was going to "insult his way into the presidency."

A local pastor told me that seven hundred people come to his church every Sunday, and he knew of only one congregant who was supporting Trump in the caucuses.

Sioux County was by far Donald Trump's worst county in the Iowa caucuses. He finished in fourth place in Sioux County, and it was a distant fourth, raking in only 10 percent of the vote. Compare that with the results statewide, where Trump finished a close second, at 24.3 percent. The contrast is even starker when you check out the surrounding rural counties in northwest Iowa: Trump won Plymouth County, just to the south of Sioux County, with 33 percent, and did well in the other counties in that corner of the state, except for Lyon County, his second-worst county in Iowa, where he scored 15 percent. Lyon is also the second-most-Dutch county in Iowa at 33 percent.[2] Trump did not win a single precinct in either Sioux or Lyon County.[3]

Political reporters often speak of the "black vote," and the "Hispanic vote," and we even get as specific as the "Cuban vote." But never before had the "Dutch vote" come onto our radar.

In previous Republican caucuses, there were two main electorates in Iowa: the more urban and suburban vote, which would go to Mitt Romney (in both 2008 and 2012); and the more rural vote, which would go to the conservative insurgent (Mike Huckabee in 2008 and Rick Santorum in 2012). It was understood as the mainstream or pro-business Republicans (Romney) versus the "evangelical" vote (Huckabee and Santorum).

But in 2016, that former Huckabee/Santorum electorate was split. Most rural Iowa counties went for Trump, while some, particularly the Dutch ones, went for Cruz. There was something going on in these mini-Hollands in Middle America.

So when Michigan voted in its primary in early March, I trained my eyes on the western part of the state to watch the Dutch vote. Sure enough, a map of Michigan's primary results showed a cluster of six counties at the west end of the state that voted for Cruz. This Cruz cluster centered on Holland, Michigan.[4]

Albertus Christiaan Van Raalte was a Dutch Reformed pastor in the nineteenth century whose hard-core orthodox ways made him and his congregation personae non gratae in the Netherlands. He led his flock across the Atlantic and to the farm fields of western Michigan, where they created their new Holland in the 1840s.

Ottawa County, where Holland sits, is Michigan's most Dutch county at 30.4 percent. It also put Donald Trump in third place and gave Ted Cruz his largest margin of victory, 16 points over John Kasich and 20 points over Donald Trump.

Cruz hit the 35 percent mark in only five of Michigan's eighty-three counties, and those are the five most Dutch counties in the state. The most Dutch municipality in Michigan is Moline, which sits inside Allegan County's Dorr Township. That precinct of Dorr Township voted 51.23 percent for Cruz,[5] his highest total I could find in the state, which Trump won easily with 36.5 percent of the vote, while Cruz and Kasich were down around 25 percent.

And it happened again in Wisconsin, if you recall Oostburg. Oostburg, similarly, is 45 percent Dutch. Another 42 percent is German.[6]

"If you ain't Dutch, you ain't much," was a phrase the waitress taught me at Judi's Place in Oostburg. Trump, who got 35 percent statewide in Wisconsin's primary, pulled only 15 percent here in Oostburg[7]—and it certainly wasn't because Oostburg is full of moderates. The village was dubbed the most conservative town in Wisconsin during the 2012 election.[8]

The pattern was clear, if baffling. Dutch population was inversely proportional to Trump support in the early GOP primaries.

Why would this be?

I ventured to Orange City, Dordt College, Dorr Township, and Oostburg to figure it out. Maybe it was just that the Dutch are nice, and Trump's New York brashness struck them as garish. When I figured out the real cause, it was suddenly so obvious.

"Live Left"

Orange City is the happiest town in Iowa, according to one (admittedly very unscientific) study.[9] The runner-up was Sioux Center, home of Dordt College.

These Dutch towns certainly have a unique culture, and on the score of social cohesion and civil society, they're off the charts.

"There are plenty of jobs, and it'll take you five minutes to drive to work," a 2017 *New Yorker* profile of the town reported, channeling the arguments Orange City natives give for staying there. "When you have children, we'll help you take care of them. People here share your values, it's a good Christian place. And they care about you: if anything happens, they'll have your back."[10]

The strong community is the support structure that makes family rearing easier. And the locals take advantage of it. Married couples living with their children make up one-third of Orange City's households,[11] which is 10 percent higher than Iowa as a whole, and about 30 percent higher than neighboring O'Brien County.[12]

Nearly half the town is Dutch by ancestry. Another quarter is German.

Livability, a journal that studies many aspects of life in big cities and small towns, put Orange City among its one hundred best small towns. *Niche* magazine declared Orange City the best town in Iowa in which to raise a family. One reader of *Niche* anonymously wrote a telling mixed review of the town:

> *The area I currently live in is a very conservative place—Orange City, Iowa. This place is one of the towns known for new families moving here to find a "safe" and "good" town to start a family. Don't get me wrong, this town is full of nice people who generally care about how their neighbors are doing and wanting to meet who just moved in down the street. They'll bring you that extra cup of sugar if you need it [with] a happy heart and good intentions. Nevertheless, everyone knows everything about everyone.*[13]

Up at Dordt College, after Jeb spoke, I chatted with dozens of its students, faculty, and neighbors. Jordan Helming isn't Dutch, and he's a transplant. His wife teaches at Dordt, and they moved to Sioux Center in 2013. "Around here," he told me, "people seem to vote Right and live Left."

What does "live Left" mean? Were they all vegetarians who smoked pot? "That's just what you do," Helming, himself left-leaning, explained. "You care about your neighbors, you care about your environment, but you also take care of it yourself—don't rely on the government."

I had to set aside my pique at Helming's notion that if you "care about your neighbors" you "live Left," in order to take in his broader point. Neighborliness is what makes these Dutch towns in Sioux Center so happy. Kids play freely with the neighborhood kids. Old-timers make newbies feel welcome. And when you need help, people help you out.

At Judi's Place in Oostburg, I chatted with Jenny, the waitress behind the counter, for hours. Jenny's a transplant, and she's not Dutch, but contrary to the saying, nobody actually treated her as if she's "not much," she told me. Jenny was scheduled for hand surgery later that week and would miss a few shifts. On Tuesday, while Jenny was refilling my coffee cup, a regular customer walked in with a bag that included a couple of frozen meals. "Can you stick this in the freezer back there?" the customer asked, handing it to Jenny. "This is for you."

It was a prepared dinner, three courses, for Jenny to heat up and eat while recovering from her surgery. Jenny thanked the lady and held herself together until she left. Then Jenny lost it and walked over to me, teary but smiling. "That's Oostburg."

One local man had carved wooden toys to leave at Judi's so that the little kids coming in with their families, often after church, would have entertainment while adults chatted with neighbors for hours. On Tuesday, there was at least one crew of old men, retirees, who came after the early rush for their regular rendezvous over coffee, and scrambled plates of cheese, meat, and potatoes.

Sitting next to me one day at Judi's was Mike Reedyk, whose parents also are transplants to Oostburg. They came here precisely because of the sense of welcoming and charity in the village. Mike, in his twenties, is disabled, and his parents found Oostburgers eager to help the family and include Mike. The Reedyks took the love the villagers gave them and multiplied it. Now they run a charity called Our Home Christian Ministries, which turns Oostburg homes into homes for the disabled, and works to help the disabled "to develop their abilities to their maximum potential" and find "meaningful work." Where do they get the homes? Sometimes elderly Oostburgers just hand over their houses to OHCM. The State Bank of Oostburg has contributed.

"What I really like about this community is they stick together," Dan, the mechanic at the nearby farm, told me over lunch at Judi's. Dan's the one who told me about the overcrowded school Christmas concert where the whole village showed up to see "our kids."

In western Michigan, I found the same thing. In fact, when I showed up in Moline—the Dutchest municipality I could find in America—I almost found myself quoting *Field of Dreams*, looking around and asking, "Is this heaven?"

Follow some dirt roads into a forest in Moline and suddenly you come to a clearing with an amazing sight: three softball diamonds, batting cages, bull pens, a clubhouse that sells food, kids playing Wiffle ball off to the side while families picnic.

Ken Ritz runs the softball operation in Moline. He was born here and has lived here all his life. "On any given night, you can come up here and know half the people." (Ritz, by the way, is of German descent.)

Why does a tiny town have a big softball program for adults and children? Why does Ritz spend his time this way? "I love to see people having fun. That's what I do." And he's not doing it alone. "I got ten people who I can turn to and say, 'Can you do this?' And they say, 'Yes.'"

How do you get this magic "strong community" vibe? It's not mystical, and it's not just luck. Institutions are the key.

The colleges in Orange City and Sioux Center help. But in all of these mini-Hollands in the Midwest, the central institution is the church.

"Connecting People to Christ and One Another"

When I asked Helming and some of the Dordt faculty about the spirituality and the social teachings of the Reformed church, they immediately noted the diversity in worship styles even in the small town of Sioux Center. "There are nineteen of them in this town—a town of seven thousand has nineteen churches."

In all of Iowa, no county has a higher portion of self-described evangelicals than does Sioux County, according to the Association of Religion Data Archives. But Sioux County's 35 percent evangelical population understates, by about half, the religiosity of the county. ARDA lists twenty-three religions or denominations adhered to in Sioux County, and the single largest, with more than eleven thousand people, is the Reformed Church in America, which ARDA counts among the mainline churches—these are the folks who self-deprecatingly call themselves "the frozen chosen." Lutherans (particularly the more orthodox Missouri Synod) were the next biggest group. In all, 85 percent of Sioux County's population were counted as adherents of Christianity. Nationally, less than half of the country are adherents of *any* religion.[14]

The most prominent citizen of Sioux Center to ask a question at the Jeb Bush event was Pastor John Lee of Bethel Christian Reformed Church on Main Street in Sioux Center. The congregation's website[15] blared the motto, "Connecting People to Christ and One Another." His question was about immigrants and compassion. (He's the pastor who told me that he knew of only one Trump caucuser in his congregation.)

Over in Moline, Michigan, two Reformed churches sit across the road from each other. Friendship Christian Reformed Church has a pristine campus, with perfect grass, a repaved parking lot, and a crisp, humble chapel.

Friendship takes pride in being very welcoming. "It's in our name," says Paul, the plumber, who showed up with his daughter to help out by unclogging a church drain on a Saturday morning.

The Religious

The happiness in these places doesn't depend on the name of the church or on the Dutch blood. It's directly tied to the strong institutions of civil society held together by a common higher purpose. The institutions are rooted in the church, and the purpose is defined and articulated by the church.

Helping people, primarily by bringing them physically together with other people, is central to the churches in small rural Dutch towns. It's also central to the good life, especially for those who can't afford a membership at the Chevy Chase Club.

"Some research suggests that least- and moderately-educated Americans," sociologist Brad Wilcox wrote, "are especially likely to benefit from the social support and civic skills associated with religious institutions."

In other words, church acts like both a finishing school and a social network for a lot lower tuition than Georgetown Prep.

You may recall the studies mentioned earlier that found a higher level of self-reported happiness—satisfaction with one's life—among the wealthy. When my AEI colleague Nick Saffran ran a regression analysis of the data from the American Time Use Survey, he found that much of that difference in happiness could be explained by the greater social engagement of the wealthy. When you look at *religious activity*, specifically, you get an even stronger correlation.[16]

This bears directly on Oostburg, Moline, and Orange City, where the Reformed churches hold services on Sunday morning *and* Sunday evening.

According to our analysis of the American Time Use Survey, spending two or more hours devoted to religious activity on a given Sunday had a stronger effect on life satisfaction than did making more than $75,000 per year. So, for someone at the national median income level of $56,500 (which is just about the median income in Oostburg, too), spending two hours a week at church is associated with more happiness in the long run than getting a $20,000 raise.

Notably, these Dutch places were voting like the elite bubbles, in one regard: They were voting, in the early primary contests, against Donald Trump. Of course, in the general election months later, the conservative Christian towns would vote Republican. In those early primaries, though, a vote for Trump was largely a vote that the American Dream was dead—a proposition that got little purchase in the church-centered small towns.

Let's take one last look at the thirty-four counties nationwide (about 1 percent of all counties) where Trump scored below 20 percent. If we discard Kenedy County, Texas (where only seventeen Republicans voted), then we see the thirty-three remaining counties break down this way:

Mormon: 21
Dutch Reformed: 4
Wealthy D.C.-area: 3
University-dominated: 3
Norwegian Lutheran: 2

Trump's worst state in the GOP primaries was Utah, where he got 14 percent. His worst county in Utah was Utah County, home of Brigham Young University, which, in addition to including a university town, is also tied for being the most Mormon county in Utah, at 89 percent of the population.[17]

Surprisingly, the most Mormon county in the nation is not in Utah. It is Madison County in Idaho. Madison includes the city of Rexburg, which is home to BYU-Idaho. Nearly everyone there is Mormon.[18] This, the most Mormon county in the country, was Trump's single worst county in the entire nation in the primaries, giving him only 7.6 percent.

The Mormons, the Dutch Reformed, and the Norwegian Lutherans are all the same in that they intentionally build tight-knit, cohesive communities, and at the heart of the community is the church.

It *Does* Take a Village

"Hillary was right," Boyd Matheson tells me over takeout in his office. I'm looking out his window at the Salt Lake Temple, which is the largest temple of the Church of Jesus Christ of Latter-day Saints (LDS). The temple sits in the middle of Temple Square, which also includes the Salt Lake Tabernacle, home to Mormon Tabernacle Choir. Just beyond the temple is the massive LDS Conference Center, where the semiannual LDS General Conference is held.

Matheson is a Republican operative and a former chief of staff to Republican senator Mike Lee. Matheson, like Lee, is not only Republican; he's also notably conservative. The same goes for the state of Utah, which has had two Republican senators continuously since 1976, and a Republican governor continuously since 1985.

So where does Matheson agree with Hillary?

"It *does* take a village to raise a child," Matheson says.

The state emblem is a beehive. The beehive adorns Utah's flag and state seal, and as a Mormon symbol it dates all the way back to the 1850s. There are few things more community-minded than a beehive. Everyone in the hive serves the greater good. Nobody says, "I *did* build that," or "I alone can fix it."

The devotion to a community is omnipresent in Salt Lake City and the LDS world. As with all strong communities, there is a shared purpose driving the community and there are strong institutions of civil society organizing and holding together the community. The "ward," or local congregation, is the primary institution of daily life in the LDS church. The ward is analogous to a Catholic parish, and the entire church structure practices what we Catholics call "subsidiarity," trying never to centralize a practical function more than is needed.

Mormons worship on Sunday at their local ward. Many wards hold occasional potluck dinners. Each ward has a bishop, who is basically a layman serving a term as a pastor. Devolving things even further, wards have a handful of "home teachers" who are each assigned a family inside the ward with which to work. If your marriage is in trouble, you can tell your home teacher. If you lose your job, your home teacher knows.

The very local ward is the avenue through which the needy get access to the safety net. The LDS man who loses his job will very soon be in touch with the ward officials who help those in material need. These, recall, will be neighbors, who have worshiped with this man for years. Together, they'll take stock of the family's reserves—literally what is in their pantry as well as what is in their bank account. When the family is in need, the church will provide for them.

Can this be intrusive? Yes, and this intrusiveness is a top complaint among former Mormons. This is always the danger of a close-knit community, as that commenter from Orange City conveyed. *Intrusive* can be understood as the opposite extreme from *neglectful*, with a proper mean somewhere in between. While closely bound communities, particularly religious ones, often err in the direction of *intrusive*, American society as a whole errs in the direction of *neglectful*.

Fasting to Feed Your Neighbors

When I visited Salt Lake City in 2016, I spent a few hours at the Bishops' Storehouse. The Storehouse is in the middle of Welfare Square and is the beating heart of the church's welfare system.

The Storehouse is a grocery store with no cash registers. Parents who cannot afford the necessities to feed their children will come to the Storehouse without cash, but with an order form filled out with a ward leader. The family will pick out the food on the order form and check out.

The localness of the whole enterprise is crucial. A family's need is assessed in meetings between ward officials and the family. This makes it less likely anyone will fall through the cracks. The intimacy of the whole matter can also be a guard against abuse. A person is less likely to game a welfare system administered and funded by his neighbors. Making matters more acute, LDS families fund the Bishops' Storehouse by fasting once a month and donating the cost of the forgone meals. This arrangement gives LDS families a concrete way in which to feed their hungry neighbors and decreases the likelihood that anyone would exploit it without real need.

Don Johnson was the welfare director at Salt Lake City's Storehouse when I visited in 2016. He told me of a family he visited back when he was a leader in his home ward, where the man had lost his job. Johnson helped take stock of what the family had in cash savings and food in the pantry. Then he told the man that he needed to be ready to sell his fishing boat.

The fishing boat wasn't some gaudy luxury, but it also wasn't a necessity—it was for family fun. But are you really going to ask your neighbors to go without food so that you can keep your fishing boat?

Potentially intrusive, yes. But compare this process with the measures that state agencies take to guard against fraud or abuse. In the Mormon welfare system, there's no peeing in a cup, no byzantine paperwork. There's an honest assessment of what you have and what you need.

More important, there's a lofty end goal: a return to "self-reliance." The LDS church preaches the communal virtues of the beehive, but these go hand in hand with self-reliance. "We cannot be self-reliant without being able to work," reads the welfare manual for church leaders. "The Lord has commanded us to work, for work is the source of happiness, self-esteem, and prosperity."[19]

Working hard enough to care for yourself and your family is the duty of every able-bodied adult in the LDS church. Raising boys and girls toward this self-reliance is a big part of the church's pedagogy.

The conservative social teachings of the church and the clear gender roles bug social liberals. Mormons' theology and salvation theory bug many Christians. And what I saw as strong community could seem to others like suffocating demands for conformity. But it's hard to disagree with the outcomes.

Utah has the highest rate of upward mobility in the country, according to Raj Chetty's study.[20] A child raised by parents in the lowest income quintile is twice as likely to reach the highest quintile as an adult (one-in-ten chance) if he grows up in Salt Lake City compared with the Milwaukee area where those struggling veterans like Gary LuMaye and CJ LaRocke live (one in twenty). The reasons for this mobility, Chetty's research suggests, are the high portion of intact families and the robust civil society.

The LDS church works hard to foster that civil society. Potlucks, schools, and community engagement all originate from the church. When I spoke with former bishop Skip Christiansen in downtown Salt Lake City, he told me a majority of people in his ward volunteered their time, either for charitable work or for community activities. As a Catholic, I looked at this world with envy.

The lesson I took from Salt Lake City wasn't a lesson about Mormonism so much as a lesson about the indispensability of *institutions*. Jesus, in the Gospel, tells his followers to feed the hungry. This isn't always an easy thing to do. If I happen to be carrying food when I run into a homeless man, I usually offer it. But that's hardly an everyday occurrence. So many Christians fail to meet their obligation to feed the hungry not out of stinginess, but simply because they don't get their act together to make it happen.

The Mormon welfare system, acting through the institution of the ward, facilitates the feeding of the poor by every member, through fasting, through financial contributions, through volunteering in the food production that goes on at Welfare Square. The institution *facilitates* charity, and it also provides *accountability*.

The result of this dense web of institutions dedicated to a higher purpose is a place where people trust their neighbors, are trusted, and have opportunities for service, a scaffolding for family formation, and a safety net.

Jews for Cruz

Our tour of close-knit religious communities brings us back, briefly, to Montgomery County, Maryland. While John Kasich had Chevy Chase as his home base here, Ted Cruz had a sweet spot a lot closer to my house.

A road called Arcola Avenue T-bones into University Boulevard in Silver Spring, a couple of miles outside the Capital Beltway. Towering over that intersection are four behemoth apartment buildings. The Warwick is one, and two are called University Towers. Arcola Towers is another. These four buildings constitute an election precinct. And Cruz, who got only 22 percent countywide in the three-man race, pulled in 50 percent in this precinct.[21] Just across University Boulevard, in the precinct centered in the Kemp Mill neighborhood, Cruz pulled in a similar 45 percent.[22]

Most of Silver Spring went to Trump. What explains these polling places that went overwhelmingly to Cruz?

You could see a hint if you stepped inside the lobby of University Towers on a Saturday: One elevator in each tower operates automatically, stopping on each floor, no matter what. This allows residents to get an elevator without needing to press a button. These are the Shabbat elevators of University Towers.[23]

University Towers stands right next to Young Israel Shomrai Emunah of Greater Washington. This is an Orthodox synagogue. The Kemp Mill neighborhood, just across University Boulevard, mostly looks like the rest of Silver Spring, with middle-class single-family houses. But if you drive through Kemp Mill on an early Friday evening, you will see large families walking together to Shabbat service. In fact, on the far side of the Kemp Mill neighborhood from Young Israel Shomrai Emunah is the Kemp Mill Synagogue, also Orthodox.

There's a very physical—but easy to miss—demarcation of these neighborhoods, too. In a large polygon (on a map it vaguely resembles a bear cub looking toward Baltimore) is a neighborhood of religious significance known as an *eruv*. In short, an *eruv* is an area designated by a rabbi as a semiprivate property. This matters, because on the Sabbath, Orthodox rules prohibit carrying *anything* in public. This includes house keys, or even a baby. These two synagogues, along with University Towers, my house, and much of Silver Spring, are inside the Silver Spring *eruv*. The *eruv* is demarcated by a wire around the boundary—a wire indistinguishable from a utility wire.

The two election precincts described above are within the *eruv*. They are overwhelmingly Orthodox because they are the precincts closest to the two synagogues. Because of the Orthodox proscription on operating machinery during the Sabbath, you have to be able to walk to synagogue. This means there's a kosher supermarket at the Kemp Mill Shopping Center, and Ben Yehuda Pizza, a kosher pizzeria. And again, there's the political result: two election precincts where the Republican primary voters had little interest in Trump in 2016.

Even if the wires are hard to spot, these *eruvs* around the country could be spotted on the map if you looked for precincts where Cruz unexpectedly trounced Trump.

The week before, Trump dominated New York City, with 64 percent of the vote, while Cruz got 13.7 percent. Cruz, who barely campaigned in New York, managed to clean up in Brooklyn's Borough Park and in Far Rockaway in Queens, two Orthodox neighborhoods.

Why? Because in these tight-knit neighborhoods, where neighbors know one another, have families, stay married, look after one another's kids, and share a common, higher purpose, the American Dream is alive and well.

Muslims in America

"Why did I come to Toledo?" Zaheer Hasan says after *Jummah* (Friday services) in this storefront mosque. "I came here one stormy dark windy night in January 1988." Hasan is a neurologist, and back in 1988 he was in training, interviewing for jobs. "Driving through Perrysburg, I was hit by a huge white building. It was the Islamic

Center of Greater Toledo. I'd never seen something like it at that time. All I did was, until the next exit, I cried."

From the hotel, Hasan called his wife. "We're coming to Toledo."

"What do you mean? You haven't even interviewed."

"No, we're coming to Toledo."

Just the words *Islamic Center of Greater Toledo* can sound almost comical if you're not familiar with the area. Toledo always struck me as a plain-Jane Ohio town, and not the place I would expect to find a gleaming white dome with a minaret next to it.

It turns out Toledo has a bustling Islamic community and a large Arab population, which is both Christian and Islamic. Hasan is a senior member of his mosque community, which in 2017 was meeting in a strip mall. A decent contingent of students from the University of Toledo were there for *Jummah*, along with many older worshippers who had been together for decades.

Over in Perrysburg, a suburb of Toledo, is the impressive Islamic Center of Greater Toledo. The Islamic Center of course is a mosque, but it's more than that. "We really focused on this being a community center," Nadia Ashraf-Moghal, the Islamic Center's president, tells me, "not just a *masjid*," she says, using the Arab word for an Islamic house of worship.

The basement of the building has a kitchen and a large dining area, and on the day I visit, a family is using it to prepare dinner to celebrate their son's *Ameen* (his first full study of the Koran). Family, neighbors, and much of the mosque community are invited.

That's also where the Islamic Center has weekly brunch as part of a large community Sunday activity. It includes "weekend school for the kids," Ashraf-Moghal tells me; a sermon, often from a visiting imam; and the community meal. Because the Muslims' holy day, Friday, is a school day and workday in the United States, community and family gatherings around *Jummah* are tough. That's why these Toledoans launched this Sunday event.

A weekly, reliable social event with food and discussion on religious and moral matters steeped in shared moral and theological beliefs— that's a pretty powerful institution. It helps Muslims who move to Toledo in turn to find community. "They come to town," Ashraf-

Moghal says, "and you say, 'Oh, just go to the mosque on Sunday, you'll meet everyone.'"

This is a perfect example of why religious institutions are the most important institutions of civil society for the nonelites and non-wealthy. A new person in town can simply show up on Sunday morning at the Islamic Center. There will be food. There will be discussion. There will be a community that in all likelihood will welcome the stranger. The requirement for admission into the full community is that you practice its religion. The charge is zero dollars, and there is no credentialing you must go through. (That said, MDs seemed to be pretty common at both these mosques—both Hasan and Ashraf-Moghal are physicians.)

And the rest of the activities at the Islamic Center show the value of *institutions*. The Islamic Center operates a Muslim food bank in downtown Toledo. It's open to everyone, but it serves only halal food. The Social Services Committee also runs a blood drive. One day a month the Islamic Center brings volunteers to man a local soup kitchen.

The power of the institution—having a kitchen on-site, operating a food bank downtown, having a professional staff and a well-organized platoon of super volunteers—makes this a much more effective tool for serving the sick and the hungry than mere individuals would be. Just as important, as with the Mormons, this makes it easy for Muslims to volunteer, to find purposeful work in serving their fellow man. "I get a text every other day," Ashraf-Moghal tells me, from someone looking for volunteer activities.

Ashraf-Moghal's father had recently died when I visited. Muslim funeral rites involve a specific ritual for preparing the body. The Islamic Center has a team of men and a team of women who volunteer to prepare the body for every funeral there—often for complete strangers. They know they'll get a call when a local worshipper dies. At her father's funeral, when the Islamic Center's mosque was packed to capacity, and the congregation was praying, and the men of the community had prepared his body for the afterlife, she felt the uplift that only a community like this can provide.

The support provided by the religious community may explain the relative optimism of American Muslims. A Pew poll of American

Muslims in the summer of 2017 showed that while most were concerned about the Trump presidency, the majority were nevertheless optimistic about life in America.[24]

Nine in ten Muslims said they were proud to be American. Eight in ten were satisfied with their own lives. Seven in ten said that in America, you can get ahead if you work hard.

Here's the thing: Muslims gave more positive answers to these questions than did the general public.[25] Especially considering that average income is lower for Muslims than for the U.S. general public, this belief in the American Dream is extraordinary.

Hasam thinks being a Muslim in America is the best of both worlds. The Muslim community in Toledo is tight-knit, he says. "A lot of people here are cousins." But he thinks the United States is extraordinary in having the necessary conditions for strong community.

"People think that we come here to get rich," the Pakistani immigrant tells me. "We have a very decent and good living. But people over there," meaning Pakistan, "are far richer than us. They have more real estate . . . they have domestic servants working for them. They travel all over the world. . . . It's not the money. I come here, I like it because people treat me well. People deal with me well."

Specifically, he means, there are strong bonds of social trust. "People don't try to cheat each other or take advantage of each other." He was the second immigrant Muslim in Toledo that day who made exactly that observation to me: You can let down your guard more in the United States because there are stronger norms of trust. This was what Tocqueville wrote of. This is what people in strong communities— whether they be elite communities, religious communities, or a combination—feel, even if they don't put it that way.

Another Muslim man in America, Raisuddin Bhuiyan, came to understand this the hard way. The very hard way.

The American and the Immigrant

Bhuiyan was a Muslim immigrant from Bangladesh, working in a Dallas mini-mart. Shortly after 9/11, Mark Stroman—a white Texan, native-born, fueled by anti-Islamic rage—entered the mini-mart and opened fire, shooting Bhuiyan and his two fellow clerks.

The other two died, but Bhuiyan survived. As he recovered, Bhuiyan learned more about Stroman and the world from which Stroman came. Soon, the immigrant came to a surprising realization: He, as an immigrant practicing a minority religion, lived in a more connected, supportive, communal world than his native-born attacker. Many parts of working-class white rural America were places of alienation and anomie, while as a religious immigrant, he enjoyed institutions and connections to help him.

Anand Giridharadas, a journalist who wrote a book on these two men, put it well: Stroman had arrived at his evil place from "a battered working class" that "was suffering from a dearth of work, community and hope, with many people failing to form strong bonds and filling the void with escapist chemicals."[26]

And as Bhuiyan recovered in Texas, Giridharadas wrote, "in America it was his takes-a-village embeddedness that enabled his revival: Immigrant friends gave him medicine, sofas to sleep on, free I.T. training and job referrals."

The Bhuiyan-Stroman story is extraordinary in an obvious way—an attempted murder and a victim who set out to understand the shooter—but it is ordinary in another. Immigrants in this country often do better than noncollege natives. In poor parts of the country, immigrants earn more than natives, are less likely to be divorced, and generally have better outcomes.[27] Some working-class whites think this reflects favoritism for immigrants. Bhuiyan's story shows a better explanation: Wherever you come from, if you have a community around you, especially a religious community, then the American Dream is within reach.

American Religion

These Muslim stories elucidate an important aspect of all religious communities in America. Because these are stories of people blending two cultures—their Pakistani or Bangladeshi Islam with American community and capitalism—these communities highlight a fact that could be hidden when we look at Oostburg, Salt Lake City, Kemp Mill, or any other religious community.

This particular recipe for a strong community has two main ingredients: a faith community and America.

One aspect of this mix is the combination of social cohesion and rugged individualism. The LDS welfare system, which steadfastly tries to tie mutual aid to self-reliance, manifests this.

There's another combination here: The faith, which involves belief in a truth grand and universal, combines with the deeply local and particular—the parish, the ward, the *masjid*, the *eruv*. Those local institutions of civil society that Tocqueville found to be America's defining traits—those "little platoons" that exist everywhere but also define the United States—are a crucial element in making religion so conducive to good results.

Remember that it is *attendance* more than anything else that makes religion so correlated with charity, trust, mobility, and optimism. The local parish, mosque, or synagogue forms the scaffolding that aids in the hard work of raising a family. The local community of worship is what forms the safety net and, on the flip side, provides the opportunity to serve others.

When the church manifests itself on the local level, on the human scale, it becomes the tool for lifting up us fallen humans from what we are in nature to what we are called to be.

ה

Seek the *shalom* of the city to which I have carried you into exile.
Pray to the Lord for it, for in its *shalom* will be your *shalom*.

Your present city, your *ir*, may seem ill-fitting. It is not your destination. That is very obvious in Jeremiah, who is writing to Jews exiled from Jerusalem into Babylon.

But this same tension exists in the New Testament. "My Kingdom is not of this world," Jesus says. Yet, when asked how to attain eternal life, Jesus says, "Love your neighbor." The story of neighbor-love that Jesus tells is of a foreigner who, by chance, is nearby when another man is in need.

In these biblical tales, we do not choose the neighbor whom we are to love or the city whose flourishing we are to seek. They are given to us.

CHAPTER 13

Overcoming Alienation

Problems and Solutions

S adly, the American Dream is dead."

Here we return to the lobby of Trump Tower, and that central premise of Donald Trump's presidential run—"the American Dream is dead." That was the message that resonated across the social capital deserts of southwestern Pennsylvania, Appalachia, and "Counciltucky." The death of the American Dream was an obvious truth acknowledged in the emptied-out VFW lounges, the rotting former Main Streets, and the defunct union halls from Maine to California, yet denied by the cheery talk of every other candidate.

While Trump's message would change a bit in the general election as he tried to rally the entire Republican and conservative base to his side against Hillary Clinton, and while it would change again during his presidency, Trump's early support came from those who heard and agreed with his words, "The American Dream is dead."

In Trump Tower, in June 2015, Trump paused after saying those words. One woman, standing in that lobby, filled the silence with a scream, "Bring it back!"

The demand seemed so absurd it was sad. To my conservative ears, the idea that a president could *bring back the American Dream* was fantasy. After traveling the country and studying the nature of the problem, I find that idea even more impossible.

Our current economic and social woes are precisely the sort of thing that cannot be solved or even significantly ameliorated by any president, or by the central government at all.

This is not fatalism or pessimism. The roadblock isn't our "stupid politicians" or our corrupt or broken political system. The roadblock is that America's illness—the condition making the American Dream seem dead to so many—is by its nature a local malady.

The alienation described herein is particularly immune to any big solutions. No central solution can fix a problem caused in large part by centralization.

Looking at two specific symptoms here reminds us how little central government can do.

Factory Jobs and Economic Mobility

The laments about the "death of the American Dream" place the disappearance of factory jobs at the root. It's true that the shuttering of a factory was (a) often driven in large part by international trade, and (b) a first domino to fall, leading to a collapse of communities. That collapse of community is the root problem.

So it's natural to ask: If we restore factory jobs, can we restore communities, and thus restore the American Dream?

But as with dominoes, this disaster is not reversible: a single domino falling may knock down the others, but lifting one back up doesn't necessarily lift the others.

The experience of Williston, North Dakota, suggests as much. Blue-collar jobs flowed into this fracking town, but marriage and family formation didn't return. Bad economics can help kill a community, but good economics cannot, alone, rebuild one. And if you're not building community, you're not getting close to fixing what ails us.

Analogously, even if public policy and international trade helped kill factory jobs in the United States, reversing those policies and choking off international trade won't restore the factory jobs.

Low wages in China have been the main reason companies have moved manufacturing out of the United States. With all those jobs going to China, wages there have been rising, thus mitigating the draw of offshoring. Throw in bountiful energy in the United States, and you've gotten more and more American companies setting up manufacturing right here at home.

This hasn't put the blue-collar guy back to work, though. Ben Casselman at *FiveThirtyEight* explains:

> *Since the recession ended in 2009, manufacturing output—the value of all the goods that U.S. factories produce, adjusted for inflation—has risen by more than 20 percent, because of a combination of "reshoring" and increased domestic demand. But manufacturing employment is up just 5 percent.*[1]

What's going on? In short, robots rather than blue-collar workers are getting the new jobs at the U.S. factories. So slapping tariffs on goods imported from China will not create jobs. To the extent that it will draw manufacturing back here, protectionism will make jobs for robots. At the same time, trade protectionism can *cost* jobs. Most American goods are inputs into other manufacturing—such as steel from China going into cars assembled in Ohio. Driving up the price of those inputs through tariffs or quotas can actually *constrict* manufacturing jobs here.

Paltry mobility is probably the problem in this book that seems most tied to public policy, and thus most fixable by it. There's reason to doubt even that, though. Three economists at Brigham Young University tried to find the effect on mobility of various state-level policies, such as education spending, tax rates, and welfare spending. How to determine the effects of those policies, as opposed to the effects of culture, population, and unrelated economic characteristics?

The BYU economists compared counties. For starters, they found that two neighboring counties in two different states were far more similar on the score of mobility than two counties chosen at random. This suggests that the local variations in mobility that Chetty found are affected by geography, but not simply by state.

Then, they tried to find differences in mobility between counties in states with higher per-pupil spending, higher welfare spending, more progressive taxation, lower taxes, et cetera. Their conclusion: "We find little statistical evidence that either state public education investments, state investments in broader social welfare spending, or tax rate differences affect mobility."[2]

More fundamentally, the forces that have left so much of America alienated are cultural forces. Culture, as they say, is upstream from politics. Our current politics are determined by culture more than culture is determined by politics. It's difficult, then, to come up with the politics that will reverse the erosion of civil society.

When the cultural change is one of coming apart and alienation, it's even tougher to turn it around. "Declines in social capital tend to be self-intensifying," Yuval Levin writes in *Fractured Republic*. "[A]s people come to have less in common with their fellow citizens, they find it more difficult to cooperate and identify with one another, which brings a further weakening of remaining social bonds."[3]

This echoes Nisbet's definition of alienation. It's not simply that individuals find themselves detached from civil society, it's that they cannot see the point of it.

And you can see the self-perpetuating mechanism at work in families. Weaker communities make it harder to have strong families, and without intact families, it's much harder to have strong communities. Look at public schools. By and large, "good public schools" are schools with involved families. The children who arguably "need" good public schools the most, though, are the children of single mothers or the children in the low-mobility areas that Raj Chetty's research suggested were characterized by single motherhood and a breakdown of family.

It's the same with any institution. An alienated landscape is one where the land is infertile for the planting of institutions of civil society, but the alienation is a result of the absence of institutions of civil society.

This is why, in this book, we've so often said the causal arrows point both ways. It's why this predicament is so self-reinforcing. As people don't see community around them, they put their hopes for help, their sense of purpose, and their sense of identity onto the stage of national politics. Alienation begets centralization, which exacerbates alienation.

When the solution is twenty thousand towns each taking steps to revitalize their community and one million little platoons forming and deploying on their little patches, it's not possible or productive to write the typical "solutions" section.

You can't write that chapter when the "solution" is mostly:

You should go to church.

Also, *You should start a T-ball team.* You should create an institution, such as a weekly coffee meeting with other old guys in your town. You should attach yourself to a little platoon and volunteer there. You should spend less time watching the cable networks and more time asking after your neighbors.

Are there public policies that could make this easier? Sure. But again, the value of civil society is directly tied to its not being centralized, and usually to its *not* being governmental. So while there are no big policy solutions, there are definitely smaller solutions.

Small Solutions

While we don't want to further entangle central government with local institutions, there are some preexisting connections between these institutions and state and federal government. The policies governing those connections can be reformed in ways that would juice civil society and alleviate the alienation felt by so much of our working class.

Labor unions, for instance, could be reinvigorated if the legal regime around them changed. Currently, unions get what strength they have from a patchwork of federal laws that more or less require employers to deal with them, and nearly coerce workers to join a union if it has organized at their employer. Pro-business politicians respond to these laws with their own heavy-handed legislation called "right-to-work laws." It's that same old spiral of aggression met with aggression.

But if we imagine labor unions as institutions of civil society rather than as creatures of the state, they would be organized differently. Workers would join them because they saw immediate benefit in joining them, and then they generate even more benefits for themselves and for the others in that same institution—as well as for the broader community.

How would that work? Some of northern Europe seems to have the proper framework. In Sweden, Denmark, Finland, and Belgium the unions have a powerful draw: They run the unemployment insurance system.[4]

Just as the diner gets you in the door with coffee and breakfast, unions in this "Ghent System" (named after the Belgian city where it was crafted) get you in the door with an insurance product.

Conservatives can get behind this idea because it decentralizes unemployment insurance and takes it to the private sector. Liberals can cheer it because they like unionization.

Unions re-created as worker-support systems would still take up the role of collective bargaining, but they would also naturally take up training roles, other insurance, or mutual-aid roles. They would be true institutions of civil society.

With so much to offer workers, such unions would swell in their ranks, advocates of this plan argue, and thus would command greater leverage in negotiations. Less coercion, more mutual aid, more solidarity—this is a model of reinvigorating civil society.

Public schools need to be reexamined. In some parts of the country, local public schools really are *local* and *public*. That is, the people of the town have control over the school curriculum and mission. In many places, "public schools" are better called "government schools." A state or county board of education, insulated from the public, hands down one-size-fits-all rules. If the people actually had power to shape the local schools, that could reinvigorate schools, families, and communities.

While there are plenty of other examples that we could find, the biggest thing Washington, D.C., and state governments could do for civil society would be to get out of the way. This would be no cure-all. Even where centralized government has *caused* the problem by smothering civil society, there's no guarantee that removing the giant footprint of Big Government will cause a community to pop back up. Where paving stones have killed grass, removing the stones doesn't guarantee the grass will come back. The soil may be too beaten down for anything to grow. Or weeds may sprout instead.

Strong communities have to grow up organically, but they don't spring up automatically. There are conditions—physical, personal, spiritual, economic, cultural—necessary for strong communities to grow. When people have been alienated from their communities for too long, they are not necessarily predisposed to forming and strengthening institutions of their own.

But still, the first step in regrowing the grass will be removing the paving stones. There's a lot the federal government can do in that re-gard. For one thing, get rid of the Michael Bloomberg–like regulations that regulate charities out of business.

Mostly, though, government needs to give up its culture war on the fundamental institution of American civil society: religious congrega-tions. All politicians ought to ask themselves, "What is government doing that constrains religious congregations?"

Plenty, to be honest. The mind-set that religion ought to be a private concern, hidden behind church doors or bedroom doors, is directly antithetical to the fact of churches, synagogues, and mosques as civil society institutions. Recall the American Civil Liberties Union's lawsuit to force Catholic hospitals to perform abortions. It's a statement that you can't be Catholic and a hospital.

The various assaults on religious liberty aimed at driving religion into solely the private sphere—out of the civic square, out of the marketplace, out of politics—need to end if we hope for civil society in America to have a chance.

Centralized safety-net programs need to be reconsidered, too, through the lens of subsidiarity. Which programs can be done better by states than by Washington? Which programs currently admini-stered by state or local governments are more fittingly done by non-profits, by voluntary groups, and by churches? Can the central government shift to being a safety net for safety nets, letting civil society be the front line in the effort, with government as the auxiliary safety net, or the reinsurance program?

Local and state governments can help civil society by building towns and cities in ways more conducive to neighborliness and community building. Walkability is a big thing. Mixing residential and commercial development would create real neighborhoods where people can walk to the corner store for a gallon of milk and run into their neighbors. It could allow for "third places" like neighborhood pubs, barbershops, and sandwich shops. Of course, it would also help if counties, states, and cities stopped giving lavish corporate welfare deals to shopping centers that help kill Main Street.

Car-centric development was largely a Big Idea by planners with grand master plans, and it has isolated families and individuals from one another.

The tax code plays a role in leaving Americans and American families abandoned. The largest single tax deduction for families is the deduction for mortgage interest. Studies suggest that this subsidy doesn't really lead to more home ownership, but instead drives up prices and leads people to buy bigger homes.[5]

More expensive homes and bigger homes are a recipe for eroding community. People spend more time inside because the house is bigger. People are more spread out. Thanks to costlier real estate, people find it harder to form neighborhoods by, say, moving in next door to their brother or within walking distance of their synagogue. Housing-price booms mean less family formation. The more dramatic the increase in home prices, the less young people start families.[6] Getting rid of the policies that make homes costlier and bigger will nudge things a bit in the direction of stronger communities.

These nudges of course can't make communities come back. Only individuals and families, coming together, can do that.

Problems with Civil Society

Erosion of civil society, leaving individuals adrift and families isolated, is at the core of America's social, economic, and political tumult. That doesn't mean there's no downside to civil society.

Strong religious communities are the best example of a reinvigorated civil society that brings to the working class the modeling, support structure, and sense of purpose that only local, human-level community can bring. That doesn't mean that tight-knit religious communities don't come with their own risks and dangers.

My own church is infamous for how its structure, including its nature as a trusted and feared institution, allowed for horrific abuses, including sexual abuse of minors, teenagers, and young men, with cover-ups by bishops. Subsequent sexual abuse scandals in college football, in women's gymnastics, in media, and in Hollywood demonstrate the greatest risks of strong institutions: The powerful in these institutions can become unaccountable, and the instinct of institutional self-preservation can override concern for individual welfare.

Resisting civil society because of the worst abuses by its institutions, however, makes no more sense than becoming an anarchist because of slavery, the Holocaust, or internment. But even short of the worst abuses, there are reasons to worry about overbearing institutions. Homogeneity and uniformity are two reasons.

Recall Robert Putnam's findings that diversity seems to undermine social cohesion. The strong communities we've discussed in this book all are fairly homogeneous in one way or another.

Oostburg is Dutch American Christians. Kemp Mill is Orthodox Jewish. Chevy Chase is almost all white, college educated, and wealthy. Salt Lake City is mostly white and Mormon. You can find tight-knit black communities all over America, often built around Protestant churches. Same with Hispanic communities, and Polish or Russian neighborhoods.

What we don't have much of in the United States is strong communities that are diverse along multiple dimensions. And that uniformity can create problems.

The term *tight-knit* has a positive connotation, but those same communities can look to others as "suffocating." Certainly, plenty of Catholic-school alumni, former Mormons, former Muslims, or refugees from Orange City, Iowa, tell stories about conformist cultures in which intellectual freedom and self-expression were stultified by explicit rules or clear cultural norms.

Shared moral values, enforced by publicly expressed norms and clear expectations, are crucial to any strong community. But if these rules are not freely chosen, they become simply *strictures* instead of *norms*. Heavy-handed enforcement actually erodes the shared values and common purpose of a community, because then the rules reflect the values and norms only of the rule makers and not of those expected to follow the rules.

How to mitigate this potential "suffocation"?

American exceptionalism, once again, is the key. There's something about the blend of America and religion that creates the best environment for the mutual flourishing of shared norms and individual liberty. It's always a difficult balance to maintain, but the rugged individualism of America, the multilayered nature of our civil society, and probably the diversity of religious groups make it more possible. More important here may be America's historic tendency toward localism:

One way to allow creative minds to flourish in a community with a set code of morals and a fixed purpose is through local variety—sometimes very local. Oostburg, as tiny as it is, has public schools and private schools. It has a First Reformed church, a Christian Reformed church, a First Presbyterian church, and a Bethel Orthodox Presbyterian church in addition to a couple of non-Reform churches. This may not sound like variety to you, but the worship styles are different, and to some extent the teachings and the expected conduct are different. More important, the churches are small enough that a motivated individual can make an impact on his community—thus mitigating the stultifying feeling that close communities can have.

Us and Them

Another problem with strong civil society is that an "us" is invariably defined in opposition to a "them." This isn't always a bad thing. Often this differentiation is perfectly peaceable. Maybe it's a friendly rivalry between Newton and Needham. Maybe it's a friendly and admiring distance between the Orthodox Jews of Kemp Mill, and St. Andrew Apostle Catholic Parish.

But far too often in America, differences have meant hatred and discord, and the commonality of close community makes it hard for outsiders to enter. Most obviously, there's our country's history of neighborhood segregation by race.

"Everybody knew pretty much everybody else," Chris, the grandmother smoking on the front stoop in Fishtown, told me. "Our kids knew all the other kids, and their parents. You know, community strength."

Institutions like the Fishtown Athletic Association, Holy Name, St. Laurentius, and the neighborhood pool ("the swimmy," the old-timers call it) bound Fishtown close together. "It was just the good old days, man," said Mike Quinn, a fifty-year-old homeless man who was drinking malt liquor when I met him in Palmer cemetery one morning.

"Close-knit," Bubbles, the morning bartender at Les & Doreen's, said.

Fishtowners had much in common, had a shared purpose, were dedicated to raising their kids. But one of the things they had in common, besides being middle-class or poor, besides sports, besides mostly being Catholic, besides having kids, was being white. "It was the last completely white enclave in the city," Chris told me.

"There was a house for sale about a block and a half away from here," Chris recalled, speaking of the 1970s, "and a black family moved in." The Fishtowners didn't appreciate that. "The city had the big Civil Disobedience truck out there for a couple of weeks," she explained as she ashed on her brick stoop, "and then they moved."

She went on, gesturing with her shoulder back to the small brick town house. "Our house, before we bought it," in 1970, "apparently a Hispanic family had tried to move in, and there was a lot of disruption about that."

This is one of America's oldest stories: racially segregated neighborhoods, resulting in invisible lines that deny opportunities to racial minorities or other out-groups. Reminiscing about "the good old days," of white working-class neighborhoods full of stickball and everyone walking to Mass, risks blurring over what it means for outsiders.

And this isn't a problem limited to the distant past.

Oostburg, the model I've used for tight-knit religious communities, also has a dark episode of exclusion along both racial and religious lines.

In 2010, Dr. Mansoor Mirza acquired a health-food store just outside Oostburg, in the town of Wilson. His plan for the property: create the Islamic Society of Sheboygan. (Sheboygan is the name of the county, and of the city to the north of Wilson.)

Not everyone in Oostburg or Wilson reacted positively. Some, as told by the minutes of the Wilson Planning Commission, were worried about terrorists setting up shop there. Others had more fundamental objections: "The basis of this community is on Christ and Christ alone," one local objected at the meeting. "Do we really want this in our backyard?"[7]

"If they're against Christianity," another said, "I don't want them coming after my kids." The pastor of one of Oostburg's churches joined in the opposition to the center.

For all the beautiful things brought to Oostburg by the centrality of the church and the Dutch heritage, there are evils. Now, a few dozen loud objectors and one pastor may not have spoken for the village. Wilson's planning commission unanimously approved the center. But the factors that create cohesiveness can sometimes lead to a hostility and prejudice toward the *others*, especially if the *others* are sufficiently different.

Again, though, this is another story where American exceptionalism points us toward the answer. Dr. Mirza got his permit, in part because of our civic setup, and our attitudes toward property rights. First, he wasn't going to be doing anything illegal in there, and so how could anyone deny him those rights? Second, while the folks of Oostburg had their say, the planning commission of Wilson—where the property actually sat—got the vote. It was localism in service of diversity. Third, while the community is built around the Dutch Reformed churches, the churches don't run the town—civic governments do.

The fourth aspect of small-town America's virtue shows up in the *Time* magazine story on the whole Sheboygan fracas:

*In late June, a Muslim child who was vacationing with her fam-
ily, Sofia Khan, 9, disappeared while enjoying the waters by Lake
Michigan in the Oostburg area. Rita Harmeling saw the commotion
from her home. A congregant of the First Reformed Church, she
immediately opened her home in what was first a rescue attempt
and later a recovery effort. But Harmeling took another step. "I
thought, If this had happened to someone in my family, I would
want to have my spiritual needs met." And so she contacted Hamad,
after getting his number through her pastor, the Rev. Wayne
DeVrou, who had originally opposed the mosque.*

*While the mosque provided a place for spiritual comfort, local
residents opened their homes to Sofia's extended family. A neighbor
who lived near the mosque, who had once been suspicious, told the
imam to let the girl's family use his front yard for their gathering.
Says Mirza: "Her family was taken care of by the same churches
that were against the mosque."*

Where civil society is strong, you find the American tradition of
individuals taking responsibility on themselves rather than waiting
for the authorities. This is exactly the story of the Good Samaritan—
someone of another race and creed is in need, and the person physically
proximate sees it as her own duty to provide the needed care.

This happy ending isn't intended to diminish the damage of bigotry
or to deny its prevalence in the United States. Instead, the ending of
this story reminds us how the special blend of America's peculiarities
and religion's virtues can be the building block for a robust civil
society not just for the Dutch in rural Wisconsin, but anywhere, with
any people.

Build a City of God

Now, at last, after visiting the Oostburgs, the Salt Lake Citys, and the
Orange Citys; after popping into Glory Days Sports Bar and Grill in
Counciltucky, Smitty's in Uniontown, and DK's in Williston; after

the stops in Langley and Chevy Chase, we bring this story home, to my own small patch off Georgia Avenue in Silver Spring, Maryland.

Glenmont ain't Mayberry. It's no dream of social capital or small-town community. Glenmont's central institution is a metro stop to which most people drive and park in one of two looming concrete garages. The closest thing to a town square in Glenmont is a vast—monstrous, in fact—asphalt lot taking up most of the footprint of a dreary strip mall at the totally inhumane, nearly unwalkable intersection of Randolph Road, Georgia Avenue, and Layhill Road. Heck, my own house is basically behind other houses and thus set way back from the sidewalk, which, being narrow with no separation from my street, is not an inviting place to stop and meet a neighbor.

But a bit off Georgia, below Randolph, nestled between the two Orthodox synagogues is St. Andrew Apostle Catholic Church, my home parish.

I want to end our journey here, not because St. Andrew's is the ideal, but because every good story should come home in the end. And if you are serious about addressing America's social problems, you have to begin where you are. While it's not perfect, around the reality of my parish we can build, with a bit of imagination, the model of a revitalized civil society.

My parish comes to mind because it has something that is rare: a combination of diversity and cohesion. We have multiple families from West Africa, many from East Africa, and some parishioners from down in Malawi. We have plenty of Italian Americans and Irish Americans, but also Mexicans, Salvadorans, and Colombians. Filipinos, Indian Americans, Vietnamese all come to Mass every Sunday and send their kids to school there. There's a dad from Dominica. The best pure shooter on the kindergarten girls' basketball team I coached is Native American, and our parish has half a dozen mixed-race couples by my count. We've got it all. A Friday fish fry in the multipurpose room looks like the United Nations.

There's also social and economic diversity. There are more than a few couples with three or four advanced degrees between them, but also quite a few couples with no college degrees. There are lobbyists with beach houses and luxury cars, and there are schoolteachers and African immigrant families dropping off their kids in beaters that were donated to them.

This racial and socioeconomic diversity rarely exists in cohesive communities, which makes our parish extraordinary. An unfortunate accident made this one happen: A Hispanic parish to the west and a mostly black parish in downtown Silver Spring both closed their schools a few years back. Some of the most motivated parents in those parishes found St. Andrew's and planted their kids there.

A shared faith is the main unifying factor. But because some of the families most involved in the school are non-Catholics, there's another unifier, which is dedication to educating the parish's kids and forming their characters.

Now, St. Andrew Apostle is no dream of new urbanism or pinnacle of social capital. Almost nobody lives within walking distance of the parish, and many folks who attend Sunday Mass will tell you they find it hard to meet people if they don't have kids at the school.

So I cannot hold up my parish as the model for civil society in twenty-first-century America, but we can use it as the foundation stone for a model.

Imagine more neighborhoods built with blends of single-family homes with yards, but also town houses, duplexes, and garden apartments, bringing in socioeconomic diversity. Also, let's weave this housing together with retail, shopping, and nice sidewalks for walking and tricycle riding.

In each of the thousand neighborhoods like this, imagine a small St. Andrew's, a small Islamic center, a small Young Israel Shomrai Emunah, a small First Reformed Christian church, or a small LDS ward. Now consider these churches not as solely *masjids*, or places to "do your religion on Sunday" or Saturday or Friday, but as core institutions of civil society.

If you belong to an active congregation, you have little trouble imagining this.

At St. Andrew's, for instance, we've begun our own version of a tradition at nearby St. Bernadette parish, called "Friday Night on the Field." These gatherings are built around T-ball and coach-pitch baseball and softball. Grills churn out burgers and dogs while younger kids climb in the playground and older kids shoot hoops, toss footballs, or just meander and chat. It fills a core need of modern suburban parents: a place to bring your children and forget about them, while they safely hang out with other kids, and you socialize with other adults.

Meeting that need alone can make a local congregation immensely valuable for promoting family formation and strengthening marriage. The nuclear family isn't meant to be self-contained, and so much of what makes modern family life difficult is the isolation of parents, especially in these days when free-range parenting is nearly illegal.

On this score, our parish also acts as a babysitting resource, sometimes more formally than others—in past years, the school has compiled and published a list of older kids and young adults available for babysitting. Two of our regular babysitters are the daughters of the second-grade teacher. Our kids' piano teacher is a cantor at the parish.

And now let us expand on what exists to consider what *could* exist, beginning with what exists elsewhere.

Across the street is a Dutch Reformed church that every Wednesday morning has a coffee for stay-at-home moms, combined with story hour for the little ones. Mom gets adult conversation and maybe some faith formation, while kids get play and stories.

Now imagine expanding this. First off, many Catholic schools offer day care that runs parallel to the school year. Expand this to become a drop-in day care at the local church or synagogue. If the basement floods while Mom's away, Dad can drop off the kids while he tries to right the problem. If a job interview arises at the last second, or the babysitter cancels right before Mom's shift begins, a place to drop the kids is of immense value, especially if the on-site babysitters are your neighbors' kids and people generally subscribed to the same values. Our old YMCA had something like this, where membership fees covered the drop-in babysitting. That meant low-income families who got free YMCA membership were also getting free drop-in babysitting, adding the flexibility that parents need.

Our parish has a baseball field, and we've leveraged that to start a T-ball program and a baseball team. It's fairly modest, but other churches have expanded the idea. In elite suburbs, so much of youth sports is high-stakes, high-cost, high-commitment "travel ball." A lower-key opportunity for sports, geared at learning the game, healthy competition, getting the kids active, fostering virtues—that's not always on offer in places like Montgomery County. One nearby church responded to this gap by launching a league that goes to extremes in being noncompetitive.

Now imagine plugging in the Mormons' welfare system. Not every little independent congregation could run this—it needs a more regional institution to house it. But if the Islamic Center of Greater Toledo can operate a food bank, and if the Mormon stakes can operate their bishops' storehouses, this notion can be transformed into something grander.

Hungry people in a neighborhood would know they could get a meal at the nearby church. But this is different from a soup kitchen. It starts with something like a Friday fish fry, but it extends past the Lenten season. Then it expands over the course of the week to the point where a church meal is available for the general public every night—maybe the neighborhoods' churches each take one evening a week. It's not gourmet. It's probably less tasty than a home-cooked meal or fast food, but it provides camaraderie, including interdenominational and cross-religious camaraderie.

If the mosque, the Catholic parish, the Protestant church, the synagogue, and the Mormon ward are all involved, then a family in one of these congregations, if in the habit of popping in when Dad gets home too late to cook anything, is suddenly exposed to the diversity of the community. Seating is arranged so as to optimize adult mingling, and kids are encouraged to run around.

But now, make it free or discounted for the poor. Maybe run it entirely on donations. Maybe ticket booklets have been bought at the beginning of the month, for use at any venue on any night, and so the poor family's free tickets look no different from some other family's paid-for tickets.

And if the destitute and homeless walk in, all the better. Especially among the religious minded, the discomfort of this situation will press them to recall the command to feed the hungry, and as Pope

Francis says, to "include the poor." What better represents inclusion than breaking bread together?

We could go on. I know of some churches that offer transportation for families who need it, and take up collections to help the needy pay their electricity bills. Boy Scout and Girl Scout troops, and similar organizations, often operate out of local congregations already.

Like the Scouts, other institutions will spring from the church congregations, many of them with no direct religious purpose. In different towns, the mix of institutions will be different. Some towns, like Fishtown of old, will be focused on youth sports. Others will develop an emphasis on food. In some places, the civil society atmosphere will be mostly secular, while in others, religion will be more up-front.

Here some reader might object: *Why tie this to religious institutions at all? So much of these goods are perfectly secular.*

My first answer is, *What else do you got?*

Chevy Chase can do fine built around secular institutions. The upper middle class, the enclaves of college-educated married parents can afford other institutions and keep them going. What the last sixty years in America have proved is that for the middle class and the working class, the options are (a) strong religious communities or (b) alienation and collapse.

It's possible that secular analogues can be built, and we ought to encourage these institutions, however we can. But in many middle-class or working-class towns, the strongest institutions are built around churches. This bothers some, because there persists in parts of American culture antipathy toward church as a central institution of civil society. That antipathy must not creep into our policy making, because policies that obstruct the growth of religious congregations as institutions of civil society are policies that will be deadly to the working class.

Sure, many of these functions can and should belong to secular institutions—the American Legion runs successful baseball leagues in many towns—but many of these functions get a boost from being tied in with the moral values preached on Friday, Saturday, or Sunday. More important, being part of a preexisting institution would help such programs grow more organically, and even in the abandoned parts of America, there still stands a church, and it's still open one day a week. In this vision, we're just talking about making it operative every day.

These everyday things like babysitting, T-ball, and plates of fish sticks may seem banal. But they can be the glue that pulls people together and forms an institution of civil society. Thus you've erected the scaffolding of life, which offers a mini–safety net, role models, and a sense of purpose.

Churches, synagogues, and mosques will do this best because these institutions operate with a divine mandate to care for God's creations. Also, the practices that yield the best outcomes are imbued with extra significance in a religious setting. School, for instance, becomes a place not merely for education but for *formation*.

Such a supportive community makes the hard things in life easier. That includes catching people when they fall, but it also includes pointing people in the right direction in the first place. A religious community worthy of the name will point individuals toward love for their neighbor and toward sacrificial work. And through setting norms, providing meeting grounds, and, most important, offering lifelong support, such a community will point its members down the aisle toward the fundamental institution, the building block of civic life—marriage and the creation of a family.

Acknowledgments and Dedication

A wise woman, my freshman-year instructor in ancient Greek, told the class a story of when she published her book on the works of Aeschylus, Euripides, Shakespeare, and Machiavelli. As the book went to press, her husband, also an academic, asked her how she felt about it.

"I'm afraid there's nothing *new* in it," she fretted.

"Oh, Mera, dear," her husband Harvey said as he comforted her, "if there were anything *new*, that would be a sure sign it was wrong."

That story, planted in my brain more than twenty years ago, has comforted me throughout the writing of this book. As my travels, my columns, and my arguments have led me to find truths and connections that seemed my own discoveries, my research showed me I was uncovering things that previous authors, thinkers, and academics had demonstrated and elaborated for their entire careers.

Robert Putnam, William Julius Wilson, and Charles Murray are the three contemporary writers who have done the most scholarship on social capital. I have not tried to match their level of original research, but instead to illustrate and synthesize their findings and arguments. Because I believe the localized erosion of civil society is the fundamental problem in our country today, I believe the work of these men to be the most important social science of contemporary America.

Raj Chetty's groundbreaking research on economic mobility tied together and advanced this research on social capital. Melissa Kearney,

Brad Wilcox, and Andrew Cherlin have further illuminated the relationships among family structure, community, and social well-being.

Michael Barone and Yuval Levin were the first I noticed to lay out the centrality of social connectedness—or the lack of it—to the Trump phenomenon.

I could credit the old authors whose ideas are dimly reflected in this book—such as Tocqueville, Nisbet, Burke, Kirk—but the list would be long, boring, and still incomplete.

These authors, their books, and their words were my intellectual companions in writing this book, but as Johnny Cash says, "Flesh and blood needs flesh and blood." And many friends and colleagues and family were indispensable in their support while I wrote this.

First and foremost, my bride Katie pushed me to write this book, listened to my endless talk about it, and carried our family on her back as I sneaked away to read volumes and pound out chapters. Katie's love for me holds me up like nothing else in the world can.

Our kids—Lucy, Charlie, Brendan, Meg, Sean, and Eve—bore some of the sacrifice in the months when this book was being created. They got less Daddy time than they or I wanted, and they had to help their mother take up the slack.

My brothers were my constant advisers on this and on every undertaking of my life. I also must thank my parents—my community-organizer mom and small-town mayor dad.

And, of course, there were the institutions. The first indispensable institution in this book's creation is the American Enterprise Institute, where I am a visiting fellow. It was a conversation with Arthur Brooks in the halls of the old Seventeenth Street building that first planted the seed of this book. It was in a speech in San Antonio to AEI's Values and Capitalism program that I first sketched out the outline of this book.

My friend at AEI Stan Veuger first pointed me to Chetty's research on mobility's connection with family strength and social capital. My friend Michael Strain regularly guided me toward the proper research, while providing professional and personal support. My supervisors

Karlyn Bowman and Ryan Streeter also provided academic and professional support.

Nick Saffran, my research assistant at AEI, spent many hours on this book. He carried out the original research, cleaned up my manuscript, and straightened out some of my facts.

My full-time employer, the *Washington Examiner*, also has my sincere thanks. My boss, Hugo Gurdon, gave me the green light, permitting my repeated leaves of absence, and my occasional civil-society-themed editorial. My friends and coeditors Dave Freddoso and Jason Russell cheerfully covered for me on "book days." My colleagues on the Commentary Page—Freddoso, Russell, Emily Jashinsky, Tom Rogan, Becket Adams, Siraj Hashmi, Philip Wegmann, and Dan Allott—were my most constant sounding boards for my book theme.

Some friends and colleagues read early drafts and provided crucial feedback: Veuger, Wilcox, Murray, Emma Green, Peter Suderman, Tyson and Julie Marx, to name a few.

Annette Kirk and the Russell Kirk Center hosted me for a very productive and inspiring writing retreat. Emily Ekins provided me with raw data to crunch.

The indispensable people for this book, though, were Andrew Duda Jr. and Sr. in Fayette City; Dave and Frank and the barmaid at Smitty's; Tracy Pritchard and Joe Adams in Bloomington; Jeff Mason in South Carolina and Drew Brandenburg in North Carolina; CJ LaRocke, Dan Suminski, and Gary LuMaye outside Milwaukee; Julia Shindel and Sinead Lamel in Zuccotti Park; and dozens of other Americans left alienated, without a community in which to live out their lives as God intended. The foregoing was my effort to tell their story, and I dedicate this book to them.

Notes

Preface

1. J. D. Vance, *Hillbilly Elegy* (New York: HarperCollins, 2016), 215.

Chapter 1: It Takes a Village

1. Jenna Johnson, "These Are the Towns That Love Donald Trump," *Washington Post*, January 8, 2016, www.washingtonpost.com/politics/2016/01/08/f5d7c5a2 -b48d-11e5-a76a-0b5145e8679a_story.html?utm_term=.0662cc9f1719.

2. U.S. Census Bureau, "2011–2015 American Community Survey 5-Year Estimates, Selected Economic Characteristics of Chevy Chase Village, MD," https://factfinder .census.gov/bkmk/table/1.0/en/ACS/15_5YR/DP03/1600000US2416787.

3. Ibid.

4. Hillary Clinton Campaign, https://web.archive.org/web/20170612092243/www .hillaryclinton.com/page/hillblazers/.

5. "What Are the Most Educated Counties in the U.S.?" *Decision Science News*, April 15, 2016, www.decisionsciencenews.com/2016/04/15/educated-counties-us/.

6. U.S. Census Bureau, "2011–2015 American Community Survey 5-Year Estimates, Selected Housing Characteristics of Oostburg Village, WI," https://factfinder .census.gov/bkmk/table/1.0/en/ACS/15_5YR/DP04/1600000US5560100.

7. Ibid.

8. "Is Oostburg the Most Conservative Community in Wisconsin?" *Retiring Guy's Digest*, June 25, 2014, http://paulsnewsline.blogspot.com/2014/06/is-oostburg -most-conservative-community.html.

9. Raj Chetty, Nathaniel Hendren, Patrick Kline, and Emmanuel Saez, "Where Is the Land of Opportunity? The Geography of Intergenerational Mobility in the United States," *Quarterly Journal of Economics* 129, no. 4 (2014): 1553–1623, https://doi.org/10.1093/qje/qju022.

10. The one exception is Story County, Iowa, home to Iowa State University.

11. Emma Green, "The Death of Community and the Rise of Trump," *Atlantic*, March 5, 2017, www.theatlantic.com/politics/archive/2017/03/religiously -unaffiliated-white-americans/518340/.

12. Yuval Levin, "Conservatism in an Age of Alienation," *Modern Age* 59, no. 2 (2017): 19.

13. Anne Case and Angus Deaton, "Mortality and Morbidity in the 21st Century," *Brookings Papers on Economic Activity* (March 2017): 33, www.brookings.edu /wp-content/uploads/2017/03/6_casedeaton.pdf.

14. Robert Nisbet, *The Quest for Community* (Wilmington, DE: Intercollegiate Studies Institute, 2010), xxiii.

Chapter 2: Progress at a Price

1. Historic Structures, "Pittsburgh Steel Company Monessen Works, Monessen Pennsylvania," June 23, 2016, www.historic-structures.com/pa/monessen /monessen_steel.php.
2. Raj Chetty, David Grusky, Maximilian Hell, et al., "The Fading American Dream: Trends in Absolute Income Mobility since 1940" (working paper 22910, National Bureau of Economic Research, Cambridge, Massachusetts, 2016), www .equality-of-opportunity.org/papers/abs_mobility_paper.pdf.
3. Brink Lindsey, "The End of the Working Class," *American Interest* 13, no. 3 (2017), www.the-american-interest.com/2017/08/30/end-working-class/.
4. Charles Murray, *Coming Apart* (New York: Crown Forum, 2012), 273.
5. "Men Adrift," *Economist*, www.economist.com/news/essays/21649050-badly -educated-men-rich-countries-have-not-adapted-well-trade-technology -or-feminism?fsrc=scn/tw/te/bl/ed/manhood.
6. The Chartbook of Economic Inequality, "Economic Inequality in USA," 2017, www.chartbookofeconomicinequality.com/inequality-by-country/usa/.
7. Murray, *Coming Apart*, 270.
8. U.S. Census Bureau, "Trends in Premarital Childbearing," October 1999, www .census.gov/prod/99pubs/p23-197.pdf.
9. Robert Putnam, *Bowling Alone* (New York: Simon & Schuster, 2001), Kindle, 16.
10. Douglas S. Massey, Jonathan Rothwell, and Thurston Domina, "The Changing Bases of Segregation in the United States," *Annals of the American Academy of Political and Social Science* 626, no. 1 (2009), www.ncbi.nlm.nih.gov/pmc /articles/PMC3844132/.
11. Putnam, *Bowling Alone*, 16.
12. Daniel Bell and Virginia Held, "The Community Revolution," *Public Interest*, no. 16 (Summer 1969): 142.
13. Historic Structures, "Complete History Part 3 Pittsburgh Steel Company Monessen Works, Monessen Pennsylvania," June 23, 2016, www.historic -structures.com/pa/monessen/monessen_steel3.php.
14. U.S. Census Bureau, 2012 Economic Census of the United States, "Geographic Area Series: Economy-Wide Key Statistics," https://factfinder.census.gov/bkmk /table/1.0/en/ECN/2012_US/00A1/E600000US4200361000.
15. Tom McCarthy, "'Outmoded, Irrelevant Vision': Pittsburghers Reject Trump's Pledge," *Guardian*, June 2, 2017, www.theguardian.com/us-news/2017/jun/02 /pittsburgh-trump-paris-climate-deal?CMP=share_btn_tw.
16. Anne Hidalgo and William Peduto, "The Mayors of Pittsburgh and Paris: We Have Our Own Climate Deal," *New York Times*, June 7, 2017, www.nytimes .com/2017/06/07/opinion/the-mayors-of-pittsburgh-and-paris-we-have-our -own-climate-deal.html.
17. "Byron York Interviews Donald Trump," *Washington Examiner*, January 13, 2016, www.washingtonexaminer.com/exclusive-byron-york-interviews-donald-trump.
18. George Borjas, "Immigration and the American Worker," Center for Immigration Studies, April 9, 2013, https://cis.org/Report/Immigration-and-American -Worker.
19. Paul Krugman, "What Should Trade Negotiators Negotiate About? A Review Essay," *Journal of Economic Literature* 35, no. 1 (1997): 113–20, http://web.mit .edu/krugman/www/negot.html.
20. Gary Clyde Hufbauer and Zhiyao (Lucy) Lu, "The Payoff to America from Globalization: A Fresh Look with a Focus on Costs to Workers," Peterson Institute for International Economics, Policy Brief, May 2017, https://piie.com/system /files/documents/pb17-16.pdf.

21. U.S. Census Bureau, "2011–2015 American Community Survey 5-Year Estimates: Selected Economic Characteristics," https://factfinder.census.gov/bkmk/table /1.0/en/ACS/15_5YR/DP04/0100000US.

22. Trading Economics, "United States Consumer Sentiment 1952–2018," www .tradingeconomics.com/united-states/consumer-confidence.

Chapter 3: "They've Chosen Not to Keep Up"

1. Aaron Blake, "Hillary Clinton Takes Her 'Deplorables' Argument for Another Spin," *Washington Post*, March 13, 2018, www.washingtonpost.com/news/the-fix /wp/2018/03/12/hillary-clinton-takes-her-deplorables-argument-for-another -spin/.

2. Sean Illing, "A Princeton Sociologist Spent 8 Years Asking Rural Americans Why They're So Pissed Off," Vox, March 13, 2018, updated June 30, 2018, www.vox.com/2018/3/13/17053886/trump-rural-america-populism-racial -resentment.

3. Sean McElwee and Jason McDaniel, "Economic Anxiety Didn't Make People Vote Trump, Racism Did," *Nation*, May 8, 2017, www.thenation.com/article /economic-anxiety-didnt-make-people-vote-trump-racism-did/.

4. German Lopez, "Survey: The Poor White Working Class Was, If Anything, More Likely Than the Rich to Vote for Clinton," Vox, May 9, 2017, www.vox .com/policy-and-politics/2017/5/9/15592634/trump-clinton-racism-economy -prri-survey.

5. Chauncey DeVega, "It Was the Racism, Stupid: White Working-Class 'Economic Anxiety' Is a Zombie Idea That Needs to Die," *Salon*, January 5, 2017, www .salon.com/2017/01/05/it-was-the-racism-stupid-white-working-class-economic -anxiety-is-a-zombie-idea-that-needs-to-die/.

6. Josh Barro, Twitter, July 22, 2016, https://twitter.com/search?f=tweets&q =thinner%20from%3Ajbarro&src=typd.

7. U.S. Department of Labor, Bureau of Labor Statistics, TED: The Economics Daily, "Women's Earnings, 1979–2012," November 4, 2013, www.bls.gov/opub /ted/2013/ted_20131104.htm.

8. National Center for Education Statistics, Postbaccalaureate Enrollment, last updated May 2018, nces.ed.gov/programs/coe/indicator_chb.asp.

9. Juliana Menasce Horowitz, Kim Parker, and Renee Stepler, "Wide Partisan Gaps in U.S. over How Far the Country Has Come on Gender Equality," Pew Research Center, October 18, 2017, www.pewsocialtrends.org/2017/10/18 /wide-partisan-gaps-in-u-s-over-how-far-the-country-has-come-on-gender -equality/#roughly-a-third-of-adults-say-men-have-it-easier-in-our-country -these-days-9-say-women-do.

10. Yuval Levin lays out this argument at length in his book *The Fractured Republic* (New York: Basic Books, 2016).

11. Illing, "A Princeton Sociologist Spent 8 Years Asking Rural Americans Why They're So Pissed Off."

12. Michelle Goldberg, "Tyranny of the Minority," *New York Times*, September 25, 2017, www.nytimes.com/2017/09/25/opinion/trump-electoral-college-minority .html.

13. "Men Adrift," *Economist*, www.economist.com/news/essays/21649050-badly -educated-men-rich-countries-have-not-adapted-well-trade-technology -or-feminism?fsrc=scn/tw/te/bl/ed/manhood.

14. Donald Trump, speech in Monessen, Pennsylvania, June 28, 2016, transcript at www.politico.com/story/2016/06/full-transcript-trump-job-plan-speech -224891.

15. Martin Neil Baily and Barry P. Bosworth, "US Manufacturing: Understanding Its Past and Its Potential Future," *Journal of Economic Perspectives* 28, no. 1 (2014): 3–26, www.brookings.edu/wp-content/uploads/2016/06/us-manufacturing -past-and-potential-future-baily-bosworth.pdf.

16. National Association of Manufacturers, "Top 20 Facts about Manufacturing," www.nam.org/Newsroom/Top-20-Facts-About-Manufacturing/.

17. Federal Reserve Bank of St. Louis, "Percent of Employment in Manufacturing in the United States," https://fred.stlouisfed.org/series/USAPEFANA.

18. Michael J. Hicks and Srikant Devaraj, "The Myth and the Reality of Manufacturing in America," Ball State University Center for Business and Economic Research, June 2015 and April 2017, http://conexus.cberdata.org/files/Mfg Reality.pdf.

19. Federica Cocco, "Most US Manufacturing Jobs Lost to Technology, Not Trade," *Financial Times*, December 2, 2016, www.ft.com/content/dec677c0-b7e6-11e6 -ba85-95d1533d9a62?mhq5j=e2.

20. Hal Sirkin, Michael Zinser, and Justin Rose, "How Robots Will Redefine Competitiveness," Boston Consulting Group, September 23, 2015, www.bcg .com/publications/2015/lean-manufacturing-innovation-robots-redefine -competitiveness.aspx.

21. Tyler Cowen, *Average Is Over* (New York: Penguin Group, 2013), 57.

22. Ibid., 164.

23. Charles Murray, *Coming Apart* (New York: Crown Forum, 2012), 68.

24. Ibid., 124.

25. Ibid., 116.

26. Virginia Postrel, "Can You Pass the 'Beverly Hillbillies' Test?" *Bloomberg*, Opinion, View, February 9, 2012, www.bloomberg.com/view/articles/2012-02-10/can -you-pass-a-beverly-hillbillies-test-commentary-by-virginia-postrel.

27. "Men Adrift," *Economist*.

28. Elizabeth Warren, "Law, Politics, and the Coming Collapse of the Middle Class," interview with Harry Kriesler, Institute of International Studies at UC Berkeley, March 8, 2007, http://globetrotter.berkeley.edu/people7/Warren/warren-con3 .html.

29. Daron Acemoglu, David H. Autor, and David Lyle, "Women, War, and Wages: The Effect of Female Labor Supply on the Wage Structure at Midcentury," *Journal of Political Economy* 112, no. 3 (June 2004): 497–551, www.journals .uchicago.edu/doi/abs/10.1086/383100.

30. U.S. Department of Labor, Bureau of Labor Statistics, "Local Area Unemployment Statistics, Labor Force Data by County, 2016, Annual Averages," www.bls.gov /lau/laucnty16.xlsx.

31. Timothy P. Carney, "In Rural Pa., Jobs Flee, Communities Crumble, and Trump's Message Rings Loudly," *Washington Examiner*, October 18, 2016, www.washingtonexaminer.com/in-rural-pa-jobs-flee-communities-crumble -and-trumps-message-rings-loudly.

32. Pennsylvania Department of State, "2008 General Election Returns, Fayette County," available via www.electionreturns.pa.gov/.

33. Ibid.

34. Jessica Contrera, "Closing of Western Pennsylvania Power Plants Leaves Workers at a Loss," *Pittsburgh Post-Gazette*, July 21, 2013.

35. David H. Autor, David Dorn, and Gordon H. Hanson, "The China Syndrome: Local Labor Market Effects of Import Competition in the United States," *American Economic Review* 103, no. 6 (2013): 2121–68, www.aeaweb.org/articles ?id=10.1257/aer.103.6.2121.

36. *Analysis of Overdose Deaths in Pennsylvania, 2016*, DEA Philadelphia Division and the University of Pittsburgh, July 2017, www.dea.gov/docs/DEA-PHL-DIR -034-17%20Analysis%20of%20Overdose%20Deaths%20in%20Pennsylvania %202016.pdf.

Chapter 4: American Decay

1. U.S. Census Bureau, American FactFinder, "Census 2010 Total Population, Fayette City, PA Population," https://factfinder.census.gov/bkmk/cf/1.0/en/place/Fayette City borough, Pennsylvania/POPULATION/DECENNIAL_CNT.
2. Greg Reinbold, "End of Steel Era in Monessen Recalled," *Mon Valley Independent*, June 28, 2016, http://monvalleyindependent.com/2016/06/end-steel-era -monessen-recalled/.
3. Ibid.
4. Chris Arnold, "China Killed 1 Million U.S. Jobs, but Don't Blame Trade Deals," NPR, *All Things Considered*, April 18, 2016, www.npr.org/2016/04/18/474393701 /china-killed-1-million-u-s-jobs-but-don-t-blame-trade-deals.
5. David H. Autor, David Dorn, and Gordon H. Hanson, "The China Syndrome: Local Labor Market Effects of Import Competition in the United States," *American Economic Review* 103, no. 6 (2013): 2121–68, www.aeaweb.org/arti cles?id=10.1257/aer.103.6.2121.
6. Jeff Madrick and Nikolaos Papanikolaou, "The Stagnation of Male Wages," Schwartz Center for Economic Policy Analysis, The New School, May 2008, www.economicpolicyresearch.org/images/docs/research/employment /Madrick_Nicolas.pdf.
7. Phillip Longman, "Wealth and Generations," *Washington Monthly*, June– August 2015, https://washingtonmonthly.com/magazine/junejulyaug-2015/wealth -and-generations/. Cited in Arlie Russell Hochschild, *Strangers in Their Own Land* (New York: The New Press, 2016), 141.
8. Lenny Bernstein, "U.S. Life Expectancy Declines for the First Time since 1993," *Washington Post*, December 8, 2016, www.washingtonpost.com/national /health-science/us-life-expectancy-declines-for-the-first-time-since -1993/2016/12/07/7dcdc7b4-bc93-11e6-91ee-1adddfe36cbe_story.html?utm _term=.d74778199e5d.
9. Anne Case and Angus Deaton, "Rising Morbidity and Mortality in Midlife among White Non-Hispanic Americans in the 21st Century," *Proceedings of the National Academy of Sciences* 112, no. 49 (2015): 15078–83, www.pnas.org /content/112/49/15078.full.
10. Ibid.
11. Shannon M. Monnat, "Drugs, Alcohol, and Suicide Represent Growing Share of U.S. Mortality," Carsey School of Public Policy, University of New Hampshire, January 31, 2017, https://carsey.unh.edu/publication/drugs -alcohol-suicide.
12. Alison Burke, "Working Class White Americans Are Now Dying in Middle Age at Faster Rates Than Minority Groups," *Brookings Now*, March 23, 2017, www .brookings.edu/blog/brookings-now/2017/03/23/working-class-white-americans -are-now-dying-in-middle-age-at-faster-rates-than-minority-groups/.
13. U.S. Department of Justice, Drug Enforcement Administration, *2015 National Drug Threat Assessment Summary*, www.dea.gov/docs/2015%20NDTA%20 Report.pdf.
14. U.S. Social Security Administration, "Selected Data from Social Security's Disability Program," www.ssa.gov/oact/STATS/dibStat.html.
15. U.S. Department of Labor, Bureau of Labor Statistics, "Labor Force Statistics

from the Current Population Survey," July 29, 2018, https://data.bls.gov
/timeseries/LNS14000000.

16. Nicholas Eberstadt, *Men without Work: America's Invisible Crisis* (West
Conshohocken, PA: Templeton Press, 2016), 40.

17. Ibid., 62.

18. Ibid.

19. George Borjas, *Labor Economics*, 7th ed. (New York: McGraw-Hill Education,
2016), 25, www.hks.harvard.edu/fs/gborjas/publications/books/LE/LEChapter
2.pdf.

20. Alan Krueger, "Where Have All the Workers Gone? An Inquiry into the
Decline of the U.S. Labor Force Participation Rate," *Brookings Papers on
Economic Activity* (August 26, 2017), www.brookings.edu/wp-content/uploads
/2017/09/1_krueger.pdf.

21. Ibid.

22. Nicholas Eberstadt, "Where Did All the Men Go?" *Milken Institute Review*,
April 28, 2017, www.milkenreview.org/articles/where-did-all-the-men-go.

23. Nate Silver, "The Mythology of Trump's 'Working Class' Support," *FiveThirtyEight*,
May 3, 2016, https://fivethirtyeight.com/features/the-mythology-of-trumps
-working-class-support/.

24. Mark Muro and Sifan Liu, "Another Clinton-Trump Divide: High-Output America vs Low-Output America," *Brookings*, November 29, 2016, www.brookings
.edu/blog/the-avenue/2016/11/29/another-clinton-trump-divide-high-output
-america-vs-low-output-america/.

25. Ben Casselman, "Stop Saying Trump's Win Had Nothing to Do with Economics,"
FiveThirtyEight, January 9, 2017, https://fivethirtyeight.com/features/stop
-saying-trumps-win-had-nothing-to-do-with-economics/.

26. Jeff Guo, "Death Predicts Whether People Vote for Donald Trump," *Washington
Post*, March 4, 2016, www.washingtonpost.com/news/wonk/wp/2016/03/04
/death-predicts-whether-people-vote-for-donald-trump/?utm_term
=.6356723a1e14.

27. "Illness as Indicator," *Economist*, November 19, 2016, www.economist.com
/news/united-states/21710265-local-health-outcomes-predict-trumpward
-swings-illness-indicator?fsrc=scn%2Ftw_ec%2Fillness_as_indicator.

28. Douglas S. Massey, Jonathan Rothwell, and Thurston Domina, "The Changing
Bases of Segregation in the United States," *Annals of the American Academy of
Political and Social Science* 626, no. 1 (2009): 74–90, www.ncbi.nlm.nih.gov/pmc
/articles/PMC3844132/.

29. U.S. Department of Agriculture, Economic Research Service, "Rural Employment
and Unemployment," www.ers.usda.gov/topics/rural-economy-population
/employment-education/rural-employment-and-unemployment/#emp.

30. Economic Innovation Group, "The New Map of Economic Growth and Recovery,"
May 2016, http://eig.org/wp-content/uploads/2016/05/recoverygrowthreport.pdf.

31. Mike Allen, "1 Big Thing: America's Great Divide," *Axios*, www.axios.com
/axios-am-2489291938.html.

32. Quoted in Annie Lowrey, "2016: A Year Defined by America's Diverging
Economies," *Atlantic*, December 30, 2016, www.theatlantic.com/business
/archive/2016/12/2016-diverging-economies/511838/.

33. Quoted ibid.

34. Raj Chetty, Nathaniel Hendren, Patrick Kline, and Emmanuel Saez, "Where Is the
Land of Opportunity? The Geography of Intergenerational Mobility in the United
States" (working paper 19843, National Bureau of Economic Research, Cambridge,
Massachusetts, 2014), www.rajchetty.com/chettyfiles/mobility_geo.pdf.

35. Laura Dwyer-Lindgren et al., "Inequalities in Life Expectancy among US Counties, 1980 to 2014: Temporal Trends and Key Drivers," *JAMA Internal Medicine* 177, no. 7 (2017): 1003–11, https://doi.org/10.1001/jamainternmed.2017.0918.

36. Jeff Guo, "The Places That Support Trump and Cruz Are Suffering. But That's Not True of Rubio," *Washington Post*, February 8, 2016, www.washingtonpost .com/news/wonk/wp/2016/02/08/the-places-that-support-trump-and-cruz -are-suffering-but-thats-not-true-of-rubio/?utm_term=.1e23af9ee128.

37. Guo, "Death Predicts Whether People Vote for Donald Trump."

38. Shannon M. Monnat, "Deaths of Despair and Support for Trump in the 2016 Presidential Election," Pennsylvania State University, Department of Agricultural Economics, Sociology, and Education, Research Brief, December 4, 2016, http://aese.psu.edu/directory/smm67/Election16.pdf.

Chapter 5: "I Don't"

1. Jonathan Vespa, Jamie M. Lewis, and Rose M. Kreider, "America's Families and Living Arrangements: 2012," U.S. Census Bureau, August 2013, www.census .gov/prod/2013pubs/p20-570.pdf.

2. Kim Parker and Renee Stepler, "As U.S. Marriage Rate Hovers at 50%, Education Gap in Marital Status Widens," Pew Research Center, September 14, 2017, www.pewresearch.org/fact-tank/2017/09/14/as-u-s-marriage-rate-hovers -at-50-education-gap-in-marital-status-widens/.

3. Richard Fry, Ruth Igielnik, and Eileen Patten, "How Millennials Today Compare with Their Grandparents 50 Years Ago," Pew Research Center, March 16, 2018, www.pewresearch.org/fact-tank/2018/03/16/how-millennials-compare -with-their-grandparents/.

4. Joyce A. Martin, Brady E. Hamilton, Michelle J. K. Osterman, et al., "Births: Final Data for 2016," U.S. Department of Health and Human Services, Centers for Disease Control and Prevention, Division of Vital Statistics, *National Vital Statistics Reports* 67, no. 1 (2018): 1–55, www.cdc.gov/nchs/data/nvsr/nvsr67/nvsr67_01 .pdf.

5. U.S. Census Bureau, "Percent Childless and Births per 1,000 Women in the Last 12 Months: CPS, Selected Years, 1976–2016," www.census.gov/data/tables /time-series/demo/fertility/his-cps.html#par_list.

6. Sezin Koehler, "8 Reasons Why I'm Not Having Children," *Huffington Post*, November 15, 2014, www.huffingtonpost.com/sezin-koehler/8-reasons-why -im-not-having-children-childfree_b_5705311.html.

7. Matthew Yglesias, "The 'Decline' of Marriage Isn't a Problem," Vox, March 25, 2015, www.vox.com/2015/3/25/8285169/marriage-decline-causes.

8. YouGov, survey conducted August 2017, question 66, http://csed.byu.edu/wp -content/uploads/2017/11/BYUC0014_Toplines.pdf.

9. Arlie Russell Hochschild, *Strangers in Their Own Land* (New York: The New Press, 2016), 202.

10. Mark Regnerus, "Cheap Sex and the Decline of Marriage," *Wall Street Journal*, September 29, 2017, www.wsj.com/amp/articles/cheap-sex-and-the-decline-of -marriage-1506690454.

11. Kay Hymowitz, "Marriage and Caste," *City Journal*, Winter 2006, www.city -journal.org/html/marriage-and-caste-12908.html.

12. Richard V. Reeves, Isabel V. Sawhill, and Eleanor Krause, "The Most Educated Women Are the Most Likely to Be Married," Brookings Institution, August 19, 2016, www.brookings.edu/blog/social-mobility-memos/2016/08/19/the -most-educated-women-are-the-most-likely-to-be-married/?utm_medium=social &utm_source=twitter&utm_campaign=es.

13. Andrew J. Cherlin and W. Bradford Wilcox, "The Marginalization of Marriage in Middle America," Brookings Institution, August 10, 2011, www.brookings .edu/research/the-marginalization-of-marriage-in-middle-america/.

14. Parker and Stepler, "As U.S. Marriage Rate Hovers at 50%, Education Gap in Marital Status Widens."

15. Megan McArdle, "The Many Cases for Getting Married Young," *Newsweek*, May 30, 2013, www.newsweek.com/2013/05/29/many-cases-getting-married -young-237436.html.

16. Isabel V. Sawhill and Ron Haskins, "Work and Marriage: The Way to End Poverty and Welfare," Brookings Institution, September 1, 2003, www.brookings.edu /research/work-and-marriage-the-way-to-end-poverty-and-welfare/.

17. Yglesias, "The 'Decline' of Marriage Isn't a Problem."

18. Melissa S. Kearney and Phillip B. Levine, "The Economics of Nonmarital Childbearing and the Marriage Premium for Children," *Annual Review of Economics* 9, no. 1 (2017): 340, www.annualreviews.org/doi/pdf/10.1146 /annurev-economics-063016-103749.

19. Robert I. Lerman, Joseph Price, and W. Bradford Wilcox, "Family Structure and Economic Success across the Life Course," *Marriage and Family Review* 53, no. 8 (2017): 744–58, www.tandfonline.com/doi/abs/10.1080/01494929.201 7.1316810.

20. Charles Murray, *Coming Apart* (New York: Crown Forum, 2012), 158.

21. Raj Chetty, Nathaniel Hendren, Patrick Kline, and Emmanuel Saez, "Where Is the Land of Opportunity? The Geography of Intergenerational Mobility in the United States" (working paper 19843, National Bureau of Economic Research, Cambridge, Massachusetts, 2014), Online Appendix Table VIII, www.equality -of-opportunity.org/assets/documents/mobility_geo.pdf.

22. Kate Antonovics and Robert Town, "Are All the Good Men Married? Uncovering the Sources of the Marital Wage Premium," *American Economic Review* 94, no. 2 (2004): 317–21, www.jstor.org/stable/3592902.

23. David Autor, David Dorn, and Gordon Hanson, "When Work Disappears: Manufacturing Decline and the Falling Marriage-Market Value of Young Men" (working paper 23173, National Bureau of Economic Research, Cambridge, Massachusetts, 2017), 2, https://gps.ucsd.edu/_files/faculty/hanson /hanson_research_WhenWorkDisappears.pdf.

24. Ibid., 6.

25. Melissa S. Kearney and Riley Wilson, "Male Earnings, Marriageable Men, and Nonmarital Fertility: Evidence from the Fracking Boom" (working paper 23408, National Bureau of Economic Research, Cambridge, Massachusetts, 2017), www.nber.org/papers/w23408.pdf.

26. Danielle Paquette, "Women Just Aren't That into the 'Marriageable Male' Anymore, Economists Say," *Washington Post*, *Wonkblog*, May 16, 2017, www.washingtonpost.com/news/wonk/wp/2017/05/16/women-just-arent -that-into-the-marriageable-male-anymore-economists-say/?utm_term =.701458aeedf0.

27. Chetty, Hendren, Kline, and Saez, "Where Is the Land of Opportunity? The Geography of Intergenerational Mobility in the United States," 1, 42.

28. Melissa Kearney, comment at "Improving Economic Opportunity in America: A Discussion with Raj Chetty," American Enterprise Institute, March 17, 2017, Washington, DC, www.aei.org/wp-content/uploads/2017/02/170317-AEI -Improving-Economic-Opportunity.pdf.

29. Chetty, Hendren, Kline, and Saez, "Where Is the Land of Opportunity? The Geography of Intergenerational Mobility in the United States," 3.

30. Ibid., 39–40.
31. Susan Elizabeth Shepard, "Wildcatting: A Stripper's Guide to the Modern American Boomtown," *BuzzFeed*, July 25, 2013, www.buzzfeed.com/susan elizabethshepard/wildcatting-a-strippers-guide-to-the-modern-american -boomtow?utm_term=.tqNqKrXpm#.pvxKB3R8d.
32. "When Marriage Disappears: The New Middle America," National Marriage Project, December 2010, http://nationalmarriageproject.org/wp-content/uploads /2012/06/Union_11_12_10.pdf.

Chapter 6: Bowling Alone

1. Alexis de Tocqueville, *Democracy in America*, trans. and ed. Harvey C. Mansfield and Delba Winthrop (Chicago: University of Chicago Press, 2000), 489–95.
2. Robert Frost, *The Poems of Robert Frost* (New York: Random House, 1946), 377.
3. Yuval Levin, *The Fractured Republic* (New York: Basic Books, 2016), 4.
4. L. J. Hanifan, "The Rural School Community Center," *Annals of the American Academy of Political and Social Science* 67, no. 1 (1916): 130, www.jstor.org /stable/1013498, cited in Robert D. Putnam, *Bowling Alone* (New York: Simon & Schuster, 2001), 19. Special thanks to AEI research assistant Nick Saffran for finding the original, which has ended up a bit misquoted in other works.
5. Putnam, *Bowling Alone*, 60.
6. Ibid., 55.
7. Vice Chairman's Staff of the Joint Economic Committee, *What We Do Together: The State of Associational Life in America*, May 2017, www.lee.senate.gov /public/_cache/files/b5f224ce-98f7-40f6-a814-8602696714d8/what-we-do -together.pdf.
8. Ivaylo D. Petev, "The Association of Social Class and Lifestyles: Persistence in American Sociability, 1974 to 2010," *American Sociological Review* 78, no. 4 (2013): 633–61, www.jstor.org/stable/23469230.
9. American Psychological Association, "So Lonely I Could Die," August 5, 2017, www.apa.org/news/press/releases/2017/08/lonely-die.aspx.
10. Charles Murray, *Coming Apart* (New York: Crown Forum, 2012), 267.
11. Anne Case and Angus Deaton, "Mortality and Morbidity in the 21st Century," *Brookings Papers on Economic Activity* (March 2017): 2, www.brookings.edu /wp-content/uploads/2017/03/6_casedeaton.pdf.
12. Centers for Disease Control and Prevention, "Age-Adjusted Suicide Rates, by State—United States, 2012," November 14, 2014, www.cdc.gov/mmwr/preview /mmwrhtml/mm6345a10.htm.
13. Murray, *Coming Apart*, 266–67.
14. Ibid.
15. Case and Deaton, "Mortality and Morbidity in the 21st Century," 34.
16. James S. House, Karl R. Landis, and Debra Umberson, "Social Relationships and Health," *Science* 241, no. 4865 (1988): 540–45, http://science.sciencemag .org/content/241/4865/540.long.
17. Julianne Holt-Lunstad, Timothy B. Smith, and J. Bradley Layton, "Social Relationships and Mortality Risk: A Meta-Analytic Review," *PLOS Med* 7, no.7 (2010): e1000316, https://doi.org/10.1371/journal.pmed.1000316.
18. Billy Baker, "The Biggest Threat Facing Middle-Age Men Isn't Smoking or Obesity. It's Loneliness," *Boston Globe*, March 9, 2017, www.bostonglobe.com /magazine/2017/03/09/the-biggest-threat-facing-middle-age-men-isn-smoking -obesity-loneliness/k6saC9FnnHQCUbf5mJ8okL/story.html.
19. Aaron Kheriaty, "Dying of Despair," *First Things*, August 2017, www.firstthings .com/article/2017/08/dying-of-despair.

20. "Toward a Conservatism of Connection: Reclaiming the American Project," June 27, 2018, Pepperdine University, Malibu, California.

21. Murray, *Coming Apart*, 262.

22. Ibid., 248.

23. Robert Putnam, *Our Kids* (New York: Simon & Schuster, 2015), 207.

24. Ibid.

25. J. D. Vance, *Hillbilly Elegy* (New York: HarperCollins, 2016), 214.

26. Ibid., 215.

27. Sandra Navidi, "Why 'Hillbillies' Don't Do Networking," *Daily Beast*, March 28, 2017, www.thedailybeast.com/why-hillbillies-dont-do-networking.

28. Ibid.

29. Robert J. Sampson, *Great American City: Chicago and the Enduring Neighborhood Effect* (Chicago: University of Chicago Press, 2012), 356, cited in Putnam, *Our Kids*, 217.

30. Raj Chetty, Nathaniel Hendren, Maggie Jones, and Sonya R. Porter, "Race and Economic Opportunity in the United States: Executive Summary," March 2018, www.equality-of-opportunity.org/assets/documents/race_summary.pdf.

31. Brink Lindsey, "The End of the Working Class," *American Interest* 13, no. 3 (August 2017), www.the-american-interest.com/2017/08/30/end-working-class/.

32. Salena Zito, "The Day That Destroyed the Working Class and Sowed the Seeds of Trump," *New York Post*, September 16, 2017, https://nypost.com/2017/09/16/the-day-that-destroyed-the-working-class-and-sowed-the-seeds-for-trump/.

33. Nicholas Eberstadt, "Our Miserable 21st Century," *Commentary*, February 15, 2017, www.commentarymagazine.com/articles/our-miserable-21st-century/.

34. Lindsey, "The End of the Working Class."

35. Navidi, "Why 'Hillbillies' Don't Do Networking."

36. Emma Green, "The Death of Community and the Rise of Trump," *Atlantic*, March 5, 2017, www.theatlantic.com/politics/archive/2017/03/religiously-unaffiliated-white-americans/518340/.

37. Patrick Sharkey, Gerard Torrats-Espinosa, and Delaram Takyar, "Community and the Crime Decline: The Causal Effect of Local Nonprofits on Violent Crime," *American Sociological Review* 82, no. 6 (2017): 1217, http://journals.sagepub.com/doi/abs/10.1177/0003122417736289#articleCitationDownloadContainer.

38. Michael Kruse, "Johnstown Never Believed Trump Would Help. They Still Love Him Anyway," *Politico*, November 8, 2017, www.politico.com/magazine/story/2017/11/08/donald-trump-johnstown-pennsylvania-supporters-215800.

39. Margaret Talbot, "The Addicts Next Door," *New Yorker*, June 5, 2017, www.newyorker.com/magazine/2017/06/05/the-addicts-next-door.

40. Homer, *Odyssey* 9.110–115.

41. Michael Barone, "Does Lack of Social Connectedness Explain Trump's Appeal?" *Washington Examiner*, March 27, 2016, www.washingtonexaminer.com/does-lack-of-social-connectedness-explain-trumps-appeal/article/2586842.

42. Green, "The Death of Community and the Rise of Trump."

43. Yoni Appelbaum, "Why Donald Trump Supporters Are Voting Alone," *Atlantic*, April 7, 2016, www.theatlantic.com/politics/archive/2016/04/voting-alone/477270/.

44. Daniel Cox and Robert P. Jones, "Two-Thirds of Trump Supporters Say Nation Needs a Leader Willing to Break the Rules," Public Religion Research Institute, April 7, 2016, www.prri.org/research/prri-atlantic-poll-republican-democratic-primary-trump-supporters/.

45. Edmund Burke, *Select Works of Edmund Burke* (Indianapolis: Liberty Fund, 1999), vol. 2, http://oll.libertyfund.org/titles/656.

46. Emily Ekins, "The Five Types of Trump Voters," Voter Study Group, June 2017, www.voterstudygroup.org/publications/2016-elections/the-five-types -trump-voters.

47. "County-Level Measures of Social Capital," Penn State College of Agricultural Sciences, http://aese.psu.edu/nercrd/community/social-capital-resources.

48. Association of Religion Data Archives, Evangelical Lutheran Church in America (Minnesota), Adherence Rate (2010), www.thearda.com/mapsReports/maps /2010/MN_D207_10R.asp.

49. Tess Gruber Nelson, "Memorial Baptist Church Closes Its Doors in Shen," *Valley News* (Shenandoah, Iowa), October 13, 2013, www.valleynewstoday.com /news/local/memorial-baptist-church-closes-its-doors-in-shen/article _4e019e6a-328b-11e3-9cf5-0019bb2963f4.html.

50. Tess Gruber Nelson, "130-Year-Old Church to Close in June," *Valley News* (Shenandoah, Iowa), November 8, 2014, www.valleynewstoday.com/news/local /year-old-church-to-close-in-june/article_5fc21e2e-66a4-11e4-94c8-072e9c3d dad9.html.

51. Kristan Gray, "Norwich United Methodist Church to Close," *Valley News* (Shenandoah, Iowa), June 22, 2016, www.valleynewstoday.com/news/local /norwich-united-methodist-church-to-close/article_87030fde-3885-11e6 -8192-ab6441ab9191.html.

52. Ted Mellnik, Dan Keating, Kevin Schaul, Denise Lu, and Samuel Granados, "These Maps Explain How Rural Voters Gave Ted Cruz the Win in Iowa," *Washington Post*, February 2, 2016, www.washingtonpost.com/graphics/politics /2016-election/primaries/iowa-results-precincts/.

53. Tess Nelson, "Despite Uncertainty, Officials Hopeful Shen Will Survive," *Valley News* (Shenandoah, Iowa), February 6, 2016, www.valleynewstoday.com /news/local/despite-uncertainty-officials-hopeful-shen-will-survive/article _1477991a-cc62-11e5-b66c-97853742dff1.html.

54. Aristotle, *Politics*, 1253a1-2.

55. Kheriaty, "Dying of Despair."

56. Vice Chairman's Staff of the Joint Economic Committee, *What We Do Together: The State of Associational Life in America.*

57. Tocqueville, *Democracy in America* II:5, 491–92.

58. Shanker Satyanath, Nico Voigtländer, and Hans-Joachim Voth, "Bowling for Fascism: Social Capital and the Rise of the Nazi Party," *Journal of Political Economy* 125, no. 2 (2017): 478–526, www.journals.uchicago.edu/doi/abs /10.1086/690949.

Chapter 7: It's about Church

1. Gregory A. Smith and Jessica Martínez, "How the Faithful Voted: A Preliminary 2016 Analysis," Pew Research Center, November 9, 2016, www.pewresearch .org/fact-tank/2016/11/09/how-the-faithful-voted-a-preliminary-2016 -analysis/.

2. Mayhill Fowler, "Obama: No Surprise That Hard-Pressed Pennsylvanians Turn Bitter," *Huffington Post*, November 17, 2008, www.huffingtonpost.com /mayhill-fowler/obama-no-surprise-that-ha_b_96188.html.

3. CNN, Exit Polls, House of Representatives, November 23, 2016, www.cnn.com /election/results/exit-polls/national/house.

4. Smith and Martínez, "How the Faithful Voted: A Preliminary 2016 Analysis."

5. Emily Ekins, "The Five Types of Trump Voters," Voter Study Group, June 2017, www.voterstudygroup.org/publications/2016-elections/the-five-types -trump-voters.

6. Geoffrey Layman, "Where Is Trump's Evangelical Base? Not in Church," *Washington Post*, March 29, 2016, www.washingtonpost.com/news/monkey-cage/wp/2016/03/29/where-is-trumps-evangelical-base-not-in-church/?utm_term=.f11fff8df9bc.

7. Peter Beinart, "Breaking Faith," *Atlantic*, April 2017, www.theatlantic.com/magazine/archive/2017/04/breaking-faith/517785/.

8. Bob Davis and Rebecca Ballhaus, "The Place That Wants Donald Trump Most," *Wall Street Journal*, April 17, 2016, www.wsj.com/articles/the-place-that-loves-donald-trump-most-1460917663.

9. Pew Research Center, "U.S. Public Becoming Less Religious," November 3, 2015, www.pewforum.org/2015/11/03/u-s-public-becoming-less-religious/.

10. Robert D. Putnam and David. E. Campbell, *American Grace: How Religion Divides and Unites Us* (New York: Simon & Schuster, 2010), 79.

11. Raphaël Franck and Laurence Iannaccone, "Why Did Religiosity Decrease in the Western World during the Twentieth Century?" (2018), http://citeseerx.ist.psu.edu/viewdoc/download?doi=10.1.1.544.2005&rep=rep1&type=pdf.

12. Mary Eberstadt, *How the West Really Lost God* (West Conshohocken, PA: Templeton Press, 2013), 38.

13. W. Bradford Wilcox, "The Latest Social Science Is Wrong. Religion Is Good for Families and Kids," *Washington Post*, December 15, 2015, www.washingtonpost.com/posteverything/wp/2015/12/15/the-latest-social-science-is-wrong-religion-is-good-for-families-and-kids/.

14. W. Bradford Wilcox, "Religion Is Good for Families and Kids," Institution for Family Studies, December 15, 2015. https://ifstudies.org/blog/religion-is-good-for-families-and-kids.

15. Robert Putnam, *Our Kids* (New York: Simon & Schuster, 2015), 224.

16. Frank Newport, Dan Witters, and Sangeeta Agrawal, "Religious Americans Enjoy Higher Wellbeing," *Gallup News*, February 16, 2012, http://news.gallup.com/poll/152723/religious-americans-enjoy-higher-wellbeing.aspx.

17. Beinart, "Breaking Faith," citing data from the Public Religion Research Institute.

18. Ellen Idler, John Blevins, Mimi Kiser, and Carol Hogue, "Religion, a Social Determinant of Mortality? A 10-Year Follow-Up of the Health and Retirement Study," *PLOS ONE* 12, no. 12 (2017): e0189134, http://journals.plos.org/plosone/article?id=10.1371/journal.pone.0189134.

19. Aaron Kheriaty, "Dying of Despair," *First Things*, August 2017, www.firstthings.com/article/2017/08/dying-of-despair.

20. Pew Research Center, "U.S. Muslims Concerned about Their Place in Society, but Continue to Believe in the American Dream," July 26, 2017, www.pewforum.org/2017/07/26/findings-from-pew-research-centers-2017-survey-of-us-muslims/.

21. Filipe Campante and David Yanagizawa-Drott, "Does Religion Affect Economic Growth and Happiness? Evidence from Ramadan," *Quarterly Journal of Economics* 130, no. 2 (2015), academic.oup.com/qje/article/130/2/615/2330341.

22. Pew Research Center, "'Nones' on the Rise: One-in-Five Adults Have No Religious Affiliation," October 9, 2012, www.pewforum.org/2012/10/09/nones-on-the-rise-demographics/.

23. Emma Green, "The Non-Religious States of America," *Atlantic*, September 6, 2017, www.theatlantic.com/politics/archive/2017/09/no-religion-states-prri/538821/.

24. Beinart, "Breaking Faith."

25. Philip Schwadel, John D. McCarthy, and Hart M. Nelsen, "The Continuing Relevance of Family Income for Religious Participation: U.S. White Catholic

Church Attendance in the Late 20th Century," *Social Forces* 87, no. 4 (2009): 1997–2030, www.jstor.org/stable/40345006.

26. Putnam, *Our Kids*, 225.

27. W. Bradford Wilcox, Andrew J. Cherlin, Jeremy E. Uecker, and Matthew Messel, "No Money, No Honey, No Church. The Deinstitutionalization of Religious Life among the White Working Class," *Research in the Sociology of Work* 23 (2012): 227–50, www.ncbi.nlm.nih.gov/pmc/articles/PMC4 315336/.

28. Ibid.

29. J. D. Vance, *Hillbilly Elegy* (New York: HarperCollins, 2016).

30. Idler, Blevins, Kiser, and Hogue, "Religion, a Social Determinant of Mortality?"

31. Schwadel, McCarthy, and Nelsen, "The Continuing Relevance of Family Income for Religious Participation."

32. Robert Putnam, *Bowling Alone* (New York: Simon & Schuster, 2001), 66.

33. Matthew 16:18–19.

34. Alexis de Tocqueville, *Democracy in America*, trans. and ed. Harvey C. Mansfield and Delba Winthrop (Chicago: University of Chicago Press, 2000), 280–81.

35. Russell Kirk, *Redeeming the Time*, ed. Jeffrey O. Nelson (Wilmington, DE: ISI Books, 1996), 3–15.

36. Putnam and Campbell, *American Grace*, 444.

37. Ibid., 445.

38. Ibid., 446.

39. Ibid., 454.

40. Ibid., 444.

41. Ibid., 460.

42. Matthew 25:40.

43. Putnam and Campbell, *American Grace*, 467.

44. David Clingingsmith, Asim Ijaz Khwaja, and Michael Kremer, "Estimating the Impact of The Hajj: Religion and Tolerance in Islam's Global Gathering," *Quarterly Journal of Economics* 124, no. 3 (2009): 1133–70, https://academic.oup .com/qje/article-abstract/124/3/1133/1905120.

45. W. Bradford Wilcox, "Faith and Marriage, Better Together?" *Principles* 3, no. 3 (2017), www.getprinciples.com/faith-and-marriage-better-together/.

46. Robert Nisbet, *The Quest for Community* (Wilmington, DE: Intercollegiate Studies Institute, 2010), xxiii.

47. Pew Research Center, "'Nones' on the Rise."

48. Putnam and Campbell, *American Grace*, 454.

49. Matthew 18:20.

50. Genesis 2:18.

51. Eberstadt, *How the West Really Lost God*.

52. Ibid., 22.

53. Wilcox, Cherlin, Uecker, and Messel, "No Money, No Honey, No Church. The Deinstitutionalization of Religious Life Among the White Working Class."

54. Fred Donovan Hill, "Robert Nisbet and the Idea of Community," *University Bookman* 18, no. 3 (Spring 1978), www.kirkcenter.org/bookman/article/robert -nisbet-and-the-idea-of-community.

55. Matthew 13:3–9.

56. Dale McDonald and Margaret Schultz, *U.S. Catholic Elementary and Secondary Schools 2016–2017: The Annual Statistical Report on Schools, Enrollment and Staffing*, National Catholic Education Association, 2017.

57.   Margaret F. Brinig and Nicole Stelle Garnett, *Lost Classroom, Lost Community* (Chicago: University of Chicago Press, 2014).

58.   Ibid., 68.

59.   Ibid., 69.

60.   Ibid., 70.

Chapter 8: Overcentralization

1.   Yuval Levin, *The Fractured Republic* (New York: Basic Books, 2016), 34.

2.   Robert Nisbet, *The Quest for Community* (Wilmington, DE: Intercollegiate Studies Institute 2010), 101.

3.   Levin, *Fractured Republic*, 38–39.

4.   Ibid., 41.

5.   Barack Obama, "Remarks by the President to the City Club of Cleveland," March 18, 2015, https://obamawhitehouse.archives.gov/the-press-office/2015/03/18 /remarks-president-city-club-cleveland.

6.   Mike Konczal, "Conservatives Don't Get That Some Problems Are Public, and It's Hurting Them," *Washington Post*, August 17, 2013, www.washingtonpost .com/news/wonk/wp/2013/08/17/conservatives-dont-get-that-some-problems -are-public-and-its-hurting-them/?utm_term=.639c8b8db43f.

7.   Arlie Russell Hochschild, *Strangers in Their Own Land* (New York: The New Press, 2016), 99.

8.   Ibid., 235–36.

9.   Albin Krebs and Robert McG. Thomas, "Notes on People; Some Disunity along the United Way," *New York Times*, September 19, 1981, www.nytimes .com/1981/09/19/nyregion/notes-on-people-some-disunity-along-the-united -way.html.

10.   Alexis de Tocqueville, *Democracy in America*, trans. Harvey Mansfield and Delba Winthrop (Chicago: University of Chicago Press, 2000), II 4.5.

11.   Franklin Delano Roosevelt, "A Social Security Program Must Include All Those Who Need Its Protection," Radio Address on the Third Anniversary of the Social Security Act, August 15, 1938, www.ssa.gov/history/fdrstmts .html#radio.

12.   Jonathan Gruber and Daniel Hungerman, "Faith-Based Charity and Crowd-Out during the Great Depression," *Journal of Public Economics* 91, nos. 5–6 (2007): 1043–69, www.sciencedirect.com/science/article/pii /S0047272706001526.

13.   Daniel M. Hungerman, "Are Church and State Substitutes? Evidence from the 1996 Welfare Reform," *Journal of Public Economics* 89, nos. 11–12 (December 2005): 2245–67.

14.   Charles Murray, *In Pursuit: Of Happiness and Good Government* (New York: Simon & Schuster, 1988), 234.

15.   Francis, *Evangelii Gaudium*, Apostolic Exhortation, Vatican website, November 2013, http://w2.vatican.va/content/francesco/en/apost_exhortations/documents /papa-francesco_esortazione-ap_20131124_evangelii-gaudium.html.

16.   John Paul II, *Sollicitudo Rei Socialis*, Papal Encyclical, Vatican Website, December 30, 1987, http://w2.vatican.va/content/john-paul-ii/en/encyclicals/documents /hf_jp-ii_enc_30121987_sollicitudo-rei-socialis.html.

17.   Benedict XVI, *Caritas in Veritate*, Papal Encyclical, Vatican Website, July 7, 2009, http://w2.vatican.va/content/benedict-xvi/en/encyclicals/documents/hf_ben -xvi_enc_20090629_caritas-in-veritate.html.

18.   Luke 10:25–37.

19.   Weather History for Chicago, DuPage, Illinois, *Weather Underground*, www

.wunderground.com/history/airport/KDPA/2017/12/25/DailyHistory
.html?req_city=Elgin&req_state=IL&req_statename=Illinois&reqdb
.zip=60120&reqdb.magic=1&reqdb.wmo=99999.

20. "Elgin Man Told to Stop 'Slumber Parties' for Homeless During Cold, He Says,"
NBC 5 Chicago, January 2, 2018, www.nbcchicago.com/news/local/elgin-greg
-schiller-slumber-parties-homeless-cold-467714563.html.

21. Johnny Sanphillippo, "Mind the Gap," Blog post at *Granola Shotgun*, November
13, 2017, https://granolashotgun.com/2017/11/13/mind-the-gap-2/.

22. John Carney, "Surprise! Dodd-Frank Helps JPMorgan Chase," CNBC, February
4, 2013, www.cnbc.com/id/100431660.

23. Marshall Lux and Robert Greene, "The State and Fate of Community Banking"
(associate working paper series no. 37, Cambridge, Massachusetts, Harvard
Kennedy School, Mossavar-Rahmani Center for Business and Government,
2015), www.hks.harvard.edu/sites/default/files/centers/mrcbg/files/Final
_State_and_Fate_Lux_Greene.pdf.

24. "Bloomberg Strikes Again: NYC Bans Food Donations to the Homeless,"
CBS New York, March 19, 2012, http://newyork.cbslocal.com/2012/03/19
/bloomberg-strikes-again-nyc-bans-food-donations-to-the-homeless/.

25. Laurie Roberts, "Ducey Orders Cosmetology Cops to Cut It Out," *AZCentral*,
February 15, 2017, www.azcentral.com/story/opinion/op-ed/laurieroberts/2017
/02/15/roberts-ducey-orders-cosmetology-cops-cut-out/97954152/.

26. Levin, *Fractured Republic*, 36.

27. Joe Weisenthal, "The 4 Things That Worry Jamie Dimon . . . ," *Business Insider*,
February 4, 2013, www.businessinsider.com/the-four-things-that-worry
-jamie-dimon-2013-2#ixzz2JwOrqfGg.

28. Frederick Winslow Taylor, *The Principles of Scientific Management* (New York:
Harper & Brothers, 1915), 38–39.

29. Credit for this passage goes to Brian M. Carney and Isaac Getz, *Freedom, Inc.:
Free Your Employees and Let Them Lead Your Business to Higher Productivity,
Profits, and Growth* (New York: Crown Business, 2009).

30. Louis Hyman, "The Myth of Main Street," *New York Times*, April 8, 2017,
www.nytimes.com/2017/04/08/opinion/sunday/the-myth-of-main
-street.html.

31. Ray Oldenburg, *The Great Good Place: Cafés, Coffee Shops, Community Centers,
Beauty Parlors, General Stores, Bars, Hangouts, and How They Get You Through
the Day* (New York: Paragon House, 1989), 205.

32. Ibid., 9.

Chapter 9: Hyper-Individualism

1. Barack Obama, "Remarks by the President at a Campaign Event in Roanoke,
Virginia," July 13, 2012, https://obamawhitehouse.archives.gov/the-press-office
/2012/07/13/remarks-president-campaign-event-roanoke-virginia.

2. Tom Wolfe, "The 'Me' Decade and the Third Great Awakening," *New York
Magazine*, August 23, 1976.

3. Alexis de Tocqueville, *Democracy in America*, trans. Harvey Mansfield and
Delba Winthrop (Chicago: University of Chicago Press, 2000), 484.

4. Patrick Deneen, interviewed by Rod Dreher, "Classical Liberalism Strikes
Out," *American Conservative*, January 9, 2018, www.theamericanconservative
.com/dreher/patrick-deneen-classical-liberalism-strikes-out/.

5. Robert Putnam, *Our Kids* (New York: Simon & Schuster, 2015), 205.

6. American Psychological Association, "So Lonely I Could Die," August 5, 2017,
www.apa.org/news/press/releases/2017/08/lonely-die.aspx.

7.   Robert Putnam, *Bowling Alone* (New York: Simon & Schuster, 2001), 44–45.

8.   Yuval Levin, *The Fractured Republic* (New York: Basic Books, 2016), 63.

9.   Michael R. Strain, "Do Volatile Firms Pay Volatile Earnings?" *AEIdeas Blog*, January 17, 2017, www.aei.org/publication/earnings-instability-volatile-firms -volatile-earnings/.

10. Danny Vinik, "The Real Future of Work," *Politico*, January/February 2018, www.politico.com/magazine/story/2018/01/04/future-work-independent -contractors-alternative-work-arrangements-216212.

11. Tyler Cowen, *Average Is Over* (New York: Penguin Group, 2013), 62.

12. J. D. Vance, *Hillbilly Elegy* (New York: HarperCollins, 2016), 12.

13. Ibid., 30.

14. Ibid., 32.

15. Ibid.

16. Quoted in Ramesh Ponnuru, "The Social Fabric Frays. The Patches Aren't Obvious," *Bloomberg*, Opinion, View, May 15, 2017, www.bloomberg.com/view/articles /2017-05-15/the-social-fabric-frays-the-patches-aren-t-obvious.

17. Ray Oldenburg, *The Great Good Place*, (Cambridge, MA: Da Capo Press, 1999), xxix.

18. Ibid.

19. Mark J. Perry, "Today's New Homes Are 1,000 Square Feet Larger Than in 1973, and the Living Space per Person Has Doubled over Last 40 Years," *AEIdeas*, February 26, 2014, www.aei.org/publication/todays-new-homes -are-1000-square-feet-larger-than-in-1973-and-the-living-space-per-person -has-doubled-over-last-40-years/.

20. Oldenburg, *The Great Good Place*, 9.

21. Elle Hardy, "Alone in America," *Current Affairs*, March 31, 2018, www.current affairs.org/2018/03/alone-in-america.

22. Christopher Lasch, *The Culture of Narcissism: American Life in an Age of Diminishing Expectations* (New York: W. W. Norton, 1978), 191.

23. George A. Akerlof and Janet L. Yellen, "New Mothers, Not Married: Technology Shock, the Demise of Shotgun Marriage, and the Increase in Out-of-Wedlock Births," *The Culture of Narcissism*, September 1, 1996, www.brookings.edu /articles/new-mothers-not-married-technology-shock-the-demise-of-shotgun -marriage-and-the-increase-in-out-of-wedlock-births/.

24. Anthony Giddens, *The Transformation of Intimacy: Sexuality, Love and Eroticism in Modern Societies* (Cambridge: Polity Press, 1992).

25. Mark Regnerus, *Cheap Sex: The Transformation of Men, Marriage, and Monogamy* (New York: Oxford University Press, 2017).

26. Mary Eberstadt, *How the West Really Lost God* (West Conshohocken, PA: Templeton Press, 2013), 39.

27. Michelle Boorstein, "After 25 Years on the Culture War's Front Lines, This Prominent Pastor-Activist Thinks Liberals Are Winning," *Washington Post*, Novemeber 27, 2017, www.washingtonpost.com/news/acts-of-faith/wp/2017 /11/27/after-25-years-on-the-culture-wars-front-lines-this-prominent-pastor -activist-thinks-liberals-are-winning/?utm_term=.cfa371b8485d.

28. Kevin Drum, "If You Take Taxpayer Money, You Have to Follow Taxpayer Rules," *Mother Jones*, January 30, 2012, www.motherjones.com/kevin-drum/2012 /01/if-you-take-taxpayer-money-you-have-follow-taxpayer-rules/.

29. For a comprehensive study of the studies, see Bruno Mozzanega, Salvatore Gizzo, Stefania Di Gangi, et al., "Ulipristal Acetate: Critical Review about Endometrial and Ovulatory Effects in Emergency Contraception," *Reproductive Sciences* 21,

no. 6 (2014): 678–85, http://journals.sagepub.com/doi/abs/10.1177/1933719113519178, which concludes, "Our evaluation suggests that UPA succeeds in preventing the clinical appearance of pregnancies mainly by its negative effects on endometrial receptivity, which is a postfertilization mechanism" (p. 5).

30. Brief for the Petitioners in *Sebelius v. Hobby Lobby*, 573 US (2014) No. 13-354, http://sblog.s3.amazonaws.com/wp-content/uploads/2014/01/01.12.14_brief_for_petitioners_doj.pdf.

31. *Real Clear Politics*, "Pelosi on Contraception & Faith: 'I Do My Religion on Sundays, in Church,'" www.realclearpolitics.com/video/2012/06/07/pelosi_on_contraception__faith_i_do_my_religion_on_sundays_in_church.html.

32. Levin, *Fractured Republic*, 4.

33. GOP War Room, "DNC Video: 'The Government Is the Only Thing We All Belong To,'" YouTube, September 4, 2012, www.youtube.com/watch?v=6gLa9Te8Blw.

34. Tocqueville, *Democracy in America*, 644.

35. Lasch, *The Culture of Narcissism*, 231.

36. Philippe Aghion, Yann Algan, Pierre Cahuc, and Andrei Shleifer, "Regulation and Distrust," *Quarterly Journal of Economics* 125, no. 3 (August 2010): 1019, https://academic.oup.com/qje/article-abstract/125/3/1015/1903634.

Chapter 10: The Alienated

1. Daniel Cox, Rachel Lienesch, and Robert P. Jones, *Beyond Economics: Fears of Cultural Displacement Pushed the White Working Class to Trump*, PRRI /Atlantic Report, May 9, 2017, www.prri.org/research/white-working-class-attitudes-economy-trade-immigration-election-donald-trump/.

2. Alex Wagner, "The Church of Trump," *Atlantic*, August 14, 2018, www.theatlantic.com/politics/archive/2018/08/the-church-of-trump/567425/.

3. Philip Bump, "Places That Backed Trump Skewed Poor; Voters Who Backed Trump Skewed Wealthier," *Washington Post*, December 29, 2017, www.washingtonpost.com/news/politics/wp/2017/12/29/places-that-backed-trump-skewed-poor-voters-who-backed-trump-skewed-wealthier/?utm_term=.e497f80f9eb7.

4. Data provided by the Center for the Study of Elections and Democracy.

5. Emma Green, "The Death of Community and the Rise of Trump," *Atlantic*, March 5, 2017, www.theatlantic.com/politics/archive/2017/03/religiously-unaffiliated-white-americans/518340/.

6. Aristotle, *Politics* 1.1253a.

7. Genesis 2:18.

8. Emily Ekins, "The Five Types of Trump Voters," Appendix D, Voter Study Group, June 2017, www.voterstudygroup.org/publications/2016-elections/the-five-types-trump-voters.

9. I reported much of my Occupy experience at the time here: "A Libertarian Camps Out with Wall Street Occupiers," *Washington Examiner*, October 12, 2011, www.washingtonexaminer.com/a-libertarian-camps-out-with-wall-street-occupiers/article/910826.

10. Charles Murray, *In Pursuit: Of Happiness and Good Government* (New York: Simon & Schuster, 1988), 234.

11. Arlie Russell Hochschild, *Strangers in Their Own Land* (New York: The New Press, 2016), 228.

12. Rod Dreher, "Classical Liberalism Strikes Out," *American Conservative*, January 9, 2018.

13.   Ryan Streeter, "Localism vs. the Politics of Abstraction," American Project, January 3, 2018, www.americanproject.org/localism-vs-politics-abstraction/.

14.   Erick Erickson, video published on Facebook: www.facebook.com/ewerickson .personal/videos/vb.509431837/10155783725331838/?type=2&theater.

15.   Scott Clement, "Veterans Are Voting Republican. And That's Not Likely to Change," *Washington Post*, November 11, 2014.

16.   Benjamin Sledge, "Today's Problem with Masculinity Isn't What You Think," *Medium*, April 5, 2018, https://medium.com/s/story/todays-problem-with -masculinity-isn-t-what-you-think-b43e80edcf60.

17.   I originally wrote of these legion halls in "Changing of the Guard," *Philanthropy*, July 2015, www.philanthropyroundtable.org/topic/excellence_in_philanthropy /changing_of_the_guard.

18.   Karen Ann Cullotta, "An Aging American Legion Fights for Relevancy," *New York Times*, March 16, 2013, www.nytimes.com/2013/03/17/us/an-aging -american-legion-fights-for-relevancy.html.

19.   Candace Smith and John Santucci, "Trump Calls on Working Class to 'Strike Back' in Final Day of Campaigning," ABC News, November 8, 2016.

20.   This is my extrapolation from exit polls; www.cnn.com/election/2016/results /exit-polls.

21.   "Donald Trump Announces Presidential Bid," June 16, 2015, www.washingtonpost .com/news/post-politics/wp/2015/06/16/full-text-donald-trump-announces -a-presidential-bid/?utm_term=.790e458bd378.

22.   Donald Trump, Tweet, July 28, 2015, https://twitter.com/realdonaldtrump/status /626140315116830721?lang=en.

23.   Neil Irwin and Josh Katz, "The Geography of Trumpism," *New York Times*, March 12, 2016, www.nytimes.com/2016/03/13/upshot/the-geography-of -trumpism.html?ref=politics&_r=1.

24.   Virginia also has independent cities, which count as counties in most measures. Trump lost some independent cities in Virginia by more than 15 points, and also he lost Albemarle County, surrounding the University of Virginia, by 12.
          Data for Loudoun: https://factfinder.census.gov/bkmk/cf/1.0/en/county /Loudoun County, Virginia/ORIGINS_AND_LANGUAGE/FOREIGN_BORN.
          Data for Fairfax: https://factfinder.census.gov/bkmk/cf/1.0/en/county/Fairfax County, Virginia/ORIGINS_AND_LANGUAGE/FOREIGN_BORN.

25.   "Virginia Primary Results," *New York Times*, www.nytimes.com/elections /2016/results/primaries/virginia.

26.   Brian Arbour and Jeremy M. Teigen, "These Two Maps Are Incredibly Revealing about Who's Voting for Trump, and Why," *Washington Post*, April 5, 2016, www.washingtonpost.com/news/monkey-cage/wp/2016/04/05/these-two -maps-are-incredibly-revealing-about-whos-voting-for-trump-and-why /?noredirect=on&utm_term=.496c2cf215b5.

27.   Pew Forum, "Religious Landscape Study," www.pewforum.org/religious-land scape-study/; and Pew Forum, "The Religious Affiliation of U.S. Immigrants: Majority Christian, Rising Share of Other Faiths," May 17, 2013, www.pew forum.org/2013/05/17/the-religious-affiliation-of-us-immigrants/.

28.   Robert D. Putnam, "*E Pluribus Unum*: Diversity and Community in the Twenty-First Century: The 2006 Johan Skytte Prize Lecture," https://macaulay.cuny .edu/eportfolios/benediktsson2013/files/2013/04/Putnam.pdf.

29.   Daisy Grewal, "Does Diversity Create Distrust?" *Scientific American*, November 29, 2016, www.scientificamerican.com/article/does-diversity-create-distrust/.

30.   American Community Survey, https://factfinder.census.gov/bkmk/table/1.0 /en/ACS/16_5YR/DP02/1600000US5560100.

31. American Community Survey, https://factfinder.census.gov/bkmk/table/1.0 /en/ACS/16_5YR/DP02/0500000US51059.

32. Arbour and Teigen, "These Two Maps Are Incredibly Revealing about Who's Voting for Trump, and Why."

33. American Community Survey, https://factfinder.census.gov/bkmk/table/1.0 /en/ACS/16_5YR/DP02/0500000US51027.

34. Peter Beinart, "Breaking Faith," *Atlantic*, April 2017, www.theatlantic.com /magazine/archive/2017/04/breaking-faith/517785/.

35. Association of Religion Data Archives.

36. Ross Douthat, "Theocracy, Theocracy, Theocracy," *First Things*, August 2006, www.firstthings.com/article/2006/08/theocracy-theocracy-theocracy.

37. Beinart, "Breaking Faith."

38. Neli Esipova, Anita Pugliese, and Julie Ray, "Europeans Most Negative toward Immigration," *Gallup*, October 16, 2015, http://news.gallup.com/poll/186209 /europeans-negative-toward-immigration.aspx.

39. Inae Oh, "Spike Lee's Incredible Gentrification 'Rant' Is Backed by Solid Facts," *Huffington Post*, February 26, 2014, www.huffingtonpost.com/2014/02/26 /spike-lee-gentrification-_n_4856847.html.

Chapter 11: The Elites

1. "The Inauguration of President Andrew Jackson, 1829," EyeWitness to History, www.eyewitnesstohistory.com/jacksoninauguration.htm (2007).

2. U.S. Census Bureau, American Community Survey 2015, https://factfinder.census .gov/bkmk/table/1.0/en/ACS/15_5YR/S1501/1600000US2416787.

3. U.S. Census Bureau, American Community Survey, https://factfinder.census .gov/bkmk/table/1.0/en/ACS/16_5YR/S1501/1600000US5148376.

4. Ibid.

5. Fairfax County, January 12, 2010 Special Election, Official Returns, www.fairfax county.gov/elections/sites/elections/files/assets/result/previous%20election %20results,%202010%20-%202017.pdf.

6. Median household income data and educational attainment data come from the United States Census Bureau's American Community Survey.

7. "What Are the Most Educated Counties in the US?" *Decision Science News*, April 15, 2016, www.decisionsciencenews.com/2016/04/15/educated-counties-us/.

8. Charles Murray, *Coming Apart* (New York: Crown Forum, 2012), 52.

9. Ibid., 61.

10. Douglas S. Massey, Jonathan Rothwell, and Thurston Domina, "The Changing Bases of Segregation in the United States," *Annals of the American Academy of Political and Social Science* 626, no. 1 (2009): 74–90, www.ncbi.nlm.nih.gov /pmc/articles/PMC3844132/.

11. Murray, *Coming Apart*, 73.

12. Ibid., 26.

13. Chevy Chase home values from American Community Survey, national data from Federal Reserve Bank of St. Louis, Median Sales Price for New Houses Sold in the United States, https://fred.stlouisfed.org/series/MSPNHSUS.

14. Robert Putnam, *Our Kids* (New York: Simon & Schuster, 2015), 217.

15. Belinda Luscombe, "Do We Need $75,000 a Year to Be Happy?" *Time*, September 6, 2010, http://content.time.com/time/magazine/article/0,9171,2019628,00.html.

16. Wendy Wang and W. Bradford Wilcox, *The Millennial Success Sequence: Marriage, Kids, and the "Success Sequence" among Young Adults*, AEI, June 2017, www.aei.org/wp-content/uploads/2017/06/IFS-MillennialSuccessSequence -Final.pdf.

17. Matt Bruenig, "The Success Sequence Is about Cultural Beefs, Not Poverty," *People's Policy Project*, August 5, 2017, https://peoplespolicyproject.org/2017/08/05/the-success-sequence-is-about-cultural-beefs-not-poverty/.

18. Wang and Wilcox, *The Millennial Success Sequence*.

19. Kim Parker and Renee Stepler, "As U.S. Marriage Rate Hovers at 50%, Education Gap in Marital Status Widens," Pew Research Center, September 14, 2017, www.pewresearch.org/fact-tank/2017/09/14/as-u-s-marriage-rate-hovers-at-50-education-gap-in-marital-status-widens/.

20. U.S. Department of Labor, Bureau of Labor Statistics, "Marriage and Divorce: Patterns by Gender, Race, and Educational Attainment," October 2013, www.bls.gov/opub/mlr/2013/article/marriage-and-divorce-patterns-by-gender-race-and-educational-attainment.htm.

21. Nicholas H. Wolfinger, "Nine Decades of Promiscuity," Institute for Family Studies, February 6, 2018, https://ifstudies.org/blog/nine-decades-of-promiscuity.

22. Cari Nierenberg, "Rich Kids and Drugs: Addiction May Hit Wealthy Students Hardest," *Live Science*, June 1, 2017, www.livescience.com/59329-drug-alcohol-addiction-wealthy-students.html.

23. Sunrise House, "Evaluating an Individual's Treatment Needs: Addiction among Socioeconomic Groups," https://sunrisehouse.com/addiction-demographics/socioeconomic-groups/.

24. Melissa Silverberg, "Lower Income Equals Lower Test Scores in Our Schools," *Daily Herald*, June 25, 2015, www.dailyherald.com/article/20150622/news/150629873/.

25. Michael J. Petrilli and Brandon L. Wright, "America's Mediocre Test Scores," *Education Next* 16, no. 1 (Winter 2016), http://educationnext.org/americas-mediocre-test-scores-education-poverty-crisis/.

26. National Center for Education Statistics, "The NAEP Mathematics Achievement Levels by Grade," https://nces.ed.gov/nationsreportcard/mathematics/achieveall.aspx.

27. Putnam, *Our Kids*, 218.

28. Ibid., 219.

29. Emma Green, "The Death of Community and the Rise of Trump," *Atlantic*, March 5, 2017, www.theatlantic.com/politics/archive/2017/03/religiously-unaffiliated-white-americans/518340/.

30. Ibid.

31. Federal Reserve Bank of St. Louis, "Unemployment Rate by Educational Attainment and Age, Monthly, Not Seasonally Adjusted," https://fred.stlouisfed.org/release/tables?rid=50&eid=48713.

32. Parker and Stepler, "As U.S. Marriage Rate Hovers at 50%, Education Gap in Marital Status Widens."

33. Fairfax County Public Schools, "Student Membership Demographics and Supplemental Programs," http://schoolprofiles.fcps.edu/schlprfl/f?p=108:13:::NO::P0_CURRENT_SCHOOL_ID,P0_EDSL:020,0.

34. U.S. Census Bureau, American Community Survey.

35. Tweet since deleted, but available at https://twitter.com/alexanderrusso/status/646353372598026240.

36. David Lauter, "How Do Americans View Poverty? Many Blue-Collar Whites, Key to Trump, Criticize Poor People as Lazy and Content to Stay on Welfare," *Los Angeles Times*, August 14, 2016, www.latimes.com/projects/la-na-pol-poverty-poll/.

37. Murray, *Coming Apart*, 290.

38. Patrick Deneen, "The Ignoble Lie: How the New Aristocracy Masks Its Privilege," *First Things*, April 2018, www.firstthings.com/article/2018/04/the-ignoble-lie.

39. Francis, *Evangelii Gaudium*, Vatican website, November 2013, http://w2 .vatican.va/content/francesco/en/apost_exhortations/documents/papa -francesco_esortazione-ap_20131124_evangelii-gaudium.html.

40. John Paul II, *Centesimus Annus*, Vatican website, September 1991, http:// w2.vatican.va/content/john-paul-ii/en/encyclicals/documents/hf_jp-ii _enc_01051991_centesimus-annus.html.

41. Pew Research Center, "Religious Tradition among Adults with a Household Income of $100,000 or More," www.pewforum.org/religious-landscape-study /religious-tradition/among/income-distribution/100000-or-more/.

42. Pew Research Center, "Religious Tradition among Adults with a Household Income of $100,000 or More," www.pewforum.org/religious-landscape -study/religious-tradition/among/income-distribution/100000 -or-more/#age-distribution-trend.

Chapter 12: The Church People

1. U.S. Census Bureau, American Community Survey, https://factfinder.census .gov/bkmk/table/1.0/en/ACS/16_5YR/B04006/0500000US19167.

2. U.S. Census Bureau, American Community Survey, https://factfinder.census .gov/bkmk/table/1.0/en/ACS/15_5YR/DP02/0500000US19119.

3. Ted Mellnik, Dan Keating, Kevin Schaul, et al., "These Maps Explain How Rural Voters Gave Ted Cruz the Win in Iowa," *Washington Post*, February 2, 2016, www.washingtonpost.com/graphics/politics/2016-election/primaries /iowa-results-precincts/.

4. Timothy P. Carney, "Cruz Wins the Dutch Vote in Michigan," *Washington Examiner*, March 9, 2016, www.washingtonexaminer.com/cruz-wins-the-dutch -vote-in-michigan.

5. Statement of Votes Cast, Allegan County, MI, 2016 Presidential Primary, http:// cms.allegancounty.org/sites/Office/Elections/201603/Results%20Reports /Statement%20of%20Votes%20Cast%20-%20UNOFFICIAL.pdf.

6. U.S. Census Bureau, American Community Survey, https://factfinder.census .gov/bkmk/table/1.0/en/ACS/16_5YR/B04006/0500000US19167|160000 0US5560100.

7. E-mail from Jill Ludens, Clerk/Treasurer, Village of Oostburg, April 6, 2016.

8. "Is Oostburg the Most Conservative Community in Wisconsin?" *Retiring Guy's Digest*, June 25, 2014, http://paulsnewsline.blogspot.com/2014/06/is -oostburg-most-conservative-community.html.

9. Only in Your State, "Here Are the 10 Happiest Cities in Iowa," January 10, 2016, www.onlyinyourstate.com/iowa/10-happiest-cities-in-ia/.

10. Larissa MacFarquhar, "Where the Small-Town American Dream Lives On," *New Yorker*, November 13, 2017, www.newyorker.com/magazine/2017/11/13 /where-the-small-town-american-dream-lives-on.

11. U.S. Census Bureau, American Community Survey, https://factfinder.census .gov/bkmk/table/1.0/en/DEC/10_SF1/QTP11/1600000US1959475.

12. U.S. Census Bureau, American Community Survey, https://factfinder.census .gov/bkmk/table/1.0/en/ACS/15_5YR/S2501/0500000US19141.

13. Niche.com, "Orange City," www.niche.com/places-to-live/orange-city-sioux-ia/.

14. Association of Religion Data Archives, County Membership Report, Sioux City, Iowa, www.thearda.com/rcms2010/r/c/19/rcms2010_19167_county_name_2010 .asp.

15. Bethel Christian Reformed Church, www.bethelsc.org/pastor_john_lee.cfm, accessed April 10, 2017.

16. Sandra L. Hofferth, Sarah M. Flood, and Matthew Sobek, American Time Use Survey Data Extract Builder: Version 2.6 [dataset], College Park, MD: University of Maryland, and Minneapolis, MN: University of Minnesota, 2017, https://doi.org/10.18128/D060.V2.6.

17. Association of Religion Data Archives, The Church of Jesus Christ of Latter-day Saints (Utah), www.thearda.com/mapsReports/maps/2010/UT_D151_10R.asp.

18. Association of Religion Data Archives, The Church of Jesus Christ of Latter-day Saints (Idaho), http://thearda.com/mapsReports/maps/2010/ID_D151_10R.asp.

19. Natalie Gochnour, "Localism in America," American Enterprise Institute, February 2018, www.aei.org/wp-content/uploads/2018/02/Gochnour.7.pdf.

20. Raj Chetty, Nathaniel Hendren, Patrick Kline, and Emmanuel Saez, "Where Is the Land of Opportunity? The Geography of Intergenerational Mobility in the United States" (working paper 19843, National Bureau of Economic Research, Cambridge, Massachusetts, 2014), www.rajchetty.com/chettyfiles/mobility_geo.pdf.

21. Montgomery County 2016 Presidential Primary Results, www.montgomerycountymd.gov/Elections/Resources/Files/pdfs/2016%20Primary%20Results/13-57.pdf.

22. Montgomery County 2016 Presidential Primary Results, www.montgomerycountymd.gov/Elections/Resources/Files/pdfs/2016%20Primary%20Results/13-33.pdf.

23. David Holzel, "University Towers Gets Shabbat Elevators," *Washington Jewish Week*, February 28, 2014, http://washingtonjewishweek.com/10597/university-towers-gets-shabbat-elevators/news/local-news/.

24. Pew Research Center, "U.S. Muslims Concerned about Their Place in Society, but Continue to Believe in the American Dream," July 26, 2017, www.pewforum.org/2017/07/26/findings-from-pew-research-centers-2017-survey-of-us-muslims/.

25. Pew Research Center, "U.S. Muslims Concerned about Their Place in Society, but Continue to Believe in the American Dream," July 26, 2017, www.pewforum.org/2017/07/26/political-and-social-views/.

26. Anand Giridharadas, "The Immigrant Advantage," May 24, 2014, www.nytimes.com/2014/05/25/opinion/sunday/the-immigrant-advantage.html.

27. Ibid.

Chapter 13: Overcoming Alienation

1. Ben Casselman, "Manufacturing Jobs Are Never Coming Back," *FiveThirtyEight*, March 18, 2016, https://fivethirtyeight.com/features/manufacturing-jobs-are-never-coming-back/.

2. Lars J. Lefgren, Jaren C. Pope, and David P. Sims, "State Policies and Intergenerational Income Mobility" (working paper, April 2016), https://jarenpope.weebly.com/uploads/2/9/7/3/29731963/wp_lefgren_pope_sims.pdf.

3. Yuval Levin, *The Fractured Republic* (New York: Basic Books, 2016), 6.

4. Dylan Matthews, "Europe Could Have the Secret to Saving America's Unions," Vox, April 17, 2017, www.vox.com/policy-and-politics/2017/4/17/15290674/union-labor-movement-europe-bargaining-fight-15-ghent.

5. See Poul Hertel, "The Long-Term Effect of Capping the Mortgage-Interest Deduction," *Washington Post*, November 17, 2017, www.washingtonpost.com/opinions/the-long-term-effect-of-capping-the-mortgage-interest-deduction

/2017/11/17/e1c3e5aa-cb3d-11e7-b506-8a10ed11ecf5_story.html?utm_term=.5fd0a8066e48.

6. Jeff Tucker, "Birth Rates Dropped Most in Counties Where Home Values Grew Most," Zillow Research, June 8, 2018, www.zillow.com/research/birth-rates-home-values-20165/.

7. Barbara Abel and Julia Lieblich, "Rural Controversy: A Mosque in Sheboygan," *Time*, August 19, 2010.

Index

Page numbers in *italics* refer to illustrations.

About the Author

———————

TIMOTHY P. CARNEY is the commentary editor at the *Washington Examiner* and a visiting fellow at the American Enterprise Institute. He is the author of *The Big Ripoff: How Big Business and Big Government Steal Your Money* and *Obamanomics: How Barack Obama Is Bankrupting You and Enriching His Wall Street Friends, Corporate Lobbyists, and Union Bosses*. He lives in the Washington, D.C., area.